NORTH AMERICAN
WILLS REGISTERED
IN LONDON

1611-1857

Compiled by

Peter Wilson Coldham

Copyright © 2007
Peter Wilson Coldham
Surrey, England
All Rights Reserved
Published by Genealogical Publishing Company
3600 Clipper Mill Rd., Suite 260
Baltimore, MD 21211
Library of Congress Catalogue Card Number 2006939043
International Standard Book Number 978-0-8063-1773-1
Made in the United States of America

North American Wills Registered in London 1611-1857

Introduction

The Prerogative Court of Canterbury (PCC) was theoretically, and for the most part in practice, the only authority in England able to issue and register grants of probate and administration required by the citizens of England and Wales who died at home or abroad leaving wills or having assets worth more than £5. Fortunately for the family historian, this meant that a will drawn up by an English person anywhere in the world required legitimisation by the PCC in London if the testator wished to pass on any property he might own in the "mother country." Less fortunately for the genealogist, fewer than one in a hundred was well enough endowed to draw up a will or to benefit from the ministrations of the London court. However, the survival in London of well over 2,000 wills relating to temporary or permanent inhabitants of North America has ensured that they, their relations and descendants have not only found a permanent place in historical records but have a provable link to English ancestry.

Until very recently the establishment of such a link was usually possible, if at all, only by a lengthy and arduous examination of hundreds of unindexed probate records, and the meagre results of such research accumulated over the past 100 or more years which have been published and republished stand witness to the previous difficulty of access to the more than one million wills registered in the PCC and now held in the National Archives (TNA)[1] in London. Not only have the registry copies of all these wills (except for a few probated during the exile of the PCC in Oxford in the 1640s, PROB 10/639-642) now been made available on the internet but the names of the testators, their place of residence or death, and date of probate are accessible at the touch of a button. A difficulty remains, however, in that the movement of emigrants between two continents and within their chosen destination – often coupled to a wide variation in spellings – can obscure their true identity and place of residence.

An attempt was made to resolve some of these problems in 1989 by assembling an alphabetical compilation of American probate records to be found in the PCC[2] supplemented in 1992 by a chronologically arranged series of abstracts from American wills proved in London[3]. However the recent advent of the National Archives' on-line service referred to above now makes it imperative to issue a completely revised and comprehensive guide not only to bring within one compass the newly accessible resources of the PCC (including references to all Canadian wills proved in London up to 1857) but to correct some minor (and a few more serious) errors in transcription.

This latest compilation celebrates both the completion by TNA of its massive indexing project nearly 150 years after the PCC closed for business and the culmination of a forty-year-long endeavour by the present author to assemble from myriad published and unpublished sources an adequate guide to American probate records to be found in the mother country. This has not only offered an opportunity to include a variety of relevant notes from previously published and newly researched sources, but has facilitated the provision of complete indexes to the names of witnesses, legatees and executors to supplement the alphabetical listing of testators to be found in the main body of this work. The places and ships mentioned in the testamentary documents have also been comprehensively indexed. Used judiciously and in conjunction, these indexes can provide a unique guide to the discovery of further genealogical and historical sources.

Introduction

The National Archives itself has issued some very helpful notes on how to use the on-line service and these deserve a careful reading. It should be made clear that the service offers copies of wills as they were written into the original Registers and not the original wills. Where the latter survive they can be made available but must be quoted for and ordered separately. The current cost of the on-line service is £3.50 (British pounds, approximately US$ 6.50 at the current rate of exchange) for each download, which may be paid by debit or credit card

The only other probate courts in England known to have exercised jurisdiction over the estates of citizens dying testate overseas were two within the purview of the Bishop of London, the so-called Commissary Court and Archdeaconry Court; their archives have proved a rich source for the wills of early emigrants to America although none after the end of the 17th century. A careful examination has been made of these records held by the Guildhall Library of the City of London[4] and abstracts made of all those of American interest.

It will be appreciated that in order to keep this volume within reasonable bounds of length substantial use has been made of abbreviations (listed below) and, where printed abstracts are known to exist, reference has been made to them in the text and particularly to those included in the following works:

ACE =   *American Colonists in English Records* by George Sherwood. Baltimore: Genealogical Publishing Co., Inc., 1982. Available on CD 7364.

AM   =   *American Migrations* by Peter Wilson Coldham. Baltimore: Genealogical Publishing Co., Inc., 2000.

AWP =   *American Wills Proved in London 1611-1775* by Peter Wilson Coldham. Baltimore: Genealogical Publishing Co., Inc., 1992. Available on CD 7364.

GGE =   *Genealogical Gleanings in England* by Henry FitzGilbert Waters. Baltimore: Genealogical Publishing Co., Inc., 1997. Available on CD 7364.

NGSQ = *National Genealogical Society Quarterly,* Washington, D.C. Serial articles by Peter Wilson Coldham.

VGE =   *Virginia Gleanings in England* by Lothrop Withington. Baltimore: Genealogical Publishing Co., Inc., 1980. Available on CD 7364.

How to use the TNA online index to PCC wills

Each entry in this volume gives the name of the testator/testatrix, occupation or rank where available, place of residence or death and date of probate. This is followed in brackets by the PROB11 reference needed by TNA to identify and transmit by internet or snail mail a copy of any will you may wish to order. While the provision of an index to over a million names is a demonstrably superb achievement, what has resulted is a somewhat less than "user friendly" database. In particular, because every entry is a literal copy from an original source and no equivalent to a soundex version is provided, some perseverance and ingenuity is often necessary either to trace a particular will or to eliminate the possibility that one may exist in the archive.

Introduction

Here is a step-by-step guide to obtaining any will listed in this book.

- On your browser go to www.nationalarchives.gov.uk/documentsonline;

- In the left-hand panel of the page which follows click on **Family History>**

If you click on 'wills' on the far right hand side (under the heading 'popular content' you will be taken to the background notes as well as to a link to the search page. Just a different way of accessing the same information!

- On the next page click on **Wills>** which will bring up the following box:

Clear   Search >

Word or phrase	First name	
	Last name	
	Occupation	
	Place	
	Other Keywords	
Date range (dd/mm/yyyy or yyyy)		to

- Enter the minimum information in the appropriate boxes to identify your target; if it is an individual listed in this book the first name and surname will usually be sufficient (but please remember the possibility of alternative spellings);

- When you are sure you have the right person click on the cartouche **See details>** which will bring up a further page indicating the size of the required will and the price of an online copy;

- Click on +**Add to shipping**, then follow through to the **Checkout** page where you will be asked for your email address and choice of payment method.

Should you decide to explore some of the other riches of this archive without too much unnecessary frustration, here are more suggestions. Most commonly a researcher is trying to track down either a particular person or relations with the same surname. If the names are at all unusual you should have no problem. Conversely should you be hunting anyone with a fairly widespread combination of names – *Catherine Moore* perhaps – it will be worthwhile entering Cat* or Kat* as the first name (of which more than a dozen variants have been found) and Mo*r? as the surname: in that way you will be provided with a more comprehensive and therefore a more labour-intensive result. A large number of results can be

Introduction

sorted into date range by clicking on the 'date' heading. Again please remember there is a plethora of odd spellings to be found in this database whether caused by faulty transcriptions, human error, custom or by machine scanning. Few of the Harding family would probably expect to find an ancestor with the given name of Schabod – but see page 45.

While you are enjoying your exploration of this newly-opened resource you might also have some genealogical fun without any additional cost to yourself by examining all the wills made by the inhabitants of Great or Little Snoring, Norfolk, between 1547 and 1851. The answer is 16 if you would like to check it, slightly outnumbering the 14 male midwives to have been identified throughout the kingdom during the same period.

ABBREVIATIONS USED IN THIS VOLUME

Admon	= Administration	MO	= Missouri
AL	= Alabama	MS	= Mississippi
AWE	= Administration with will	NB	= New Brunswick
Berks.	= Berkshire	NC	= North Carolina
Bucks.	= Buckinghamshire	NH	= New Hampshire
CA	= California	NJ	= New Jersey
Chesh.	= Cheshire	NL	= Newfoundland
Corn.	= Cornwall	Northants	= Northamptonshire
cr.	= creditor	NS	= Nova Scotia
CT	= Connecticut	NY	= New York
dau(s)	= daughter(s)	NYC	= New York City
DC	= District of Columbia	OH	= Ohio
DE	= Delaware	ON	= Ontario
Derbys.	= Derbyshire	OR	= Oregon
E.FL	= East Florida	PA	= Pennsylvania
Exec	= Executor(s)	pc	= principal creditor
Exex	= Executrix	PE	= Prince Edward Island
FL	= Florida	pr.	= proved
GA	= Georgia	QC	= Quebec
Glos.	= Gloucestershire	RI	= Rhode Island
Hants.	= Hampshire	Salop.	= Shropshire
Herts.	= Hertfordshire	SC	= South Carolina
Hunts.	= Huntingdonshire	Staffs.	= Staffordshire
IA	= Iowa	Sx.	= Sussex
IL	= Illinois	Sy.	= Surrey
IN	= Indiana	TNA	= The National Archives
KY	= Kentucky	TX	= Texas
LA	= Louisiana	VA	= Virginia
LAB	= Labrador	VT	= Vermont
Leg:	= Legatee(s)	W.FL	= West Florida
Leics.	= Leicestershire	WA	= Washington
Lieut.	= Lieutenant	Warw.	= Warwickshire
MA	= Massachusetts	WI	= Wisconsin
MB	= Manitoba	Wilts.	= Wiltshire
MD	= Maryland	Wit:	= Witness(es)
Mddx.	= Middlesex	Worcs.	= Worcestershire
ME	= Maine	Yorks.	= Yorkshire
MI	= Michigan		

Introduction

[1] The National Archives, Kew, Richmond, Surrey TW9 4DU, England.
www.nationalarchives.gov.uk

[2] *American Wills and Administrations in the Prerogative Court of Canterbury 1610-1857* by Peter Wilson Coldham. Baltimore: Genealogical Publishing Co., Inc., 1989.

[3] *American Wills Proved in London 1611-1775* by Peter Wilson Coldham. Baltimore: Genealogical Publishing Co., Inc., 1992.

[4] Guildhall Library Manuscripts, Aldermanbury, London EC2P 2EJ.
www.cityoflondon.gov.uk/guildhalllibrary

Peter Wilson Coldham	Christmas 2006
Purley, Surrey, England	A M D G

NORTH AMERICAN WILLS REGISTERED IN LONDON
1611 – 1857

Abbott, Stephen of QC now in London but about to sail for QC, merchant. 18 Apr. 1765. Leg: sister Jane Collier, widow; sister Elizabeth Rutherford. Execs: Richard Gomm of Clerkenwell, Mddx., merchant, and brother William Abbott of QC. Wit: Mary Denham and John Bushnell. Pr. 9 Jul. 1766 by Richard Gomm. (PROB11/920).

Abell, George Esq. of St. George Westminster, Mddx., late of Charles Town, SC, widower. Will 19 Aug. 1737 pr. 12 Mar 1742 brother Thomas Abell of Coleshill, Warw. (PROB11/716). AWP.

Abercrombie, James of Philadelphia, mariner. Will 11 Dec. 1758 AWW 23 Jul. 1761 to William Neate, attorney for Charles and Alexander Stedman and Samuel McCall of Philadelphia. (PROB11/867). AWP.

Achley, John of London, merchant, bound on a voyage to Tangier and VA by the *Hope* but who died in VA. Will 15 Aug. 1666. Leg: brothers and sisters [unnamed]; William Martin; William Read; Samuel Booker; Capt. Richard Longman who is to have testator's goods in VA. father Anderson Achley Sr. Wit: Francis Collins and William Martin. Will pr. 6 Aug. 1667 by Dr. John Dolman of Stepney, Mddx. (PROB11/324). AWP. NGSQ 67/61.

Acrod, Benjamin of Hackney, Mddx., gent., who had lands in PA and died there. Will 12 Jan. 1683 pr. 10 Dec. 1684 by John Acrod. (PROB11/378). AWP.

Adams, Joseph of York Town, VA, seaman of HMS *Wolf.* Will 1 Oct. 1740 AWW 19 Jun. 1758 to Daniel Walton, attorney for relict Ann Adams in York Town. (PROB11/838). AWP.

Addison, Anthony of Prince George's Co., MD. Will pr. by nephew Henry Addison Callis 2 Feb. 1838. (PROB11/1890).

Aderne, John of Bickton, Chesh., gent., who died in Carolina. Will 28 Feb. 1699 pr. 28 Apr. 1715 by cousin Edward Warren of London, merchant. (PROB11/545). AWP.

Aglionby, William of Savannah, GA. Will 8 Aug. 1738 pr. 30 May 1745 by William Bradley of Savannah. (PROB11/739). AWP.

Alderne, Thomas of London, merchant, whose son Owen Alderne was to inherit a sawmill and lands belonging to the New England Co. Will 21 Apr. 1656 pr. 20 Jun 1657 by relict Dorothy Alderne. (PROB11/265). AWP.

Alexander, John of St. Olave, Southwark, Sy., bound for Carolina by the *Edward Francis.* Will 12 Sep. 1698 pr. 27 Jul. 1700 by relict Jane Alexander. (PROB11/456). AWP.

Alexander, Robert of KY. Will pr. 24 Jun. 1841 by son Robert Alexander. (PROB11/1946).

Alexander, William of St. Gregory by St. Paul's, London, gent., who died in Philadelphia. Will 17 Oct. 1707 pr. 6 Oct. 1727 by relict Mary Alexander. (PROB11/617). AWP.

Allcock, William of Mollington, Oxon., mason. Will 29 Sep. 1733. Leg: brother and sister John Farmer and Joan his wife to have lands in Mollington; nephew John Farmer; brother George Elkington and his children; children and grandchildren [unnamed] of brother George Elkington of NJ, deceased, etc. Trustees: John Gorstel and Robert Sparrow. Wit: Richard Woodward, Anthony Harris, John Burrowes, Philip Coleman, William Coleman and Alice Smith. Pr. 27 Jan. 1738 by Francis Abbitts. (PROB11/687).

Allan, Dr. Colin of Fredericton, NB, surgeon of H.M. Forces on half-pay. Will pr. 10 Mar. 1851. (PROB11/2128).

Allan, Winckworth of Halifax, NS. Will pr. 24 Dec. 1834. (PROB11/1839).

Allen, Aaron of Nether Providence, Delaware Co., PA. AWW 17 Jul. 1837 to Nathaniel Mason. (PROB11/1881).

Allen, Samuel of Boston, MA, mariner of HMS *Kent* but late of HMS *Maidstone.* Will 23 Feb. 1745 pr. 1 Jun. 1747 by Daniel Gunn of Wapping, Mddx., cordwainer. (PROB11/754). AWP.

Allen, Sarah of Ridley Township, Delaware Co., PA, widow. AWW 16 Apr. 1836 to granddaughter Elizabeth Bottomley. (PROB11/1860).

Allenby, William Charles of Baltimore, gent. Will pr. 12 Jun. 1801 by brother George Allenby. (PROB11/1359).

Allison, William. *See* **Annerson**

Allman, Susanna of NY, widow. Will pr. 24 Nov. 1806. (PROB11/1451).

Allman, formerly Douglas, Susanna of NY, widow. AWW 24 Nov. 1807 to Howard Douglas. (PROB11/1469).

Allmon, William James of Halifax, NS, physician. Will pr. 26 Jun. 1817. (PROB11/1593).

Allright, William of Arborfield, Berks., yeoman, whose eldest daughter was in New England. (PROB11/323). AWP.

Alston, David of Northfield, Richmond Co., NY, Capt. on half pay of NJ Volunteers. AWW Jul. 1806 to David Davies. (PROB11/1445).

Alvey, Henry of Halifax, NS, soldier in Capt. Barbut's Co.,15th Regiment. Will pr. 2 Nov. 1761. (PROB11/870).

Amar, John of NYC, formerly of Pensacola, master carpenter of Ordnance Board. AWW 26 Oct. 1782 to James Dewey. (PROB11/1095).

Ambrose, John of Baltimore, physician. Will pr. 3 Sep. 1803. (PROB11/1398).

Amory, Simon of Pensacola, W. FL, gent. Will 28 Aug. 1765 pr. 20 Nov. 1766 by brother Rev. Thomas Amory of St. Michael Bassishaw, London. (PROB11/923). AWP.

Amphlett, William of St. Louis, MO, Lieut. in Royal Navy. Will pr 19 Jul. 1852 by brother Richard Paul Amphlett. (PROB11/2155).

Amyand, Isaac of Charles Town, SC, gent. Will 26 Aug. 1738 pr. 20 Dec. 1739 by cousin Claudius Amyand. (PROB11/699). AWP.

Anderson, Alexander of HMS *Enterprise* of Burnt Island, NL. Will pr. 22 Apr. 1723. (PROB11/590).

Anderson, James of George Town, SC, planter. Will pr. 17 Aug. 1821 by son Richard Oswald Anderson. (PROB11/1646).

Anderson, James of NYC, merchant. AWW 18 Oct. 1832 to sons Andrew, Smith Weeks and Abel Tyler Anderson. (PROB11/1806).

Anderson, James of QC. Will pr. 6 Nov. 1837. (PROB11/1886).

Anderson, John of Boston, MA, shipwright. Will pr. 20 Feb. 1678 by John Phillips with similar powers reserved to the relict Mary Anderson. (PROB11/356). GGE.

Anderson, Julia Ann of Detroit, MI. AWW 28 Feb. 1845 to Henry Barkly and Henry John Lias. (PROB11/2011).

Andre, John of Tappen, Staten Island, [NY], Adjutant General of Army & Capt. in 54th Regiment of Foot. Will pr. 3 Jan. 1781 by uncles David Andre, Andrew Girardot and John Lewis. (PROB11/1073).

Andrews, Alexander of Kingston, [ON], Col. of 60th Regiment of Foot. Will pr. 5 Jan. 1824. (PROB11/1680).

Andrews, Samuel of Yarmouth, Shelburne Co., NS, reduced Provincial Officer. Will pr. 16 Jan. 1811. (PROB11/1518).

Andrews, William of Cote, Bishops Canning , Wilts., who died in VA, bachelor. Will 16 May 1712 pr. 7 Dec. 1721 by uncle Nicholas Nash. (PROB11/582). AWP. Further grant Aug. 1726.

Angell, John of Wapping, Mddx., and late of Winterbourne St. Martin, Dorset, but who died in VA.Will 20 Nov. 1691. Leg. & exec: Samuel Pacy of Wapping, victualler. Wit: Thomas Grandey, William Chester and Samuel Wills. Pr. 2 Apr. 1694 by Samuel Pacy. (Guildhall Ms 9171/46/109v).

Angell, Samuel of Pitty Harbour, NL. Will pr. 26 Feb. 1736. (PROB11/669).

Annely, Richard of NY, merchant. Will 25 Mar. 1737 pr. 24 Oct. 1750 by brother Thomas Annely [of Bristol]. (PROB11/782). AWP.

Annerson *alias* **Allison** *alias* **Annison, William**, carpenter of HMS *Guerriere* in Naval Hospital in Halifax, NS. Will pr. 28 Aug. 1813. (PROB11/1547).

Annison, William. *See* **Annerson.**

Anthony, David of Stepney, Mddx., mariner, who died in VA. Will 4 Jul. 1675 AWW 8 Jul 1676 to Margaret, wife of James Dicks. (PROB11/351).

Anthony, John of RI, mariner. Will 16 Jun. 1701. Leg: son John Anthony. Execs: Richard and Elinor Potts. Wit: John Wood, Mary Pinkny and John Dennis. Pr. 10 Dec. 1703 by Elinor Potts. (PROB11/473).

Anthony, John of RI, mariner. Will 16 Jun. 1701 pr. 10 Dec. 1703 by affirmation of relict. (PROB11/473). AWP.

Antill, John of New Burgh, Orange Co., NY, Major of late Regt. of NJ. AWW 20 Apr. 1819 to William Young. (PROB11/1615).

Antle, John of Cerne Abbas, Dorset, but late of New Perlican, Trinity Bay, NL, planter. Will 16 Aug. 1841. Leg: son or reputed son Joseph Antle *alias* Sullivan who is to be exec; 5 (unnamed) children of Mary Sanson. Wit: William Bullock and Mary Elizabeth Bullock. Pr. 16 Aug. 1841 by Joseph Antle *alias* Sullivan. (PROB11/1949).

Antram, William of HMS *Boyne* who died in SC on HMS *Mermaid*, bachelor. Will 31 Oct. 1743 pr. 26 Feb. 1752 by mother Mary Minor of Gosport, Hants. (PROB11/792). AWP.

Anwyl, Mary Senhouse of Charlotte Town, PE, spinster. Will pr. 4 Oct. 1850. (PROB11/2120).

Appy, John of Albany, NY, Secretary and Judge Advocate of HM Forces. Will 10 Jun. 1758 AWW 10 May 1763 to father Peter Appy. (PROB11/887). AWP.

Apthorp, John Esq. of Cambridge, MA. Will 8 Oct. 1771 pr. 22 Feb. 1773 by George Apthorp. (PROB11/984).

Arbuckle, John of NY, gunner of HMS *Daphne*. Will 11 Jun. 1779. Wit: John Chinnery and John Dykes. Pr. 9 Apr. 1788 by relict and sole legatee Mary Arbuckle. (PROB11/1164).

Archbell, John of Shadwell, Mddx., mariner who died on ship *Ephraim* in VA. Will 23 Oct. 1691 pr. 13 Nov. 1692 by Hannah Thompson. (PROB11/412). AWP.

Archer, Christopher of St. John's, NL. Will pr. 17 Mar. 1736. (PROB11/676).

Arderne, John of NC. Will 22 Oct. 1707 pr. 3 Sep. 1720 by William Duckinfield of NC. (PROB11/575). AWP.

Arey, John of City of Oxford, carpenter bound to NC and who died there in the service of Anthony Bacon of London, merchant. Will 15 Dec. 1770 pr. 4 Nov. 1771 by Henry Trenchard Goodenough. (PROB11/972). AWP.

Arlington, Michael of Stepney, Mddx., marine of HMS *Lyme*, who died in VA. Will pr. 18 Aug. 1719 by Nathan Movelty. (PROB11/569). AWP.

Armstrong, George, second mate of *Concord* bound to MD and who died there. Will 6 Mar. 1735 pr. 5 Dec. 1735 by uncle Robert Pitt of Bethnal Green, Mddx. (PROB11/674). AWP.

Armstrong, Lawrence, Lieut. Governor of NS. Will pr. 28 Nov. 1741. (PROB11/713).

Armstrong, Richard, Lieut. General of Queensbury, York Co., NB. Will pr. 4 May 1818. (PROB11/1604).

Arnall, Thomas of Goodmans Fields, Mddx., master of the *Merchants' Adventure* who died on a voyage to VA in 1693. Will 18 Nov. 1691 pr. 26 Jul. 1694 by relict Katherine Arnall. (PROB11/421). NGSQ 70/41.

Arnold, Henry of NY. Lieut. in HM Service. AWW 11 Jul. 1827 to Pownal Phipps. (PROB11/1728).

Arnold, Mary late of St. John's, NL, now of NYC. Will dated 3 Feb. 1764 witnessed by Elias Degrush, James Giles and John Woods. Leg: one shilling to eldest son William Arnold in full settlement of his claim and as a bar for ever; the same sum to daughter Dorothy Platus; to daughter Batty Branscome the plantation in St. John's, NL, received by the will of the testatrix's father William Roberts of Dartmouth, Devon. AWW 28 Feb. 1775 to James Goss, attorney for the named executrix Batty *alias* Betty Radford, formerly Branscome, wife of Henry Radford, now at St. John's. (PROB11/1004).

Arrowsmith, Hugh of NY, mariner of *Edgar*, who died at sea. Will 25 Jan. 1691 AWW 11 Sep. 1691 to Elizabeth Anger. (PROB11/404). AWP.

Arthur, Christopher of Sypruss Barony, SC, who died in Stepney, Mddx. Will 24 Oct. 1724 pr. 21 Dec. 1724 by Patrick Roche of Limerick, Ireland. (PROB11/600). AWP.

Ash, John of Danho, Colleton Co., SC, gent. Will 9 Apr. 1703 AWW 31 Jan. 1706 to William Methuen, attorney for relict Mary Ash. (PROB11/486). AWP.

Ash, John of Westfield, Colleton Co., SC. Will 30 Mar. 1711 AWW 16 Aug. 1721 to William Livingston, husband and adr. of the relict Ann Livingston *alias* Ash of Westfield, SC, who died in Wilts., England. (PROB11/581). AWP.

Ashley, John of Blackheath, Kent, late of Barbados, with lands in PA. Will 9 Oct. 1750 AWW 9 Oct. 1751 to pc. George Prescott. (PROB11/790). AWP.

Ashton, James of Stafford Co., VA, gent. Will pr. 14 Jul. 1687. (PROB11/388).

Aspden, Matthias of Philadelphia. Will pr. 27 Jul. 1825. (PROB11/1701).

Astwood, John of Milford, New Haven, CT. Will pr. 31 Aug. 1654. (PROB11/242).

Atchinson, George, late of Charles Town, SC, but late of Islington, Mddx., merchant. Will pr. 12 Sep. 1728 by brother David Atchison. (PROB11/624). AWP.

Atkins, John of VA. AWW 2 Oct. 1624 to brother William Atkins (PROB 11/144); revoked & granted to brother Richard Atkins Aug. 1626; revoked & granted to brother Humfrey Atkins Jun. 1627. (PROB11/144). VGE.

Atkinson, Francis, mariner of HMS *Deptford* who died in VA. Will 8 Sep. 1694 pr. 30 Dec. 1695 by James Bowerman. (PROB11/429). AWP.

Atkinson, George, Governor of Eastmain, Rupertsland, Hudson's Bay . Will pr. 26 Nov. 1832. (PROB11/1807).

Atkinson, Theodore of Portsmouth, NH. AWW 17 Oct. 1783 to Thomas Dickason. (PROB11/1108).

Atkinson, William of West River, Anne Arundel Co., MD, Lieut. on half pay. AWW 28 Jul. 1795 to John Clapham. (PROB11/1263). .

Auchmuty, James Smith of Shelburne, NS, gent. Will pr. 15 Dec. 1790. (PROB11/1198).

Auchmuty, John of NS, Lieut. of Regiment of Foot. Will pr. 24 Sep. 1751. (PROB11/790).

Audley, George of Annapolis Royal, NS, Ensign in Royal NL Regiment of Fencibles. Will pr. 23 Jan. 1815. (PROB11/1564).

Austell, Joseph of Boston, MA, mariner. Will 6 Nov. 1743 pr. 7 Sep. 1748 by cousin Moses Austell. (PROB11/764). AWP.

Austin, Charles surgeon to Indian Department of North America. Will pr. 7 May 1788 by sister Anna Maria Prichard. (PROB11/1165).

Austin, Dr. John of NYC. AWW 11 Jul. 1839 to Charles Dean. (PROB11/1913).

Austin, Joseph, formerly of New England but late of Shadwell, Mddx., mariner. Will 28 Sep. 1678 pr. 1 Sep 1679 by Mary Yems. (PROB11/360). AWP.

Austin, Thomas of Wapping, Mddx., mariner of HMS *Richmond* who died in NY. Will 13 Mar 1689 pr. 6 Jun. 1694 by Thomas Frampton. (PROB11/420). AWP.

Avery, John of Dorchester Co., MD, shipwright. Will 25 Apr. 1677 AWW 11 Aug. 1683 to Cuthbert Haslewood, brother of John Haslewood now overseas, husband of the relict Anne Haslewood *alias* Avery deceased. (PROB11/373). AWP.

Avery, John, formerly of CT but late of Bristol, mariner. Will 13 Mar. 1745 pr. 7 Jul. 1746 by Jane Day of Bristol, spinster. (PROB11/748). AWP.

Avory, Mary of Prince George's Co., MD. Will 26 Oct. 1766 pr. 2 Dec. 1769 by children Charles Avory and Molly, wife of Amos Elliott . (PROB11/953). AWP.

Axtell, Daniel of Stoke Newington, Mddx., who died in Carolina. Will 3 Aug. 1678 AWW 2 Jul. 1687 to Dr. Walter Needham, attorney for relict Rebecca Axtell in Carolina. (PROB11/388). AWP.

Aylward, William, formerly of VA, merchant, and late of London, but who died in France, bachelor. Will 6 Nov. 1701 pr. 20 Feb. 1707 by Robert Cary. (PROB11/492). AWP.

Ayscough, Richard of NYC, doctor of physic and surgery. Will 22 May 1760 pr. 22 Nov. 1760 by uncle Rev. Francis Ayscough. (PROB11/860). AWP. Further grant in Jan. 1768.

Baal, George of Rencontre, Fortune Bay, NL. Will pr. 23 May 1856. (PROB11/2232).

Baby *alias* Reaume, Suzanne of QC, widow. Will pr. 21 Nov. 1815. (PROB11/1574).

Bache, Thomas of Over Penn, Staffs., whose nephew Peter Bache was in VA. Will 21 Jan. 1674 AWW 2 Jul. 1674 to the daughter Mary Dyson, no executor having been named. (PROB11/345). AWP. NGSQ 62/273.

Backer, Joseph of Boston, MA, joiner. Will pr. 2 Nov. 1742. (PROB11/721)

Bacon, Richard of Stepney, Mddx., seaman of merchant ship *Thomas & Richard* bound for VA. Will 18 Aug. 1686 pr. 12 Dec. 1687 by William Chalke. (PROB11/389). AWP.

Bailey, Richard of Stoughton, MA, yeoman. Will pr. 7 Nov. 1736 by son Henry Bailey. (PROB11/1147).

Baillie, William Esq., Captain in 60th Regiment of Foot in North America. Letter dated QC 8 Oct. 1759 from William Baillie to Miss Sally Grant at Inverness, Scotland containing personal news and informing her that he has been wounded in the arm off "Sandy Shaw" and was afraid that it would have to be cut off but the danger is now over. Deposition of 1 Nov. 1764 by Sally Grant, spinster of Inverness, and William Chisholm of Inverness, surgeon, that they well know Baillie's handwriting and that the letter [to rank as a will] is his. AWW 14 Nov. 1764. granted to the aunt and only next-of-kin Anne Grant, widow. (PROB11/903).

Bailey, William Hyde of Southfield, Richmond Co., NY. Will pr. 24 May 1850 by relict Ann Taylor. (PROB11/2112).

Baird, Archibald of SC, planter. AWW 11 Mar. 1788 to William Greenwood. (PROB11/1163).

Baker, John of Stepney, Mddx., mariner who died in New England. Will 2 Nov. 1675 pr. 22 Oct. 1678 by relict Sarah Baker. (PROB11/358). AWP.

Baker, John of Fairlight, Sussex, who died in East NJ and having estate there. Will pr. 30 Jun. 1709 by brother Joseph Wakeham. (PROB11/509). AWP.

Baker, John of Bristol and late of Charles Town, SC, merchant. Will 9 Oct. 1734 pr. 23 Jan. 1736 by son Stephen Baker. (PROB11/681). AWP.

Baker, Nicholas of St. George's, MD, widower. Will 28 Feb. 1753 AWW 7 Jan. 1766 to sister Elizabeth Pell. (PROB11/915). AWP.

Baker, Richard of Chalfont St. Giles, Bucks., yeoman, who had lands in PA and NJ. Will 6 Feb. 1695 pr. 18 Nov. 1697 by daughter Rebecca Baker. (PROB11/441). AWP.

Baker, Thomas, formerly of Purbeck, Dorset, mariner, but late master of the *Elizabeth* who died in VA. Will 16 May 1693 pr. 19 Aug. 1698 by sister Mary Bennett *alias* Baker. (PROB11/447). AWP.

Bakewell, Thomas of York, [ON], gent. Will pr. 7 Mar. 1850. (PROB11/2109).

Balfoure, William of London, surgeon, who died in VA. Will 2 Apr 1685 pr. 1 Sep. 1686 by Alexander Blair. (PROB11/384). AWP.

Balgay, Frances of St. Paul, Covent Garden, Mddx., widow, whose relations John Gordon, John Ancrum and Parker Quince of Charleston, SC, sued her executors. Will pr. 31 Mar. 1763 by William Thompson and William Frankcombe. (PROB11/885). AWP. NGSQ 65/142. Further grant in 1774.

Ball, Ingram of Cape Breton Island. Will pr. 23 Jan. 1808. (PROB11/1472).

Ballaine, John of Arichat, Cape Breton Island, merchant. Will pr. 25 Nov. 1813. (PROB11/1549).

Ballett, John Esq. of Charles Town, SC, commander of HM sloop *Otter*. Will dated 28 May 1749 leaves his whole estate to his wife Mary Ballett, now in Great Britain, and appoints her with Robert Shields and Richard Stow as executors. Witnessed by Ben Lloyd, Joseph Lloyd and Charles Royse. Pr. by Mary Ballett 30 Aug. 1750. (PROB11/781).

Ballew, Abraham of merchant ship *Robert* who died in VA. Will 28 Jan. 1704 pr. 17 Jan. 1709 by relict Mary Ballew. (PROB11/506). AWP.

Bamber, William of Bermondsey, Sy., shipwright of *Five Sisters* who died in NY on the merchant ship *Bugill*, bachelor. Will 1 Apr. 1729 pr. 20 Dec. 1731 by Thomas Scott. (PROB11/648). AWP.

Banks, William of Halifax, NS, Capt. in Col. Warburton's Regiment. Will pr. 6 Dec. 1752. (PROB11/798).

Bannatyne, Francis of New Providence, NJ. Will dated 8 Aug. 1760 witnessed by G. Williams, Robert Burton Tucker and William Rose with bequests to his brother Robert Bannatyne in the East Indies, his sister Agdalon, wife of Cuthbert Stewart of Glasgow, and his brother William Bannatyne, officer in Gibraltar. His estate in the Bahamas is to be sold. Pr. 14 Feb. 1765 by Alexander Rose of Charles Town, SC, merchant, with similar powers reserved to Archibald Johnston of Charles Town, gent. (PROB11/905).

Barber, Ann of Prince George's Co., MD. Will pr. 26 Jul. 1831. (PROB11/1787).

Barbot, James of St. Margaret Westminster, Mddx., merchant who died in MD. Will 20 Mar 1703 pr. 27 Apr. 1719 by relict Mary Barbot, the brother John Barbot having died. (PROB11/568). AWP.

Barclay, John of NYC, mariner of HMS *Emerald*. Will pr. 7 Jul. 1779 by relict Ann, now wife of James Thain. (PROB11/1054).

Barclay, Thomas of NYC, HM Consul-General for Eastern States of America. AWW to John Brodribb Bergne 31 May 1831. (PROB11/1785).

Barclay, Thomas of NYC. Will 12 Nov. 1831. Leg: wife Catharine Smith Barclay; children Thomas, Walter Channing, Nancy, Henry Hothham and Cuthbert Collingwood Barclay. Wits. in NY: William H. Maxwell of 70 Liberty St., A.S. Robertson of 97 Liberty St., John Newland of 70 Liberty St., and Hugh Swinton Ball. Pr. 9 Aug. 1838 by Gerard Stuyvesant and Morris Robinson. (PROB11/1899).

Barham, Anthony of Mulberry Island, VA, gent. Will pr. 13 Sep. 1631 by Edward Major and William Butler. (PROB11/187). ACE.GGE.

Barker, Robert of London, merchant, late Collector of Customs in Burlington, NJ. Will 4 Apr. 1730 AWW 20 Dec. 1735 to sister Mary Hurdd. (PROB11/674). AWP.

Barlow, Samuel of Deptford, Kent, mariner of HMS *Montague* and late of HMS *Shoreham* who died in VA. Will 1 Mar. 1694 pr. 4 Jun. 1716 by relict Elizabeth Barlow. (PROB11/552). AWP.

Barnard, Anna of Hendon, Mddx., widow, whose sister was wife of Job Goodson of PA. Will 2 Sep. 1739 pr. 20 Nov. 1741 by William Dolley. (PROB11/713). AWP.

Barnes, John of Christ Church, Sy., dyer, who died in GA, widower. Will 15 Jun. 1733 pr. 21 Oct 1740 by William Graves. (PROB11/704). AWP.

Barnes *alias* **Lovell, John** of Placentia Island, NL. Will pr. 17 Aug., 1816. (PROB11/1583).

Barnes, Mary of Trenton, NJ, widow. Will pr. 21 Jun. 1808. (PROB11/1480).

Barnes, Thomas of HMS *Rose* who died near New England. Will 8 Apr. 1687 AWW 1 Nov. 1690 to Susan Harvison. (PROB11/402). AWP.

Barnett, Moses *alias* **Morris** of Montreal, gent. Will pr. 7 May 1857. (PROB11/2250).

Barnier, Pierre, formerly of Westminster, Mddx. but late of Philadelphia, bachelor. AWW 7 Jun. 1770 to mother Ann Barnier. (PROB11/958). AWP.

Barnsley, Thomas Esq. of Bensalem, Bucks Co., PA, Capt. in 60th Royal American Regiment of Foot. Will pr. 7 Sep. 1774 by solemn affirmation of William Redman and Gilbert Hicks. (PROB11/1001). AWP.

Barrell, Theodore of Saugerties, Ulster Co., NY. AWW 31 Aug. 1847 to Thomas Boosey. (PROB11/2060).

Barrett, William of Philadelphia, [aboard the *Venus*]. Will 15 Oct. 1790. Leg: sister Mary Barrett and friend John West. Wit: George Noble, J. Rolfe and John Brookes, surgeon of the *Venus*. Pr. 3 Feb. 1791 by John West. (PROB11/1201). NGSQ 63/42.

Barrie, Robert of St. Augustine, E. FL, assistant surgeon who died at sea on passage to England. Will 3 Apr. 1775 pr. 12 Aug. 1775 by relict Dorothy Barrie of St. Martin in Fields, Mddx.. (PROB11/1010). AWP.

Barry, Thomas of NL, servant. Will pr. 30 Apr. 1822. (PROB11/1655).

Barton, Phoebe of St. John's, NL, widow. Will pr. 5 Jan. 1803. (PROB11/1385).

Barton, Thomas of Berkeley Co., SC. Will 29 Jan. 1732 AWW 17 Jan. 1735 to Samuel Wragg, attorney for sons William and John Barton in SC. (PROB11/669). AWP.

Barton, William, mariner of HMS *Play*, who had [unnamed] children in PA. AWW 26 Jun. 1697 to John Bunce. (PROB11/440). AWP.

Battersby, Joseph of Charlestown, SC, merchant. Will pr. 6 Dec. 1854. (PROB11/2201).

Bayard, Samuel of NY, now purser of HMS *Mermaid*. Will dated 23 Apr. 1746 leaves his estate to his brothers William and Robert Bayard and appoints Richard Joneway of London, merchant, as executor. Witnesses Ann King and Martha Webber. Pr. by Richard Joneway 3 Aug. 1749. (PROB11/772).

Bayard, Samuel Vetch of Wilmot, Annapolis Co., NS. Will of 21 Mar. 1828 appoints as executrix his wife Sarah Bayard. Witnessed by William Holland, Abel Wheelock and Samuel

Wheelock. AWW granted 23 Nov. 1849 to Boulter Johnston, attorney of the relict Sarah Bayard and [sons] Robert and Samuel Bayard now in St. John, NB. (PROB10/2102).

Bayley, Barnard of Eastchester, Westchester Co., NY. Will pr. 3 Jun. 1833 by Edward Dry. (PROB11/1817).

Bayley, John of Philadelphia, mariner of HMS *Jersey*. Will 18 Oct. 1746 pr. 29 Oct. 1748 by Hugh Hagan. (PROB11/765). AWP.

Bayliff, Featherston of Frederica, GA, surgeon at Charles Town, SC. Will 14 Jun. 1748 AWW 5 Sep. 1750 to James McKay. (PROB11/782). AWP.

Beachamp, William of Bareneed, Conception Bay, NL, planter. Leg: William Henry Lacely; nephew John Beachamp. Execs: Thomas Bartlett Sr. and George Heath, both of Bareneed. Wit: Jacob Bishop and George Heath. AWW 4 Sep. 1847 to Henry Frederick Holt, attorney for Thomas Bartlett Sr. and George Heath. (PROB11/2061).

Beadle, Robert of Salem, MA, but late of London, mariner. Will 23 Mar. 1708 pr. 19 Sep. 1710 by Joanna Mann of Bermondsey, Sy., widow. (PROB11/517). AWP.

Beadon, Solomon of Twillingate, NL, merchant. Will pr. 31 Dec. 1834. (PROB11/1839).

Bealey, Thomas of NYC, mariner. Will 16 Dec. 1780. Leg: wife and sole exex. Sarah Bealey. Wit: William Durie and Charles Hart. Pr. 11 Oct. 1791 by relict Sarah Bealey. (PROB11/1209).

Beardsley, Martha. *See* **Rattry.**

Beaumont, Jacob of NY, late of HMS *Launceston* and *Chester* but after to *Mermaid*, mariner. Will pr. 8 Dec. 1848. (PROB11/766).

Beckwith, formerly Loughnan, Mrs. Clementina of Montreal. Will pr. 19 Jul. 1816. (PROB11/1582).

Bedon, Stephen of Charles Town, SC, but late of St. Clement Danes and Chelsea, Mddx. Will 20 May 1750 pr. 10 Feb. by cousin George Bedon. (PROB11/792). AWP.

Beckwith, Henry Ferdinand, of Kingston, [ON], officer in Rifle Brigade. Will pr. 10 Sep. 1847. (PROB11/2061).

Beckwith, John of Halifax, NS. Will pr. 21 Jun. 1820. (PROB11/1630).

Bedford, John of Goderich, Huron District, [ON], gent. Will pr. 4 Nov. 1850. (PROB11/2121).

Bedingfield, Thomas, gent. of Dorking, Sy., whose nephew Thomas Bedingfield Hands was in MD. Will 17 Nov. 1739 pr. 25 Feb. 1743 by niece Ann Le Counte. (PROB11/723). AWP.

Beekman, Gerard G. of Mount Pleasant, Westchester Co., NY. AWW 15 Nov. 1823 to Gabriel Shaw. (PROB11/1677).

Beere, Richard, late of Ballynahow, Co. Tipperary, Ireland, but late of Charleston, SC, reduced Ensign in Regiment of York Light Infantry. Will 31 Aug. 1821. Leg: brother Piercy Beere of Ballynahow. Execs: Rev. Henry Palmer and Lester Battersby of Caher, Co. Tipperary. Wit: Lewis Roux, John C. Duke, and Richard Maynard, all of Charleston. AWW 2 Apr. 1822 to Piercy Beere. (PROB11/1655).

Beesley, Samuel of Bristol, merchant, who died in VA. Will 13 Jun. 1726 pr. 3 Sep. 1727 by affirmation of brother William Beesley of Worcester. (PROB11/617). AWP.

Belisario, Henry Mendes of Baltimore. Will pr. 20 Jun. 1855. (PROB11/2213).

Bell, David of St. Giles in Fields, Mddx., surgeon, who died in Albany Fort, [Hudson's Bay]. Will 25 Apr. 1702 pr. 26 Jan. 1713 by relict Elizabeth Bell. (PROB11/531). AWP.

Bell, John of Newport, RI, purser of HMS *Apollo*. AWW 5 Feb. 1780 to William Roberts. (PROB11/1061).

Bell, William of Norfolk, VA, mariner. Will pr. 16 Mar. 1795 by relict Rebecca Bell and brother Henry Bell. (PROB11/1257).

Benger, John of Ferryland, NL. Will pr. 29 Jan. 1793. (PROB11/1227).

Bennett, Edmond of Boston, MA, cook of HMS *Squirrel*. Will 2 Jan. 1736 pr. 5 Oct. 1743 by Edward Westall. (PROB11/729). AWP.

Bennett, Elisha of Rumney Marsh, MA. Will 9 Apr. 1726 AWW 30 May 1727 to Henry Palmer, attorney for relict Dorothy Bennett in Rumney Marsh. (PROB11/615). AWP. Further grant in 1724.

Bennet, James of the transport ship *James* who died in NY Hospital, bachelor. Will 7 Mar. 1760 pr. 3 Apr. 1761 by John Oswald of Shadwell, Mddx., rigger. (PROB11/864). AWP.

Bennett, John of St. Gabriel, Fenchurch Street, London, merchant who had estate in MD. Will 12 Apr. 1698 pr. 14 May 1698 by mother Margery Jones. (PROB11/445). AWP.

Bennet, John of Wappoo Creek near Charles Town, SC on HM galley *Cornwallis* but late of St. George in the East, London. Wit: John Johnson and Thomas Richardson of Charleston. Will 1 Jul. 1782 pr. 25 Feb. 1783 by sole executrix and legatee Maria Hyne. (PROB11/1100).

Bennett, Richard of Nansemond River, VA. Will pr. 3 Aug. 1676 by James Joffey. (PROB11/351). GGE.

Bennett, Richard of Queen Anne Co., MD. Will 25 Sep. 1749 AWW 22 Aug. 1750 to John Hanbury and William Anderson, attorneys for cousin Edward Lloyd in MD. (PROB11/781). AWP.

Bennett, Robert of Charleston, SC. Will pr. 24 May 1817 by Benjamin Burton Johnson. (PROB11/1592).

Bennett, Thomas of NL. Will pr. 24 Dec. 1821. (PROB11/1650).

Benson, William John Chapman of QC, merchant. Will pr. 10 Jan. 1851. (PROB11/2125).

Beresford, Henry Tristram of Canada, Capt. in 71st Regiment of Foot. Will pr. 7 Sep. 1842. (PROB11/1967).

Berry, John of NYC, merchant. Will pr. 1 Jun. 1795 by Edward Cox. (PROB11/1261).

Berthon, Isaac, born at Chatellerault, [France] on 6 Aug. 1663 but late in London whose cousin Michael Berthon was in NY. Will 12 May 1746 pr. 2 May 1747 by Claude Aubert, Elias Le Clerc, Stephen Galhie and Francis Ribot. (PROB11/754). AWP.

Bessill, William of Southampton, Hants., and Westminster, Mddx., mariner who died in VA. Will 9 Jan 1707 pr. 17 Sep. 1713 by relict Mary Bessill. (PROB11/535).

Best, Ven. George of Fredericton, York Co., NB. Will pr. 3 Feb. 1830. (PROB11/1766).

Best, George of Newark, NJ. Will pr. 26 May 1842 by relict Mary Best and Thomas Colpitts Granger. (PROB11/1962).

Best *alias* May, Thomas of Trinity Island, NL, joiner. Will pr. 22 Jan. 1813. (PROB 11/1540).

Bethune, George of Cambridge, MA. Will pr. 22 Jul. 1785 by nephew Samuel Prince. (PROB11/1131).

Bethune, Rev. John of Williamstown, Charlottenburg, Glengarry Co., [ON]. Will pr. 15 Mar. 1816. (PROB11/1578).

Bevis, William of Topsham, Dev., mariner, master of the ship *Hope*, who died in VA. Will 7 Oct. 1715 pr. 26 Mar 1717 by relict Margaret Bevis. (PROB11/557). AWP.

Bew, Rigault of Ware, VA, planter who died in St. Giles Cripplegate, London, bachelor. Will 30 Dec. 1696 pr. 29 Jun. 1698 by Samuel Dawson. (PROB11/446). AWP.

Bickley, Benjamin of St. John's, NL. Will pr. 20 Apr. 1801. (PROB11/1356).

Bicknell, William of Annapolis, MD, master sailmaker of HMS *Richmond*. Will 19 Jan. 1764 pr. 22 Jun. 1764 by brother Andrew Bicknell of Yeovil, Somerset. (PROB11/899). AWP.

Biggs, Richard of West & Sherley Hundred, VA. AWW 9 Aug. 1626. (PROB11/149). ACE.VGE.

Billings, William, surgeon of HMS *Eolus* who died in Pensacola, W. FL. Will 28 Mar. 1764 pr. 2 Jun. 1767 by uncle George Billings. (PROB11/929). AWP.

Billop, Christopher, prisoner in Fleet Prison, London, gent., who had a plantation in Bentley Manor *(now Tottenville)* and other estate in Staten Island, NY. Will 25 Apr. 1724 pr. 24 Apr. 1725 by James Fittar and nephew Thomas Billop. (PROB11/602). AWP.

Billopp, Christopher of St. John, NB. Will pr. 23 Oct. 1827. (PROB11/1731).

Binney, Hon. Hibbert Newton of Halifax, NS. Will pr. 21 Oct. 1842. (PROB11/1969).

Birch, Chamberlain of Augusta, Richmond Co., GA. AWW 10 Jan. 1799 to relict Elizabeth Birch. (PROB11/1317).

Birch, Elizabeth, widow of Mathew Birch of PA deceased. Will 26 Nov.1700 pr. 29 Jan. 1701 by daughter Alice Birch. (PROB11/459). AWP.

Bird, Henry, Captain in Army of North America. Will pr. 6 Nov. 1800. (PROB11/1349).

Bird, James of Red River Settlement, Chief Factor of Hudson's Bay Co. 16 Feb. 1857. (PROB11/2245).

Bird, John of North America. Capt. in Army. Will pr. 6 Nov. 1800. (PROB11/1349).

Byrd, Mary of Westover, VA, widow. AWW 20 Sep. 1819 to William Byrd Page. (PROB11/1620).

Bird, Thomas of NYC who died at sea. AWW 12 Oct. 1808 to father William Bird. (PROB11/1486).

Birkett, Henry of IL, bachelor. Will pr. 16 Mar. 1826. (PROB11/1709).

Birston, Magnus of Red River Colony, Rupertsland, Hudson's Bay. Will pr. 22 Jan. 1838. (PROB11/1889).

Bisaker, Ambrose, corporal in 22nd Regiment who died in W. FL, bachelor. Will 3 Feb. 1765 pr. 13 Jun. 1766 by William Chipman. (PROB11/919). AWP.

Bishop, Nathaniel, Master of Prince of Wales Fort, Churchill River, Hudson's Bay. Will pr. 15 Oct. 1723. (PROB11/593).

Bishop, Thomas of Halifax, NS, Ensign in Maj. Gen. Laseulle's Regiment. Will pr. 17 Sep. 1756. (PROB11/824).

Bisuchet, Francois of Rue Dauphine, New Orleans, LA. Will 23 Nov. 1846 accompanied by autobiographical note: *I am aged 40, a native of Charin near Neufchatel, Switzerland. I was born on 3rd August 1807, the lawful son of Daniel Bisuchet and Mrs. Charlotte Amelis. The latter died in Aubonne, Canton Vaud. I am married to Miss Frederike Heinert who is now living with me but we have no issue.* Leg: wife Frederike Bisuchet who is to be exex. Wit: Ferdinand Humm, T. Burberet and R. C. Trust. AWW 12 Sep. 1849 to Philip Walther attorney for exex. (PROB11/2099).

Bize, Hercules Daniel of Newark, NJ. Will pr. 3 May 1800 by Anthony Bordenave. (PROB11/1341).

Blaau, Waldron of NYC. AWW 19 Nov. 1787 to Charles Cooke. (PROB11/1158).

Black, Catharine of Halifax, NS, widow. Will pr. 22 Jan. 1841. (PROB11/1939).

Black, James of Port Colborne, Humberstone Township, Niagara, [ON]. Will pr. 13 Dec. 1845. (PROB11/2027).

Black, John of Aberdeen, Scotland but late of St. John, NB, merchant. Will dated Stanayan(?) 24 Jul. 1835. Leg: adopted children born in North West or Indian Country named George now in Scotland and Ramloops born in Thompson's River, Columbia; three adopted females, Jean married to George Ballandyn of Red River, Elinora residing in Canada with her mother Mrs. Robert Henery, and one born in Thompson's River; mother Mary Black to have my real estate during her life and then to sisters Ann McCombie and Mary Ros, both in Aberdeen. Wit: Peter Skeen Ogden and Alexander C. Anderson. Pr. 13 Jun 1843. (PROB11/1683). Further grant 16 Apr. 1851.

Black, Samuel of Columbia River, [OR]. Will pr. 13 Jun. 1843. (PROB11/1980).

Blackalar, Philip of New England, mariner of *Ruby*. Will 26 Aug. 1708 pr 3 Feb. 1709 by relict Mary Blackalar. (PROB11/506). AWP.

Blackburn, Job of St. Clement Danes, Mddx., coal merchant, whose nephew John Richardson was resident in Charleston, SC. Will 24 Jan. 1775 pr. 24 Apr. 1775 by William Harding of Teston, Kent, yeoman, and John Maides of Lambeth, Sy., yeoman. (PROB11/1006). AWP. NGSQ 65/144.

Blackburn, William of Kemptville, Johnstown District, [ON]. Will pr. 30 Jun. 1842. (PROB11/1963).

Blacklock, Christopher of Boston, MA, mariner of HMS *Mermaid* at Nantucket. Will 23 Feb. 1747 AWW 1 Dec. 1750 to John Coles, attorney for relict Ruth Blacklock in Boston. (PROB11/784). AWP.

Blackmore, Arthur of St. Gregory, citizen and painter stainer of London, whose daughter Susan married Capt. William Corker of VA, surgeon. Will 7 Dec. 1663 pr. 31 Mar. 1664 by relict Elizabeth Blackmore. (PROB11/313). AWP.

Blackstone, Henry, Coroner of QC. Will pr. 22 Mar. 1827. (PROB11/1722).

Blair, John of Montreal, Lieut. in 15th Regiment of Foot. Will pr. 8 Oct. 1833. (PROB11/1822).

Blake, Charles of MD. Will 24 Aug. 1723 pr.14 Jan. 1734 by the son Philemon Blake with similar powers reserved to the son John Blake. (PROB11/663). AWP.

Blake, Joseph of Berkeley Co., SC., who died on the ship *Wilmington*, widower. Will 18 Dec. 1750 pr. 20 Feb. 1752 by son Daniel Blake. (PROB11/792). AWP.

Blake, Philemon Charles of Queen Anne Co., MD. Will 13 Jan. 1753 AWW 3 May 1766 to William Anderson, attorney for relict Sarah Blake in MD. (PROB11/918). AWP.

Blanchard, William of Louisville, KY. Will pr. 25 Aug. 1840. (PROB11/1932).

Bland, John of NL. Will pr. 19 Apr. 1826. (PROB11/1710).

Bland, Thomas of London, merchant who had lands in Anne Arundell Co., MD. Will 25 Jan. 1700 pr. 13 Jan 1701 by cousin Sarah Pendrill. (PROB11/459). AWP.

Blandford, Thomas of Battle Harbour, Labrador. Will pr. 26 Dec. 1833. (PROB11/1824).

Blowers, Hon. Sampson Salter, Chief Justice of NS. Will pr. 3 Mar. 1843. (PROB11/1976).

Bluck, John of Shadwell, Mddx., who died in New England on the ship *Samuel*. Will pr. 7 Feb. 1712 by Amy Bluck, mother and executrix of the named executrix Amy Bluck who died before administering. (PROB11/525). AWP.

Bludder, Thomas of Clewer, Berks., who had relations in VA but "I do not know whether any of them be living, not having heard from any of them these five years." Pr. 16 Mar. 1654 by relict Emma Bludder. (PROB11/240). AWP.

Blunt, Margaret of St. Thomas, Southwark, Surrey, widow, whose sister Mary Welch was in Martin's Hundred, VA. Will pr. 23 Sep. 1659 by cousin Sybilla Levitt. (PROB11/295). AWP.

Bocking, Thomas of London, mariner bound by the *Pilgrim* of London to Barbados and VA. Will 30 Aug. 1655. Leg: William Gayford and Sarah his wife. Pr. 7 Aug 1657 by Sarah Gayford. (PROB11/267).

Boisseau, James Edward of Cape Breton, [NS]. Will pr. 6 Feb. 1794. (PROB11/1241).

Boldry, Philip of Wapping, Mddx., mariner of merchant ship *Patsey* who died in VA, bachelor. Will 1 Feb. 1731 pr. 15 Sep. 1731 by William Greene of Wapping, victualler. (PROB11/646). AWP.

Bolland, William of Eastmain Factory, Hudson's Bay. Will pr. 11 Dec. 1804. (PROB11/1418).

Bond, Barnet of Limehouse, Mddx., but late of MD, mariner. Will 25 Jan. 1742 pr. 20 Apr. 1749 by relict Alice, now wife of William Grimes. (PROB11/769). AWP. NGSQ 62/275.

Bond, Stephen of SC, mariner. Will dated 20 Feb. 1737. Estate to go to Penelope Edgly including wages due for service in HMS *Seaforth* now in Charles Town Harbour [MA], a messuage in Neston parish and one in Westchester [NY], as well as any estate in England, and she is to be sole exex. Commission of 3 Apr. 1740 to Alexander Dingwall to act as attorney for Penelope Edgly. (PROB11/701).

Bonnell, Isaac of Digby, Annapolis Co., NS. Will pr. 4 Oct. 1808. (PROB11/1486).

Bonnifield, Abraham of Reading, Berks, distiller, who had lands in PA. Will 16 Jul. 1701 pr. 15 Apr. 1701 by affirmation of son Abraham Bonnifield. (PROB11/464). AWP.

Bonnycastle, Sir Richard Henry of Kingston, [ON], Capt in Royal Engineers. Will pr. 17 Mar. 1848. (PROB11/2070).

Booth, John of Stepney, Mddx., mariner who died on ship *Industry* in VA. Will 26 Jan. 1691 pr. 7 Apr. 1694 by relict Sarah Booth. (PROB11/419). AWP.

Bordley, Thomas of Annapolis, MD, who died in Greenwich, Kent. Will 4 Jun. 1747 pr. 19 Sep. 1747 by Martin Smith of London, haberdasher. (PROB11/756). AWP.

Borland, Francis Esq. of Boston, MA. Will 7 Mar. 1763 AWW 20 Oct. 1768 to William Mills, Edward Brice and Edward Wheeler, attorneys for son John Borland and relict Phebe Borland in Boston. (PROB11/942). AWL.

Borradale, George Aris Tilden of Montreal. Will pr. 4 Mar. 1802. (PROB11/1371).

Boswell, Walter of Cobourg, Northumberland, [ON]. Will pr. 21 Oct. 1850. (PROB11/2120).

Botetourt, Lord Norborne, of Stoke, Glos., but late of VA. Will 26 Jul. 1766 pr. 10 Jan. 1771 by Henry, Duke of Beaufort. (PROB11/963). AWP.

Bouquet, Henry Esq., Brig. Gen. of HM Forces and Lieut. Col. of Royal American Regt. who died in North America. Will dated Philadelphia 25 Jun 1765 pr. 13 Nov. 1766 by Col. Frederick Haldimand. (PROB11/923). AWP.

Bourchier, William of Canada, Commander in Royal Navy. Will pr. 26 Jan. 1848. (PROB11/2067).

Bourne, George Stuart of NYC, Capt. in Coldstream Regiment of Foot Guards. Will pr. 15 Jan. 1777 by Goalston Bruere. (PROB11/1027).

Bourne, Thomas, citizen and grocer of London who died in MD. Will 4 Aug. 1703 AWW 2 Oct. 1711 by solemn oath to Benjamin Bourne. (PROB11/523). AWP.

Boustead, James of Northern Liberties, Philadelphia, tanner and currier. Will pr. 29 Mar. 1852 by son John Boustead. (PROB11/2148).

Bowen, Goodin of Mount Pleasant near Wilmington, Cape Fear, NC. Will pr. 8 Nov. 1799 by John Younger. (PROB11/1332).

Bowen, Sarah of Bladon Co., NC, widow. AWW 26 Feb. 1793 to son Goodin Bowen. (PROB11/1228).

Bower, Joseph of Harbour Grace, NL. Will pr. 24 Apr. 1793. (PROB11/1230).

Bowers *alias* Bower, William of Bay de Verds, NL, carpenter. Will pr. 23 Nov. 1742. (PROB11/721).

Bowes, Maria. *See* **Johnson.**

Bowker, James of St. Peter's parish, New Kent Co., VA. AWW 17 Nov. 1704 to Micajah Perry. (PROB11/479). AWP.

Bowles, James of St. Mary's Co., MD, merchant. Will 13 Jun. 1727 pr. 23 Jun. 1729 by the relict Rebecca Bowles. (PROB11/630). AWP.

Bowles, Tobias of Chelsea, London, merchant, whose niece Thomazine Bowles was in VA. Will pr. 3 Jul. 1727 by Henry Alexander Primrose and John Underdowne. (PROB11/616). AWP. NGSQ 62/36.

Bowles, Tobias of St. Philip's, SC. AWW 4 Oct. 1811 to John Stevens. (PROB11/1526).

Bowring, Charles of Norfolk, VA. Will pr. 22 May 1824. (PROB11/1685).

Bowyer, William of NYC but formerly of Jamaica, merchant. Will 15 Jan. 1706 pr. 30 May 1707 by William Turner. (PROB11/494). AWP.

Boylston, Ward Nicholas of Princeton, Worcester Co., MA. AWW 17 Jul. 1828 to Petty Vaughan. (PROB11/1742 & 1743).

Boys, William of Cranbrook, Kent, clothier, part of whose lands in Cranbrook belonged to John Stow, son of Thomas Stow in New England. Will 14 Aug. 1656 pr. 24 Feb. 1657 by the relict Joane Boys. (PROB11/262). AWP.

Brabazon, Edward of Bath, Som., but late of NYC, Capt. in 22nd Regiment of Infantry. Will 24 Feb. 1781. Leg: sisters Elizabeth Brabazon and Arabella Brabazon alias Ronan, wife of George Ronan of Wicklow, Ireland; elder sister Juliana Brabazon alias Hughes; William Brabazon in Co. Louth, Ireland. AWW 29 Jul. 1789 to sisters Elizabeth and Arabella. (PROB11/1181).

Brace, Robert of St. Botolph Bishopsgate, London, cooper, bound on the *Samuel* of Newcastle in the service of the company of merchants trading to VA. Leg: mother Anne Poole, wife of John Poole of St. Botolph Bishopsgate, citizen and merchant tailor of London, to be sole attorney and exex. Wit: Christopher Mayott and John Warner. Will pr. 40 Jun. 1628 by Anne Poole. (Guildhall: Ms 9171/25/247).

Braddock, Edward Esq., Maj. General of HM Forces of expedition fitting out for America. Will 25 Nov1754 pr. 3 Sep. 1755 by John Calcraft. (PROB11/817). AWP.

Bradley, Edward of Philadelphia, glazier. Will 22 Mar. 1743 pr. 8 Nov. 1746 by nephew Edward Shepherd . (PROB11/750). AWP.

Bradley, Lewis of SC, mariner of HM sloop *Happy*. Will 4 Jul. 1734 AWW 27 Aug. 1735 to John Bryan and Paul Debell, attorneys for John Owen of Charles Town, SC, tailor, and William Mallard.. (PROB11/672). AWP.

Bradstreet, John, Lieut. Governor of H.M. Garrison of St. John's, NL. Will pr. 21 Nov. 1774. (PROB11/1002).

Bragg, Mary of Grand Bank, NL, widow. Will pr. 31 Jul. 1832. (PROB11/1802).

Brailsford, Edward of SC. Will 24 Mar. 1730 AWW 21 Apr. 1733 to Samuel Wragg. (PROB11/658). AWP. New grant 25 May 1762.

Braine, John of Wapping, Mddx., merchant who had lands in NJ. Will 12 May 1699 pr. 3 Jan. 1700 to brother James Braine and Roger Newham. (PROB11/454).

Brake, Ralph of Bay of Islands, NL, planter. Will 5 Aug. 1838. Leg: sons John Matthews Brake, Joseph Matthews Brake, Robert Matthews Brake, Ralph Matthews Brake, William Matthews Brake, Thomas Matthews Brake, James Matthews Brake, Edward Matthews Brake; daughters Elizabeth Matthews wife of Thomas Pay of Bay of Islands, and Jane Matthews wife of William Whorior of Bay of Islands. Exec: William Blanchard of Bay of Islands and Joseph Bird of East Orchard, Dorset. AWW 13 Feb. 1844 to Thomas Street Bird, attorney for son Edward Matthews Brake. (PROB11/1992). Further grant 21 Dec. 1866.

Bramble, James of Elizabeth River, America, now of HMS *Lowestoffe*. Will dated 16 Apr. 1741 appoints Thomas Stocker of Littlehampton parish near Arundel, Sussex, [England], as universal legatee and sole executor. Witnessed by John Coatsworth and John Dimend. Pr. 8 Aug. 1741 by Thomas Stocker. (PROB11/711).

Brathwaite, John Esq. of SC. Will dated 1 Apr. 1740. To his mother Mrs. Silvester Brathwaite of Dover, widow, £20 for mourning and £40 a year during her life. £1,000 to his wife [Silvia Brathwaite]. Other bequests to: his nephew Thomas Brathwaite and, if he does not get his grandfather's estate, £20 when he is 21; £20 to the daughter of Mrs. Hannah Ives when she is 21. The testator's estate in England is in the hands of Edward Jasper Esq. of Tower Hill, London, and that in Carolina in the hands of Benjamin Whittaker Esq., Chief Justice, and George Austin, merchant. Executors to be the testator's wife, Mrs. Margaret Pultney, widow of Daniel Pultney, Elizabeth Tichborne, sister of Mrs. Pultney, and Thomas Revell, M.P. Witnessed by Peter Colleton and J. Colleton. Pr. 27 Aug. 1740 by the relict Silvia Brathwaite and Elizabeth Tichborne, spinster. (PROB11/704). AWP.

Bray, Josias of Otonabee, Colborne District, [ON], Capt. in Royal Navy. Will pr. 22 Aug. 1846. (PROB11/2040).

Breach, George of QC, soldier under Capt. Lewis Kirke. Will pr. 20 Oct. 1631. (PROB11/160).

Brecken, John of Charlotte Town, PE, gent. Will pr. 28 Mar. 1827. (PROB11/1722).

Bremner, Ann of Halifax, NS. Will pr. 5 Sep. 1810. (PROB11/1515).

Bressey, John of St. Clement Danes, Mddx. gent., who died in MD, bachelor. Will 30 Jun. 1717 pr. 26 Apr. 1723 by Ellinor Lloyd. (PROB11/590). AWP.

Brewen, Hubbard of MD, merchant late in London. Will 31 May 1755 pr. 31 Jul. 1756 by John Philpot of London, merchant. (PROB11/823). AWP.

Brewer, William, of Boston, MA, but late of Titchfield, Hants., mariner. Will pr. 23 Mar. 1747 by Clement Walcot of Titchfield. (PROB11/753). AWP.

Breynton, Rev. John, Rector of St. Paul's, Halifax, NS. Will pr. 31 Jul. 1799. (PROB11/1326).

Brickell *alias* Brickland, Thomas of NY, mariner of HMS *Centaur* and HMS *Hampshire*. Will dated 10 Dec. 1754 witnessed by Thomas Chadwick and Thomas Walls. AWW granted 2 Mar. 1767 to Peter Berton, attorney for the relict Margaret Brickell, widow, now resident in NY. (PROB11/926).

Brickland, Thomas. *See* **Brickell.**

Brickleton, Edward of NS, mariner of HMS *Kinsale*. Will pr. 14 Jun. 1758. (PROB11/838).

Bridgen, Thomas of Sussex Co., NJ. AWW 6 May 1817 to Edward Winwood. (PROB11/1592).

Bridges, Robert, Capt. of King's or 8ᵗʰ Regiment of QC. Will pr. Will pr. 30 Nov. 1775. (PROB11/1012).

Brien, David of NL. Will pr. 22 Jul. 1808. (PROB11/1482).

Brinley, Francis Esq. of Boston, MA. Will 19 Oct. 1719 pr. 1 Jul. 1721 by grandson Francis Brinley. (PROB11/580). AWP.

Brinley, George of Halifax, NS, Commissary and Storekeeper-General. Will pr. 3 Oct. 1809. (PROB11/1503).

Brinley, Mary of Halifax, NS, widow. Will pr. 20 Dec. 1823. (PROB11/1578).

Britton, Robert of QC, master. Will pr. 1 Sep. 1767. (PROB11/932).

Broadhurst, John Jr. of London, factor but late of VA. Will 13 Sep. 1699 pr. 4 Dec. 1701 by relict Elizabeth Broadhurst. (PROB11/462). AWP.

Broadrick, Andrew of St. John's, NL, merchant. Will pr. 11 May 1785. (PROB11/1129).

Brocas, Thomas of Westminster, Mddx., surgeon, but late of Littleton, MA. Will 2 Apr. 1748 pr. 26 Jul. 1751 by Christopher Kilby of Spring Gardens, Mddx. (PROB11/788). AWP.

Bromfield, Thomas of Boston, MA, merchant. AWW 14 Sep. 1787 to Gilbert Harrison, John Ansley and George Bainbridge. (PROB11/1156).

Brook, John of [Trinity] Bay, NL, planter. Will pr. 21 Aug. 1834. (PROB11/1835).

Brooke, Paulin of York River, VA, bachelor. Will 4 Jul. 1746 pr. 15 Feb. 1748 by William Watts. (PROB11/759). AWP.

Brooker, Joanna of Boston, MA, widow. Will 11 May 1759 AWW 11 Aug. 1763 to Edward Pearson, attorney for Silvester Gardiner, Joshua Henshaw and John Winslow, shopkeeper, in Boston. (PROB11/890). AWP.

Brooks, Philip of 22nd Regiment of Foot who died in Mobile, W. FL, bachelor. Will 15 Nov. 1764 AWW 30 Apr. 1766 to Jane Drummon. (PROB11/917). AWP.

Brookes, Samuel of Dorchester, MA, gent. Will 20 Aug. 1757 pr. 25 Oct. 1758 by cousin Henry Norris. (PROB11/840). AWP.

Brookesbancke, Isaac, surgeon of the *Anne* who died at sea on passage to MD. Will 29 Aug. 1674 pr. 4 Aug 1675 by brother William Brookesbancke. (PROB11/348). AWP.

Brooks, Susanna. *See* **Wilson.**

Broome, Thomas of HMS *Dunkirk* bound to Boston, MA. Will 22 May 1693 AWW 5 Jun. 1695 to John Aldred. (PROB11/426). AWP.

Browne, Abraham of Shadwell, Mddx., mariner of the *Margaret* bound to Barbados and VA. Will 2 Oct. 1695. Leg: wife Margaret Browne who is to be exex. Wit: Arthur Beach, Tobias Davidson, John Rutton and Thomas Rutton. Pr. 9 May 1696 by relict Margaret Browne. (Guildhall: Ms 9171/48/99).

Browne, Benjamin of Salem, Essex Co., MA, merchant. Will 8 Nov. 1708 AWW 10 Jan. 1712 to John Ive, attorney for the nephews Samuel and John Browne in New England. (PROB11/525). AWP.

Brown, Francis of Madeira but late of Philadelphia, merchant. Will 29 Jul. 1728 AWW 30 Mar. 1738 to cr. Robert French. (PROB11/688). AWP.

Brown, Henry of Salvage, Bonavista Bay, NL, planter. Leg: wife Hannah Brown; children James, John and William Brown and 3 daughters (unnamed). Execs: John Mifflen of Bonavista Bay, merchant, and Joseph Brown of King's Cove, planter. Wit: Edward Mifflen, Abraham A. Kerman and –iennes R . Mifflen. Will pr. 4 Aug. 1846 by John Mifflen and brother Joseph Brown. (PROB11/2040).

Browne, Rev. Isaac of Annapolis Royal, NS, late chaplain of NY Volunteers at Windsor, NS. AWW 25 Sep. 1789 to David Thomas. (PROB11/1183).

Brown, Isabel of Cincinnati, OH, widow. AWW 27 Jun. 1851 to children Eliza Liddell Brown, Jane Spears Brown and Isabella Livingstone Brown. (PROB11/2134).

Brown, James of Wapping, Mddx, but late of Rotherhithe, Sy., who died on the ship *Champion* in MD. Will 17 Dec. 1724 pr. 28 Sep. 1725 by relict Abigall Brown of Wapping. (PROB11/605). AWP.

Browne, James of Philadelphia, mariner. Will 8 Mar. 1710 AWW 3 Oct. 1749 to William Lea. (PROB11/773). AWP.

Browne, Jonathan of Philadelphia, merchant. Will pr. 7 Oct. 1784 by relict Elizabeth Browne. (PROB11/1122).

Brown, Lancelot of Chester Township, West NJ, yeoman. Will pr. 24 Dec. 1744. (PROB11/736).

Browne, Robert of St. John's, NL, sailmaker. Will pr. 14 Apr. 1784. (PROB11/1115).

Browne, Sarah of Gloucester [City], widow, whose grandchild Sarah, wife of William Barnes, was in New England. Will pr. 17 Dec. 1646 by Gregory Wiltshire. (PROB11/198) GGE & NGSQ 51/115.

Brown, Thomas of NYC, merchant who died in St. Sepulchre, London. Will 19 Mar. 1768 pr. 18 Jul. 1769 by William Hardwick. (PROB11/949). AWP. New grant in Apr. 1779.

Brown, Thomas of VA in HMS *Intrepid* in E. Indies. Will pr. 2 Nov. 1803. (PROB11/1400).

Brown, Thomas of NYC, merchant. Will pr. 18 Jul. 1769. (PROB11/949).

Brown, William of Bonavista Bay, NL. Will pr. 16 Mar. 1776. (PROB11/1017).

Brown, William of Lynchburg, VA. Will pr. 3 Feb. 1815 by parents James and Margaret Brown. (PROB11/1565).

Brown, William of Halifax, NS, seaman of HMS *Narcissus*. Will pr. 1 Sep. 1823. (PROB11/1675).

Brown, William, chief trader of the Hudson's Bay Co. but late of Edinburgh, Scotland. Will 5 Feb. 1826. Leg: natural children Daniel, Elizabeth and Jenny Brown; Josette Bolion; daughter Brown; father [unnamed], etc. Execs: William Smith Esq, Secretary to the Hudson's Bay Co., and Rev. John Roxburgh in Ayrshire. AWW 4 Sep. 1827 to leg. Barbara Muir, spinster, the named execs. renouncing. (PROB11/1730).

Brownjohn, William of NYC, druggist. 14 Jun. 1785. AWW 14 Jun. 1785 to Robert Richard Randall. (PROB11/1130).

Bruce, Benjamin of North Walls, Orkney, but late of Hudson's Bay, widower. Leg: son William Bruce to have house and ground in North Walls; son James Bruce; daughters Margaret, Nancy and Matilda Bruce. Wit: John Stewart McFarlane, Patrick Cunningham and Donald Mackenzie. Affidavit by Peter Pruden chief trader of York Factory, Hudson's Bay, confirming testator's handwriting. AWW 30 Oct. 1826 to son William Bruce. (PROB11/1717).

Bruce, Charles Key of Richmond, NY. Will pr. 3 Apr. 1827 by James McKillop and Joseph Boulderson. (PROB11/1724). NGSQ 61/1.

Bruce, Frances of NYC, widow. AWW 14 Sep. 1821 to John Chambers White and John Scott. (PROB11/1647).

Brush, Ichabod late of Demarara but now of Huntingdon, Long Island, NY. Will 14 Mar. 1808. Leg: sister Fanny, wife of Joseph Tromson; children of brother John Brush named Hannah, Henrietta, Elenor, Fanny and Naomi; children of deceased sister Rebecca Young; wife Euphemia who is to have farm at Huntingdon. Execs: J. Wilkins and Luther Bradish of NYC and Archibald Nelson of London, merchant   Pr. 27 Jul. 1811 by Luther Bradish. (PROB11/1524).

Bruyeres, Ralph Henry of QC, Lieut. Col. of Royal Engineers. Will pr. 8 Sep. 1814. (PROB11/1560).

Bryan, Edward of Clements, Annapolis Co., NS. Will pr. 18 May 1833. (PROB11/1815).

Buchanan, James of Drummondville, Welland, [QC]. Will pr. 16 Feb. 1852. (PROB11/2146).

Buckley, Michael of NYC. Will pr. 24 Aug. 1840 by Jeremiah Shine. (PROB11/1932).

Budd, Elisha of Digby, Annapolis Co., NS. Will pr. 26 Aug. 1814. (PROB11/1559).

Bulkley, James of VA, mariner. Will pr. 7 May 1740. (PROB11/702).

Bulkeley, Hon. Richard of Halifax, NS. Will pr. 22 Apr. 1802. (PROB11/1372).

Bulkeley, Thomas of Montreal, surgeon of 71st Regiment of Highland Light Infantry. Will pr. 29 Sep. 1846. (PROB11/2041).

Bull, Absalom of Savannah, GA, gent. AWW 28 Jul. 1797 to Effingham Lawrence. (PROB11/1293).

Bull, Jonathan of Boston, MA, mariner. Will 2 Aug. 1727 pr. 7 Jan. 1729 by relict Elizabeth Bull. (PROB11/627). AWP.

Burges, Joseph of Marlborough, Wilts., but late of MD, merchant. Will 22 Oct. 1672 pr. 7 Nov. 1672 by John Keynes. (PROB11/340). NGSQ 62/210.

Burges, William of South River, Anne Arundel Co., MD. Will pr. 5 Jul. 1689. (PROB11/396). GGE.

Burley, William of NY, midshipman of HMS *Torbay*. Will 12 May 1727 pr. 18 Aug. 1727 by Peter Seignoret of Greenwich, Kent, and Mark Anthony Ravaud of Hammersmith, Mddx. (PROB11/616). AWP.

Burn, James of Frankford Borough, Philadelphia Co., PA, gent. Will pr.16 Aug. 1831 by Joel Roberts Poinsett. (PROB11/1788).

Burnett, John of Stanstead Abbots, Herts., but late of New England, who died abroad or at sea. Will 19 Jul. 1704 pr. 11 Jan. 1716 by Thomas Aunger of Ware, Herts. (PROB11/550). AWP.

Burnett, William, Governor of NY and NJ. Will 6 Dec. 1727 pr. 9 Jul. 1730 by Abraham and Mary Vanhorn. (PROB11/638). AWP.

Burnley, John of York River, Hanover Co., VA. Will pr. 16 Feb. 1780. (PROB11/1061).

Burnley, William Hardin late of Trinidad and one of HM Council there but then of NYC. Will 4 Dec. 1837. Leg: son William Frederick Burnley of Glasgow, Scotland, merchant; son Joseph Hume Burnley; William Eccles of Glasgow, merchant; William Brackenridge of London, solicitor; nephew Joseph Burnley Hume of London when he is 21; wife Charlotte Burnley; nephews and nieces, children of Joseph Hume and Maria his wife; Mary Augusta Farquhar of NYC, daughter of James Farquhar deceased . Will pr. 2 Jun. 1851 by son and surviving exec. William Frederick Burnley. (PROB11/2133).

Burns, Hon. William of QC. Will pr. 21 May 1830. (PROB11/1770).

Burrage, William, of Wapping, Mddx., mariner of HMS *Rupert* who died in Charles Town, MA. Will 7 Sep. 1685. Leg: wife Barbery Burrage who is to be attorney and sole exex. Pr. 2 May 1690 by relict Barbara Burrage. (Guildhall: Ms 9171/42/141).

Burrell, William of VA, planter. Will pr. 5 Aug. 1648 by brother-in-law Richard Kelley. (PROB11/205). ACE.GGE.VGE.

Burridge, Robert, boatswain of HMS *Launceston* who died in VA. Will 13 Sep. 1759 pr. 20 Jul. 1769 by relict Sarah Burridge. (PROB11/949). AWP.

Burrington, John of St. George, Hanover Square, Mddx., who had estate on Cape Fear River, NC. Will 1 Apr. 1747 pr. 14 Dec. 1747 by Esquire Cary. (PROB11/758). AWP. NGSQ 64/289.

Burry *alias* **Burrey, David** of Greenspond, NL. Will pr. 4 Jul. 1818. (PROB11/1570).

Burton, Joseph Hews of Shelburne Co., NS, merchant. Will pr. 27 Feb. 1796. (PROB11/1271).

Bushe, Mary. *See* Noel.

Butcher, James, formerly of London but late of NY, master of the *Raynham Hall*. Wit: David Mathews, William Wiseham and James Griffiths. Will 13 Dec. 1781 pr. 4 Dec. 1782 by relict and legatee Sarah Butcher. (PROB11/1097).

Butler, Charles of Newcastle District. [ON]. Will pr. 10 Oct. 1749. (PROB11/2100).

Butler, Elizabeth wife of Edmund of Cincinnati, OH. AWW 24 Jun. 1847 to Edmund Butler Jr. (PROB11/2057).

Butler, John of Newark, Lincoln Co., [ON], Lieut. Colonel of Rangers on half pay. Will pr. 26 Sep. 1797. (PROB11/1206).

Mary Buttall of Exeter, Devon, (widow of Samuel Buttall), who had plantations in NC. Will 23 Mar. 1730 pr 10 Feb. 1731 by daughter Dame Mary Hodges. (PROB11/642). AWP. NGSQ 63/294.

Buttall, Samuel of Topsham, Devon, sugar baker, who had 1,000 acres near New London, [NC]. Will 24 Jan. 1719 pr. 12 Nov. 1723 by relict Mary Buttall. (PROB11/594). AWP. NGSQ 63/294.

Buxton, John of NYC, baker. AWW 24 Apr. 1795 to Robert Rolleston. (PROB11/1259).

Buy, John Sr. of Reading, Berks., mealman, who had lands in PA. Will 4 Jul. 1707 pr. 18 Aug. 1713 by affirmation of sons John and William Buy. (PROB11/535). AWP.

Buy, Mary of Reading, Berks., widow of John Buy, who had a plantation in Ridley, PA. Will 22 Aug. 1717 pr. 11 Jun. 1719 by affirmation of son-in-law John Buy. (PROB11/569). AWP.

Byrd. *See* Bird.

Byrn, Barnaby of Jamaica Township, Nassau Island, NY, gent. AWW 18 May 1776 to James Rivington. (PROB11/1019).

Byrom, John of Hulland, Derbys., yeoman, whose son John was in VA and son Roger in Barbados. Will pr. 25 Feb. 1658 by son William Byrom. (PROB11/275).

Cable *alias* **Capell, George** of Withycombe Raleigh, Devon, mariner bound for NL by the *Pilgrim* of London. Will 1 Apr. 1651 pr. 23 Apr. 1651 by relict Joane Cable *alias* Capell. (PROB11/216).

Cade, Andrew of East Betchworth, Surrey, haberdasher of London, whose cousin Andrew Cade was in VA. Will 20 Sep. 1662. Wit: Francis Bryant, John Friday and Peter Monk. Will pr. 23 Oct. 1662 by relict Magdalen Cade.. (PROB11/309). NGSQ 69/35.

Cadwallader, Thomas of Martinsburg, Bedford Co., PA, gent. Will pr. 24 Oct. 1742 by Isaac Ironside. (PROB11/1969).

Cain, Thomas, quarter gunner of HMS *Africa* in Naval Hospital, Halifax, NS. Will pr. 6 Sep. 1813. (PROB11/1547).

Cairnes, Alexander of Islington, Mddx., who died in VA, widower. Will 1 Aug. 1760 pr. 10 Feb. 1761 by partner John Lidderdale of London. (PROB11/862). AWP.

Calder, James of Kent Co., MD. Will pr. 3 Mar. 1768. (PROB11/937).

Caldwell, James, mariner of HMS *Captain* who died in Boston Hospital, MA. Will 29 Apr. 1757 AWW 10 Sep. 1774 to Andrew Rice, attorney for relict Agnes Caldwell in Falkirk, Scotland. (PROB11/1001). AWP.

Callanan, Michael of Philadelphia, gent. AWW 23 Oct. 1807 to Robert Barclay. (PROB11/1486).

Callbeck, Phillips of Charlotte Town, [PE]. Will pr. 26 Mar. 1791. (PROB11/1202).

Calvert, Benedict Leonard Esq. of Epsom, Surrey, but at present of MD. Will 22 Apr. 1732 pr. 17 Aug. 1733. (PROB11/1660). AWP.

Calvert, Edward Henry Esq. of Annapolis, MD. Will 24 Apr. 1730 pr. 20 Nov. 1730 by relict Margaret Calvert. (PROB11/640). AWP.

Calvert, Raymond of Charles Town, SC. Will 24 Oct. 1766 pr. 22 Aug. 1767 by Emanuel Reller. (PROB11/931). AWP.

Cameron, Alexander of Savannah, GA. AWW 26 Feb. 1784 to William Ogilvy. (PROB11/1113).

Cameron, Kenneth of Montreal, QC, Assistant Commissary-General. Will pr. 21 Apr. 1756. (PROB11/2230).

Cameron, Lauchlan McLean of Thorah Township, Simcoe Co., [ON]. Will pr. 25 Sep. 1855. (PROB11/2219).

Camp, Abiather of St. John, NB, gent. Will pr. 2 Jun. 1791. (PROB11/1205)

Campbell, Alexander of Philadelphia, merchant. Will pr. 16 Feb. 1757. (PROB11/827).

Campbell, Archibald of Fredericksburgh, NY, Capt. of NY Volunteers of Brookland Fort, Long Island. AWW 15 Aug. 1781 to brothers Duncan and John Campbell. (PROB11/1080).

Campbell, Sir Donald, Lieut. Governor of PE. Will pr. 19 Mar. 1851. (PROB11/2128).

Campbell, Dr. Edward of NYC. Will pr. 5 Dec. 1822 by Alexander Campbell. (PROB11/1664).

Campbell, Patrick of NY, Maj. in 71st Regiment of Foot. Will pr. 26 Jun. 1784 by father Duncan Campbell and brother Alexander Campbell. (PROB11/1117).

Campbell, William of Wapping, Mddx., mariner of HMS *Expedition* who died on the ship *Anne* in VA. Will 6 Dec. 1691 pr. 24 Nov. 1693 by David Watson. (PROB11/417).

Capell, George. *See* **Cable.**

Capper, James of QC, merchant. Will pr. 22 Jan. 1819. (PROB11/1612).

Cargey, Hermione, wife of Capt. Robert Cargey of NY. Will 25 Jan. 1786. Lands in RI left to her by her mother Elizabeth Harrison; estate inherited by 1786 will of Dr. Thomas Moffat of Pimlico, Mddx., devised by Samuel Peters of Pimlico. Leg: nephew Norwood William Walker, son of brother Peter Walker. Wit: William Browne of Furnival's Inn and John Alexander Jr. Pr. 11 Mar. 1788 by Thomas Russell, James Longman and John Dighton. (PROB11/1163).

Carman, Robert of QC, merchant. Will pr. 27 Mar. 1846. (PROB11/2032).

Carman, William of QC, merchant. Will pr. 10 Oct. 1835. (PROB11/1852).

Carpender, Francis of London, draper, late living in Hereford, whose cousin Simon Carpender was in VA. Will 15 Mar 1660 & codicil 9 Feb. 1661 pr. 9 May 1662 by relict Helen Carpender. (PROB11/308). AWP.

Carpenter, Corynden of Launceston, Devon, gent., whose brother Nathaniel Carpenter was resident with his family in VA. Will 22 Mar. 1771 pr. 16 Jul. 1776. (PROB11/1021). NGSQ 70/115, 73/207.

Carpenter, Thomas of Lansingburgh, Rensselaer Co., NY, Assistant on half pay of De Lancey's Regiment. AWW 3 May 1832 to James Tidbury. (PROB11/1799).

Carpenter, William of St. George, Southwark, Sy, mariner of HMS *Essex* but who died in NY on HMS *Richmond*. Will 15 Jul. 1689 pr. 1 Jul. 1695 by relict Elizabeth Carpenter. (PROB11/426). AWP.

Carroll, Patrick of Aldgate, London, mariner who died on the ship *St. Thomas* in VA in May 1690. Will 2 Dec. 1689. Wit: James Frankling and Ann Black. Pr. 27 Nov. 1690 by Margaret Souldsby of Aldgate, spinster. (Guildhall: Ms 9052/28).

Carson, Robert, sergeant of 22nd Regiment who died in Mobile, W. FL, bachelor. Will 21 Feb. 1765 AWW 30 Apr. 1766 to Jane Drummon. (PROB11/917). AWP.

Carter, Christopher of Montreal, surgeon. Will pr. 7 Nov. 1823. (PROB11/1677).

Carter, William of Ferryland, NL. Will pr. 28 Aug. 1841. (PROB11/1949).

Cartwright, Timothy of Boston, MA, mariner of HMS *Renown*. AWW to Richard Prowse 23 Nov. 1787. (PROB11/1158).

Cary, Richard of Bristol, merchant who died in VA, bachelor. Will 26 Feb. 1712 AWW 24 Nov. 1730 to niece Jane Cary, spinster. (PROB11/640). AWP.

Cary, Samuel of Charles Town, Suffolk Co., MA. Will 14 Nov. 1763 AWW 8 Nov. 1770 by his solemn affirmation to Abraham Dettorne, attorney for brothers Richard and Nathaniel Cary in MA. (PROB11/961). AWP.

Carey, Thomas of Witless Bay, NL. Will pr. 3 Mar. 1783. (PROB11/1101).

Caswall, Henry of Boston, MA, merchant. Will pr. 8 Jun. 1748 by sister Susanna Allison and cousin John Caswall. (PROB11/762).

Caswall, Kezia, formerly of Boston, MA, but late of Queen Street, London, and Camberwell, Sy., widow. Will 17 Jul. 1735 pr. 5 Dec. 1740 by John Caswall. (PROB11/706). AWP.

Catherwood, Robert of St. Augustine, E. FL. Will pr. 8 Sep. 1787. (PROB11/1156).

Caulfield, Thomas, of Annapolis Royal, NS, Lieut. Governor of the Garrison. Will pr. 19 Jun. 1717. (PROB11/558).

Cay, David of Philadelphia, PA, merchant & partner of Andrew Clow in Philadelphia. Will pr. 16 May 1797 by William Cramond, John Leary and Hugh Holmes. (PROB11/1290). TNA:C33/496/337.

Cay, Jonathan, Rector of Christ Church, Calvert Co., MD. Will 24 Jun. 1714 pr. 19 Oct. 1738 by relict Dorothy Cay. (PROB11/692). AWP.

Chambers, Richard, of MD, late of London, citizen and skinner. Will 10 Dec. 1697 pr. 16 Jul. 1701 by mother Mary Chambers.

Chamier, Daniel of Baltimore. AWW 13 Oct. 1780 to brother Anthony Chamier. (PROB11/1069). NGSQ 66/229.

Chandler, Kenelm of QC, Barrack Master of QC Garrison and Store Keeper of Ordnance. Will pr. 24 Oct. 1806. (PROB11/1450).

Chandler, Nathaniel of Worcester, MA. AWW 15 Aug. 1801 to Samuel Paine. (PROB11/1361).

Chandler, Richard of Portobacco Creek, Charles Co., MD. Will 12 Apr. 1712 pr.16 Oct. 1714 by Ralph Pigott. (PROB11/542). AWP.

Chandler, Robert of New London, CT, seaman of HMS *Penelope*. AWW 20 Mar. 1801 to William Compton. (PROB11/1355).

Chapman, William of Alexandria, [DC], but formerly of Whitby, Yorks., master mariner. Letter from him to "Dear Father" dated ship *Powhatan* off North Foreland 30 Jul. 1792. "I came as a passenger in this ship to arrange my affairs for which I paid only £10. I must hold one-third of the ship and cargo worth over £1,000. I shall not proceed to New Brunswick . . . and have credits in Maryland, Georgetown and Virginia [details]. Leg: parents Isaac and Frances Chapman; sister Elizabeth Marwood. Affidavit 16 Jan. 1801 by Michael Danby of Cornhill, London, merchant, and George Moorson of South Shields, Durham, that they knew the testator and that the letter is in his hand. AWW 27 Jan. 1801 to Elizabeth, wife of John Marwood. (PROB11/1352).

Chardavoyne, Anthony of NYC, mariner and bachelor of HMS *St. Antonio* who died aboard HMS *Pheasant*. Will dated 15 Nov. 1756 witnessed by Solomon Pinto, Lawrence Wesells and Samuel Pinto. AWW granted 5 Oct. 1765 to Naphtali Hart Myers, attorney to the named executor Isaac Chardavoyne, father of the testator, now in NY. (PROB11/912).

Charles, Peter of VA, mariner of HMS *Shoreham*. Will 28 Nov. 1700 pr. 16 Oct. 1701 by Hendrick Cloyson. (PROB11/461(. AWP.

Charlett, Richard of Calvert Co., MD. Will pr. 4 Apr. 1694. (PROB11/419).

Charlton, Daniel of HMS *Garland* who died in MD. Will 5 Jul. 1753 pr. 22 Dec. 1757 by Elizabeth Dawley of Portsmouth, Hants. (PROB11/834). AWP.

Chergwind, Richard of Gravesend, Kent, but late of Churchill, Hudson's Bay. Will pr. 6 Dec. 1768. (PROB11/944).

Cherry, Robert of St. Thomas the Apostle, citizen and draper of London whose daughter Mary was wife of Samuel England of PA.. Will 27 Dec. 1704 pr. 30 Dec. 1704 by affirmation of Richard Beckett. (PROB11/480). AWP.

Cheshire, Charles of Ernest, Midland District, [ON], retired Royal Navy officer. Will pr. 22 Februry 1845. (PROB11/2012).

Chesley, Philip of York Co., VA. Will pr. 10 May 1675 by Margaret Chesley. (PROB11/347). VGE.

Cheston, Francina Augustina of Kent Co., MD, widow. Will 3 Nov. 1765 pr. 10 Feb. 1767 by William Stephenson. (PROB11/925). AWP.

Chew, John of York District, [ON], yeoman. Will pr. 22 Jul. 1854. (PROB11/2194).

Chew, Nathaniel of MD, master mariner. Will pr. 14 Dec. 1761. (PROB11/871).

Chichester, John of VA. Will 24 Sep. 1753 pr. 28 May 1763 by brother Richard Chichester. (PROB11/887). AWP. Further grant in 1803.

Chichester, Richard of Lancaster Co., VA. AWW 15 Mar. 1746 to John and Richard Tucker. (PROB11/745). VGE.

Chichester, Richard of Fairfax, VA. AWW to William Murdoch 9 Jun. 1803. (PROB11/1394).

Chichester, Sir Charles of Toronto, Col. of 81st Regimen of Foot. Will pr. 23 Aug. 1847. (PROB11/2060).

Chiene, Margaretta of Philadelphia, widow. Will pr. 7 Nov. 1834 by Peter A. Browne. (PROB11/1838).

Child, Henry of Baltimore. Will pr. 20 Oct. 1831. (PROB11/1791A).

Chisholm, Alexander of St. Antoine Suburbs, Montreal. Will pr. 16 Apr. 1818. (PROB11/1603).

Chrystie, John of Wapping, Mddx., surgeon of merchant ship *Rumsey* who died at York River, VA, bachelor. Will 25 Jul. 1716 pr. 28 Nov. 1718 by Elizabeth Grimes. (PROB11/566). AWP.

Christie, William Plenderleath of Christieville, Seigniory Bleury, [QC]. Will pr. 25 Jun. 1846. (PROB11/2037).

Claiborne, William of VA but late in London, merchant who died in Hackney, Mddx. Codicil 16 May 1746 to will made in VA pr. 17 Jul. 1746 by John Hanbury of London, merchant. (PROB11/748). AWP. NGSQ 64/290.

Clare, Alfred of Pittsburgh, PA. Will pr. 25 May 1835 by nephew George Thatcher. (PROB11/1846).

Clerke, Sir Francis Carr, Adjutant of 3rd Regiment of Foot Guards. Memorandum by him dated Camp Still Water 6 Apr. 1773 thanking his doctor and nurse for their care after his wounding. Deposition 14 May 1774 by Rev. Sir William Henry Clerke of St. George, Hanover Square, Mddx., and John Money of Trowse, Norfolk, Esq. that they knew Sir Francis before his death in Oct. 1777 and testify to his writing. AWW 18 May 1779 to the mother Susanna Elizabeth Clerke, widow. (PROB11/1053).

Clarke, Frederick of Carolina who died in Barbados, bachelor whose sister Mary Stephen was in Carolina. Will 13 Nov. 1697 AWW 20 Aug. 1700 to John Trott for brother Robert Stephen in Carolina. (PROB11/456). AWP.

Clark, George of Albany Fort, Hudson's Bay, bachelor. Will pr. 20 May 1761. (PROB11/865).

Clark, George of Brandywine Hundred, Newcastle Co., DE, Capt. of NJ Volunteers on half pay. AWW 31 Oct. 1812 to Thomas Courtney. (PROB11/1537).

Clarke, George of Hyde Hall, Springfield, Otsego Co., NY. Will pr. 13 Aug. 1838 by son George Rochfort Clarke. (PROB11/1899).

Clarke, Henry of Shadwell, Mddx., mariner who died in PA. Will 27 Jul. 1719 pr. 9 Mar. 1717 by relict Elizabeth Clarke. (PROB11/614). AWP.

Clarke, James of Preston, (East Landings), North America. Will dated 17 Apr. 1683 names his wife Catherine Grimes as legatee and sole executrix. Witnessed by Christopher Browne,

Edward Bishop and James Dixon. Pr. 15 May 1684 by Catherine Clarke *alias* Grimes. (PROB11/376).

Clarke, John Jr. of London, merchant, late of Gloucester Co., VA, bachelor. Will 31 Jan. 1749 pr. 23 Nov. 1757 by father John Clarke of Bugbrooke, Northants, merchant. (PROB11/833)> AWP.

Clarke, Jonathan, Assistant Commissary-General of QC. Will pr. Will pr. 1 Oct. 1783. (PROB11/1109).

Clarke, John of Great Yarmouth, Norfolk, master of *Unity* who died in VA having estate there. Will 30 Nov. 1657 pr. 26 May 1665 by William Clarke of Yarmouth, mariner. (PROB11/316). AWP. NGSQ 66/219.

Clerk, Matthew, bachelor of Lake George Camp [NY], Lieutenant in Col. Montagu's Regiment and engineer. Will dated Lake George, 14 Jul. 1758 and witnessed by Capt. James Abercrombie and Capt. Walter Rutherford leaves to his brothers Sir James Clerk of Pennycuick, Scotland, and John Clerk, or to his sisters, all the estate inherited by his father's will. His cousin Lieut. George Clerk is to have all his effects in America. Deposition by Thomas Clerk of All Hallows Staining, London, merchant, that in Aug. 1758 he received an attested copy of the will from America. AWW 15 Nov. 1758 to the said Thomas Clerk as attorney for Sir James and John Clerk in Scotland. (PROB11/841).

Clark, Richard of Granville, Annapolis Co., NS, farmer. Will pr. 10 Dec. 1783. (PROB11/1111).

Clark, Robert of Rotherhithe, Surrey. late resident at Boston, MA, mariner. Will 16 Sep. 1662 AWW 10 Mar. 1663 to Walter Rogers. (PROB11/310). AWP.

Clarke, Robert of St. Giles Cripplegate, London, but late of MD, planter. Will 14 Dec. 1689 pr. 20 Dec 1689 by brother John Clarke. (PROB11/397). AWP.

Clark, William of PA, Sergeant in 20th Regiment of Foot. AWW 17 Nov. 1783 to Henry Rowland. (PROB11/1110).

Clark, Sarah of Leeds, Fauquier Co., VA, widow. AWW 11 Feb. 1835 to John Birkett. (PROB11/1842).

Clarke, Thomas of York, VA. Will pr. 10 May 1670 by Peter Temple. (PROB11/332). VGE.

Clarke, William of Great Yarmouth, Norfolk, master of the *Unity* and trader in VA. Will 2 Aug. 1664 pr. 26 May 1665 by William Clarke Sr. (PROB11/316). NGSQ 66/219.

Clark, William of Burnt Prairie, Edwards Co., IL. [Will pr. 11 Oct. 1842. (PROB11/1969).

Clarkson, Freeman of NY. Will 22 Aug. 1800. Leg: wife Henrietta Clarkson who is to be exec. with brother Matthew Streatfield. Wit: Ann Browne and Cornelia Ann Clarkson. AWW 27 Jun. 1811 to Thomas B. Batard, attorney for relict residing at NY. (PROB11/1523).

Clay, Stephen, mariner of merchant ship *Anne* who died in VA., bachelor. Will 19 May 1730 pr. 22 Oct. 1734 by uncle William Norwood of Margate, Kent. (PROB11/667). AWP.

Cleare, Ambrose of Stratton Major, New Kent Co., VA. Will 28 May 1686 AWW 10 Nov 1697 to Richard Parke, merchant, attorney for relict Anne, now wife of Thomas Tea, in VA. (PROB11/441). AWP.

Cleary, Richard of QC. Will pr. Will pr. 21 May 1808. (PROB11/1479).

Cleaver, Thomas of Stepney, Mddx., mariner who died in VA. Will 5 Apr. 1693 pr. 24 Jul. 1700 by sister Mary Cleaver. (PROB11/456). AWP.

Cleghorn, John of Frederick Co., MD. Will pr. 25 May 1824. (PROB11/1685).

Clements, James of NYC. AWW 10 Jan. 1831 to John Baring. (PROB11/1780).

Clemson, Mary Jane of Kingston, [ON]. Will pr. 22 Feb. 1853. (PROB11/2166).

Clinch, John of Trinity, NL, clerk. Will pr. 28 Aug. 1820. (PROB11/1633).

Clothier, Andrew of Trinity, NL. Will pr. 23 Dec. 1844. (PROB11/2008).

Coats, Philip of Trinity, NL. Will pr. 17 Mar. 1813. (PROB11/1542).

Cochet, Robert of Mickleover, Derbys., whose sister Dorothy was wife of John Joyce of New England. Will 5 September 1657 pr. 30 Apr. 1657 by relict Anne Cochet. (PROB11/274). AWP.

Cochran, Harriet Anna of Halifax, NS, spinster. Will pr. 28 Sep. 1829. (PROB11/1760).

Cochran, Jane of Halifax, NS, widow. Will pr. 4 May 1827. (PROB11/1725).

Cochran, John of St. Bartholomew, Colleton, SC, practitioner of physic. Will dated 13 Jun. 1762 witnessed by Robert Hogg, Elisha Poinsett Jr. and Robert Wilson, leaving bequests to his brothers William and Robert Cochran and sister Catherine Cochran. Pr. 8 Sep. 1762 by the relict Margaret Cochran with similar powers reserved to the testator's brother-in-law Moses Darquier. (PROB11/879).

Cocke, Catesby Esq. of Prince William Co., VA. Will 13 Jun. 1763 AWW 1 Mar. 1773 to William Perkins and William Brown, attorneys for sons William and John Catesby Cocke in VA. (PROB11/985). AWP.

Cock, Charles of St. John's, NL. Will pr. 29 Jun. 1830. (PROB11/1772).

Cock, John of St. John's, NL. Will pr. 14 Dec. 1731. (PROB11/648).

Cockburn, Thomas of PA, mariner of the *Newberry*. Will 5 Sep. 1724 pr. 4 Jan 1725 by brother John Cockburn. (PROB11/601). AWP.

Cockshudd, Jeffery of Great Harwood, Lancs., mariner who died in VA, bachelor. Will 15 Apr. 1691 pr. 14 Jan. 1710 by brother Thomas Cockshudd. (PROB11/513). AWP.

Codenham, Robert, late of Shadwell, Mddx., but late of NY and who died there, mariner. AWW 26 Feb. 1700 to John Chapman. (PROB11/454). AWP.

Coffin, Hezekiah of Nantucket, [MA], commander of the ship *Dennis*. Will of 13 Mar. 1778, pr. 2 Jun. 1781. Leg: wife Abigail Coffin of Nantucket. Exec: Richard Coffin of London, merchant. Wit: Robert Robson and James Price. (PROB11/1079).

Cogan, William of Halifax, NS, late surgeon of 81st Regiment of Foot, now retired. Will pr. 2 Aug. 1826. (PROB11/1715).

Cogswell, Nathaniel of NYC, merchant. Will pr. 24 May 1834 by brother Jonathan Cogswell and sister Lois Cogswell. (PROB11/1831).

Cohen, Jacob Aron of Charleston, SC, shopkeeper. Will pr. 15 Jun. 1813 by John Bulow. (PROB11/1545).

Colbourne, Joseph of Twillingate, Fogo District, NL. Will pr. 23 Jul. 1853. (PROB11/2175)

Colcutt, William, seaman of the *Planter* in VA. Nuncupative will 29 Mar. 1659. Leg: if report of wife's death is true, sister Anne West to have share of estate; John Nossiter; John Frost; Patience Dandy to have residue. Wit: Thomas Prinderges and David Man. AWW 5 Aug. 1659 to Anne West, aunt of Patience Dandy, a minor. (PROB11/294). AWP.

Colden, Alexander of Brooklyn, King's Co., NY. Will pr. 16 Aug. 1784 by brother John Antill. (PROB11/1120).

Cole, formerly Hale, Elizabeth, wife of William Cole, late of Kemerton, Glos., but now residing in North America. Will 19 Nov. 1788. Leg: daughter Sarah Hale; sons Nathaniel and Thomas Hale. Wit: Henry White, George Tomkins and James Hind. Pr. 22 May 1789 by John Smith Sr., Isaac Hind and son Nathaniel Hale. (PROB11/1179).

Cole, Michael of Ratcliffe, Mddx., mariner whose bonds for £1,800 were in the hands of Col. William Rhett of SC. Will 31 Jan. 1717 pr. 3 Aug 1719 by Samuel Vaus and Jonathan Shakespeare. (PROB11/569). AWP.

Cole, Thomas of Bird Island Cove, NL, fisherman. Will pr. 21 May 1844. (PROB11/1998).

Coles, John of Exeter, Devon, cheesemonger, who had lands in PA and died there. Will pr. 17 Oct. 1693 by James Kerle. (PROB11/416). AWP.

Colles, Thomas of Deptford, Kent, shipwright of *Nicholson*, who died in VA. Will 8 Jan. 1706 pr. 5 Feb 1707 by Mary Colles. (PROB11/492). AWP.

Colleton, Charles Sackville of Canada, Lieut. of Royal Regiment of Artillery, bachelor. Will pr. 27 Jun. 1782. (PROB11/1091).

Colleton, John of Fairlawns, St. John's parish, Berkeley Co., SC. Will pr 3 Apr. 1751 by Sir John Colleton. (PROB11/ 787). AWP.

Colleton, Sir John of Withycombe Rawleigh, Devon, who had property and descendants in SC. Will 22 Apr. 1751 pr. 11 Nov. 1754 by son Robert Colleton. (PROB11/811). AWP. NGSQ 64/145. Further grants 1755 and 1759.

Colleton, Sir John of Fairlawns, St. John's parish, Berkeley Co., SC. Will pr. 3 Dec. 1779 by Elizabeth Janverin, spinster. (PROB11/1059).

Colleton, Margaret of Hanover Square, Mddx., widow of John Colleton, who had property in South Carolina. Will 13 Aug. 1779 pr. 9 Nov. 1779. (PROB11/1058). NGSQ 64/145.

Colleton, Sir Peter of St. James Westminster, Mddx., who had lands in Carolina and Barbados. Will 12 Jan. 1694 pr. 4 Apr. 1694 by daughter Katherine Colleton. (PROB11/419). AWP.

Colleton, Peter of Fairlawns, Berkeley Co., SC. Will 30 Nov. 1740 pr. 11 Nov. 1754 by brother Robert Colleton. (PROB11/811). AWP.

Collett, John of Washington, D.C. AWW 11 Jul. 1822 to Thomas Wilson. (PROB11/1659).

Collier, Alexander of St. Katherine's Precinct, London, mariner of HMS *Wolf* who died in VA, bachelor. Will 1 Jun. 1734 pr. 12 Nov. 1739 by William Culling. (PROB11/699). AWP.

Collier, Daniel, mariner of HMS *Devonshire* who died in NY, bachelor. Will 16 Nov. 1757 pr. 14 Jun. 1763 by cousin Susannah Long of Greenwich, Kent. (PROB11/888). AWP.

Collin, John of St. John's, NL, planter. Will pr. 13 May 1742. (PROB11/718).

Collingwood, Gerard of Wapping, Mddx., mariner of merchant ship *Three Brothers* who died in VA, bachelor. Will 24 Sep. 1728 pr. 20 Oct. 1732 by Eleanor Slater, widow. (PROB11/654). AWP.

Collins, Walter of Canada. belonging to HMS *Stirling Castle* in St. Lawrence River. Will pr. 6 Aug. 1760. (PROB11/858).

Collins, William of Placentia, NL. Will pr. 26 Apr. 1797. (PROB11/1288).

Collis, James of Trinity, NL. Will pr. 11 Oct. 1828. (PROB11/1746).

Collis, Thomas of Twillingate, NL, agent. Will pr. 11 Feb. 1826. (PROB11/1708).

Collyer, James of Coolspring Township, Mercer Co., PA, farmer. AWW 9 Jul. 1844 to John Goodman. (PROB11/2001).

Coltman, William of Stepney, Mddx., mariner who died in VA. Will pr. 1 Nov. 1666 by mother Alice Coltman. (PROB11/322). AWP.

Colson, Elizabeth of Bethnal Green, Mddx., late of Charles Town, SC, widow. Will dated London 1 Jun. 1744 AWW 17 Aug. 1751 to James Crockatt, attorney for son William Roper. (PROB11/789). AWP.

Colston, Rawleigh of Berkeley, VA. AWW 21 Mar. 1827 to John Dunlop. (PROB11/1722).

Colvill, John of Cranbrook, Kent, clothier, who left money to John Colvill in New England. Will 13 Aug. 1691 pr. 15 Jul. 1695 by relict Susanna Colvill. (PROB11/426). AWP.

Conner, Roger of Newport, RI, mariner, formerly of merchant ship *Caesar* but late of HMS *Vigilant*. Will dated 5 May 1745 appoints Mr. George Goulding of Newport, mariner, as sole executor. Witnesses: John Gardner, William Rogers and Jonas Lyndon. AWW 19 Mar. 1754 to James Standerwick, attorney for James Perryman, sole executor of the will of George Goulding deceased. Probate of a pretended will dated 6 Jul. 1745 witnessed by Thomas Daviss and Andrew Steward, and appointing the testator's aunt Elizabeth Buckham, widow of St. Catherine Creed, London, as sole executrix, and pr. by her on 29 Dec. 1750 now declared null and void. (PROB11/784 & 807).

Connolly, William of Montreal, gent. Will pr. 24 Feb. 1851. (PROB11/2127).

Connop, John of Ratcliffe, Stepney, Mddx., mariner of merchant ship *Olive Tree* who died in VA. Will 6 Sep. 1704 pr. 16 Dec. 1706 by Edmond Castle. (PROB11/491). AWP.

Connor, Sarah of Lawn, NL, widow. Will pr. 19 Jan. 1843. (PROB11/1073).

Conquest, George of NY, bachelor, seaman. Will undated. Leg: John Staple, innkeeper of Nottingham and Richard Shaw of Nottingham, merchant, who are to be execs; mother Ruth Conquest; sisters Mary Ann and Rebecca Conquest and [unnamed], wife of Thomas Bartlett of Ludgate Hill, London, woollen draper; brothers William Conquest of Puckeridge, [Herts.], surgeon, and John Tucker Conquest of Nottingham, M.D. Wit: Henry Carrier Steyder. AWW 13 Aug. 1835 to brother Dr. John Tucker Conquest, execs. John Staple and Richard Shaw having died. (PROB11/1850).

Constable, Peter and **William** of Shadwell, Mddx., brothers bound for Guinea and VA by the *Goodwill* of London, Mr. Humphrey Wells. Will 27 Sep. 1660. Leg: each to the other brother but, if both die, to kinsman Edward Arnold of Shadwell, mariner, and Margaret his wife who are to be execs. Wit: Grace Atkenson and John Morgan. Pr. 29 Apr. 1662 by Richard [*sic*] Arnold with powers reserved to his wife Margaret Arnold. (Guildhall: Ms 9171/31/136).

Cook, Andrew of St. Giles in Fields, Mddx., gent, who had estate in Dorchester Co., MD. Will 21 Dec. 1711 pr. 2 Jan. 1712 by children Ebenezer and Anne Cook. (PROB11/525). AWP.

Cook, Edmund of Norwich, Norf. but late of MD who died in St. John's, St. Mary Co., MD, bachelor. Will 29 Mar. 1744 pr. 19 May 1747 by Charles Martin of Norwich. (PROB11/754). AWP.

Cooke, John of St. James Santee, Craven Co., SC. Will 4 Nov. 1744 AWW 12 Jun. 1755 to Elizabeth Cooke, spinster, attorney for daughter Rebecca Cooke in SC. (PROB11/816). AWP.

Cook, Joseph of Red River, Hudson's Bay, schoolmaster. Will pr. 8 Apr. 1850. (PROB11/2111).

Cookson, George of St. Augustine, E. FL. AWW 5 Feb. 1777 to Thomas Harrison. (PROB11/1028).

Cookson, George of St. Augustine, E. FL. Will pr. 25 Feb. 1786. (PROB11/1138).

Cooper, Christopher, of St. John's, NL, planter. Will pr. 8 Jun. 1697. (PROB11/436).

Cooper, Edward of Boston, MA. Will pr. 22 Aug. 1809 by brother George Cooper. (PROB11/1501).

Cooper, James Grafton of Saltfleet, Gore District, [ON]. Will pr. 29 Aug. 1849. (PROB11/2097).

Cooper, Joseph of NYC, gent. Leg: daughter Charlotte, wife of James Borrian; daughter Rachel, wife of Samuel Pooley; daughter Rosabella Cooper. Execs: William Fosbrook and John Cauldwell of NYC. Wit: George Coldwell, James Potter and James Willett. Will pr. 19 Mar. 1818 by William Fosbrook. (PROB11/1602).

Cooper, Mary of Charleston, SC, but late of Bristol whose grandchildren Vander Horst were in Carolina. Will 19 Jul. 1796 pr. 18 May 1797. (PROB11/1290). NGSQ 63/203.

Cooper, William of NL, planter. Will pr. 14 Jan. 1729. (PROB11/627).

Cooper, William of Louisburg, NS, bachelor, Lieutenant in 28th Regiment on board transport ship *Fortitude*. Will pr. 8 Apr. 1765. (PROB11/907).

Cope, Henry of NY, Lieut. Col. of American Regiment of Foot. Will dated Jamaica 5 Mar. 1743 AWW 29 Feb. 1744 to Richard Jeneway, attorney for Stephen Bayard in NY. (PROB11/731). AWP.

Corderoy, William of VA, merchant. Will 15 Sep. 1667 pr. 10 Oct. 1667 by brother Jasper Corderoy. (PROB11/325). AWP.

Corker, Thomas of Charles Town, SC, merchant. Will 3 May 1768 AWW 4 Aug. 1772 to James Poyas, attorney for Josiah Smith Jr. of Charles Town, merchant. (PROB11/980). AWP.

Cornell, Samuel of NYC, formerly of New Bern, NC, merchant. Will pr. 2 May 1787 by daughter Susanna Chads. (PROB11/1152).

Cornock, Samuel of London, master of ship *Molly* who died in SC, bachelor. Will 31 Aug. 1730 pr. 3 Aug 1733 by affirmation of Thomas Plumsted. (PROB11/660). AWP.

Cornwall, Alexander of St. Botolph Aldgate, London, mariner of *Maryland Factor* who died in MD. Will 13 Jul. 1703 pr. 8 Aug. 1704 by William Findlason. (PROB11/477). AWP.

Cornwell, Thomas of London, merchant who died in MD, bachelor. Will 27 Mar. 1694 AWW 24 Dec. 1695 to brother Anthony Cornwell. (PROB11/429). AWP.

Corrigal, Jacob of Cobourg Town, Newcastle District, ON. Will pr. 6 Nov. 1844. (PROB11/2007).

Cosby, Henry of NYC. Captain of HMS *Centaur*. Will 6 Oct. 1753 pr. 16 Aug. 1754 by mother Hon. Grace Cosby. (PROB11/810). AWP.

Cosby, William of NY Esq., Governor of NY and NJ. Will dated 19 Feb. 1736 bequeaths his Manor of Corby on the Mohawk River to his sons William and Henry Cosby; lands at Rochester, Ulster Co., to his wife Grace Cosby; his house at St. Leonard's Hill to his wife during her life and then to his said son William. Witnessed by James de Lancey, John Felton, Joseph Murray and Charles Williams. Pr. by Grace Cosby 3 Jul. 1739. (PROB11/697).

Cote, Pascal of Commissaries Street, St. Roch, QC, traveller. Will pr. 24 Sep. 1844. (PROB11/2004).

Cotton, Richard of Camden, SC, Capt. in 33rd Regiment. Will pr. 25 May 1789. (PROB11/1179).

Coutart, Peter of Petersburg, VA. Will pr. 18 Aug. 1809. (PROB11/1501).

Coutts, Hercules of the City of London, merchant, who died in Newcastle, PA. Will 2 Sep. 1697 pr. 7 Oct. 1709 by the brother James Coutts. (PROB11/512). AWP.

Couturier, Eliza Maria of Charleston, SC, widow. Will 1 Dec. 1837. Leg: son Isaac R.E. Couturier. Wit: Anne Thompson and Daniel W. Giuliard. Pr. 5 May 1849 by son-in-law Thomas J.Gautte and Isaac R.E. Couturier. (PROB11/2092).

Couzens, John of Oswego, NY, Ensign in 57th Regiment of Foot. Will 4 Aug. 1755 AWW 1 Feb. 1757 to Henry Kidgell, attorney for father Samuel Couzens in Dublin, Ireland. (PROB11/827). AWP.

Coward, William of Boston, MA, mariner, who died on ship *Neptune* in Piscataqua, NH. Will 23 Apr. 1690 witnessed by Benjamin Bullivant, Joseph Love and James Atkins, pr. 10 Oct. 1691 by relict Christian Coward. (PROB11/406). AWP.

Cowcher, Robert of Brantford, Gore, [ON], surgeon. Will pr. 16 Jun. 1852. (PROB11/2154).

Cowman, John of NY, gent. Will pr. 7 May 1833 by James Hay and Daniel Lord Jr. (PROB11/1815).

Cox, Andrew of Suffolk, Nansemond Co., VA. Will pr. 18 Feb. 1764 by Peter Hodgson. (PROB11/895).

Cox, Isaac of Philadelphia, merchant. Will pr. 27 Jul. 1784 by son Isaac Cox and Isaac Wickoff. (PROB11/1119).

Cox, Samuel of Barbados who died in MD. Will 10 Apr. 1724 AWW 25 Jun. 1726 to Henry Palmer, attorney for relict Elizabeth Cox in Barbados. (PROB11/609). AWP.

Cox, Samuel of MD, chief mate of merchant ship *Bladen*. Will pr. 1 Jun. 1743. (PROB11/727).

Cox, Sem of St. Mary's, Richmond Co., VA. Will 18 Oct. 1710 pr. 12 Oct. 1711 by Benjamin Deverill. (PROB11/523). AWP.

Cox, Thomas, citizen and vintner of London who had lands in PA. Will 20 May 1709 pr. 14 Mar. 1712 by solemn affirmation of relict Anne Cox. (PROB11/526).

Crab, Samuel of Boston, MA, who died in Stepney, Mddx., bachelor. Nuncupative will 25 Sep. 1691 AWW 4 Sep. 1694 to William March. (PROB11/422). AWP.

Cradock, Sarah of Boston, MA, gentlewoman. AWW 4 Feb. 1799 to George Brinley. (PROB11/1319).

Craig, Archibald Cummings of Bedminster, Somerset Co., NJ., formerly of Philadelphia, AWW 12 Nov. 1802 to Rev. Joseph Anderson. (PROB11/1382).

Craig, Sir James Henry, Governor in Chief of Upper & Lower Canada, Col. of 78th Regiment. Will pr. 20 Mar. 1812. (PROB11/1531).

Craig, John of Philadelphia, merchant. AWW 13 Jan. 1810 to James Mackenzie. (PROB11/1507).

Crate, Joseph Henshaw of Middleton, Carroll Co., MA. Will pr. 30 Jun. 1856 by Sarah Nicoll, spinster, and James Abbott. (PROB11/2234).

Crawford, William, Judge of Gaspé District, [QC]. Will pr. 22 Jul. 1822. (PROB11/1659).

Crawley, John formerly of Bristol but late of Newark, NJ, widower. AWW 7 Nov. 1800 to Peter Barlow, attorney for the son John Crawley in NJ; the named executors Thomas Griffith M.D. and the wife Catherine Crawley having died and Elisha Boudinet having renounced. (PROB11/1349).

Crawley, Thomas of Sydney, Cape Breton, NS. Will pr. 21 Oct. 1851. (PROB11/2140).

Creake, Samuel of Limehouse, Mddx., master of the *Britannia* who died in MD. Will 23 Jan. 1710 pr. 1 Oct. 1716 by affirmation of relict Mary Creake. (PROB11/554).

Crease, Alfred of Philadelphia, chemist. AWW 27 Jan. 1836 to Orlando Crease. (PROB11/1856).

Creasy, Elizabeth of Twillingate, NL, widow. Will pr. 27 Jan. 1835. (PROB11/1841).

Creasey, Henry of Sturminster Newton, Dorset, but late of Bonne Bay, NL, planter. Will 23 Sep. 1809. Leg: wife Mary Creasey and daughter Mary Creasey. Execs: Mary Chauncy, William Chauncy and Lion. Chauncy. Pr. 13 Apr. 1813 by Joseph Bird. (PROB11/1543).

Creed, John of Martin's Hundred, VA. AWW 18 Apr. 1635 to Anne Faussett. (PROB11/167). ACE.VGE.

Creighton, John of Lunenburg, NS. Will pr. 4 Jul. 1808. (PROB11/1482).

Creighton, Joseph of Halifax, NS, Col. in HM Army. Will pr. 2 Dec. 1853. (PROB11/2182).

Creighton, Lucy of Lunenburg, NS, widow. Will pr. 6 Jul. 1824. (PROB11/1688).

Creteau, John of Province of ME. Will pr. 24 Oct. 1811. (PROB11/1841).

Crew, Martin of Connergie Bay, NL. Will pr. 6 Jul. 1852. (PROB11/2156).

Crispe, John of Buffalo, NY. AWW 3 Jan. 1840 to William Baxter Jr. (PROB11/1921).

Critchett, Michael of Perry Co., OH. Will pr. 3 Dec. 1851 by Charles Carter with similar powers reserved to the relict Ann, now wife of Mathias D. Stotlar. (PROB11/2143).

Crockett, William of SC, mariner of HMS *Aldborough* who died on Providence Island [Bahamas]. Will 15 Sep. 1729 pr. 13 Jun. 1730 by Thomas Vinter of London. (PROB11/628). AWP.

Crokatt, John of Charles Town, SC, and late in Lisbon, merchant. Will 21 Nov. 1738 pr. 28 Jun. 1740 by father Charles Crokatt of Edinburgh. (PROB11/703). AWP.

Cromartie, Adam of Wapping, Mddx., mariner of HMS *Colchester* who died in VA. Will 20 Nov. 1736 pr. 13 Jan. 1741 by Elizabeth Crafts. (PROB11/707). AWP.

Crommelin, Charles of NY. Will 27 May 1735 pr. 22 Apr. 1740 by son Daniel Crommelin. (PROB11/701). AWP.

Cronen, Eleanor of Philadelphia, spinster. AWW 3 Aug. 1816 to George Haslewood. (PROB11/1583).

Crook, Edward of George Town, SC. Will pr. 1 Oct. 1803 by George Lockey. (PROB11/1399).

Crow, John of Shadwell, Mddx., mariner of merchant ship *Providence* who died in VA. Will 6 Jul. 1707. Leg: Thomas and Mary Jackson of Shadwell. Wit: Henry Hewis, Edward Ivory and John Forrest. Pr. 9 Jan. 1710 by Thomas Jackson. (PROB11/513). AWP.

Cruger, Mrs. Catharine of NYC. Will pr. 24 Apr. 1840 by John Church Cruger. (PROB11/1925).

Cruger, John of NYC, merchant. Will pr. 15 Mar. 1825. (PROB11/1696).

Cruger, Nicholas of NYC, merchant. Will pr. 5 Jan. 1805 by relict Ann Rogers. (PROB11/1419).

Cull, John of St. John's, NL. Will pr. 24 Apr. 1817. (PROB11/1591).

Cullin, Thomas of Stepney, Mddx., bound for New Guinea and NL. AWW 10 Aug 1621 to attorney Agnes Gray, no executor having been named. (Guildhall: Ms 9168/17/70v).

Cully, Abraham of Stafford Co., VA, gent. Will 31 May 1692 AWW 26 Apr. 1694 to brother John Cully. (PROB11/419). AWP.

Cummings, Archibald of Philadelphia, clerk. Will 23 Mar. 1741 pr. 1 Aug. 1741 by Rev. Thomas Moore. (PROB11/711). AWP.

Cunningham, Patrick of Isle La Crosset, Hudson's Bay. Will pr. 6 Feb. 1834. (PROB11/1827).

Cuninghame, William of NYC, of HMS *Windsor*, surgeon. Will pr. 8 May 1789. (PROB11/1178).

Curle, Nicholas Wilson of Elizabeth City Co., VA, former Lieut. of HMS *Bellona*. Will pr. 12 Dec. 1772. (PROB11/983).

Currie, Ebenezer of PA but late in London. Will 28 Aug. 1746 pr. 2 Dec. 1747 by John Seton of London, merchant. (PROB11/758). AWP.

Curry, Samuel of St. Martin in Fields, Mddx., peruke maker, who died in Boston, MA. Leg: sister Ester, wife of Henry Herbert, goldsmith. Exec: John Le Sage. Wit: Ezekias Lever and John S___eer. AWW 7 Jan. 1737 to Ester Herbert. (PROB11/681). AWP.

Curtis, John of Boston, MA, bachelor, mariner of *English Tiger*. Will pr. 3 Dec. 1690 by Robert Chipchase. (PROB11/402). GGE.

Curtyce, John of Burghfield, Berks., whose sister Jane was wife of Thomas Collyer in New England. Will 20 Sep. 1660 pr. 31 Oct 1660 by John Curtyce of Tilehurst, Berks., John Curtice of Radley, Berks., John Cole of London, merchant, and James Maynard of Reading, Berks., woollen draper. (PROB11/300). AWP.

Current, Edward of Dubuque City, IA. AWW 5 Mar. 1857 to relict Eliza Susannah Current. (PROB11/2247).

Cusack, Thomas of Halifax, NS, seaman of HMS *Rainbow*. Will pr. 8 Aug. 1782. (PROB11/1094).

Custis, Hon. John of Williamsburg, James City Co., VA. Will 14 Nov. 1749 pr. 19 Nov. 1753 by son Daniel Park Custis. (PROB11/804). AWP. Further grant in 1784.

Cuyler, Abraham of Montreal. Will pr. 16 Dec. 1816. (PROB11/1586).
Cuyler, Cornelius of Montreal. Will pr. 10 Dec. 1807. (PROB11/1471).
Cuyler, Henry of Greenbush, Rensselaer Co., NY, Commissary on half pay of Staff of Martinico. AWW 15 Jul. 1806 to John Thompson. (PROB11/1446).
Cuyler, Jane, widow of St. Therese, [QC]. Will pr. 20 Jan. 1830. (PROB11/1765).

Dafforne, Ann of Shoreditch, Mddx., widow, whose son John Dafforne was resident in New England. Will 14 Oct. 1675 pr. 27 Nov. 1675 by son Benjamin Dafforne. (Guildhall: Ms 9052/19).
Dagworthy, Ely of Trenton, NJ, Capt. of 48ᵗʰ Regiment of Foot. AWW 28 Jun. 1780 to Robert Barclay. (PROB11/1066).
Dallett, Judith of Philadelphia City, widow. Will pr. 4 Jul. 1854 by son Gillies Dallett. (PROB11/2194).
Dalrumble, Alexander of HMS *Woolwich* who died in Salem, MA. Will 10 Mar 1747 pr. 12 Mar 1747 by Paul Moor of Ratcliffe, Mddx, victualler. (PROB11/753). AWP.
Dalrymple, John Esq. of Brunswick Co., NC. Will 25 Feb. 1743 AWW 8 Oct. 1767 to Alexander Duncan of Wilmington, NC, attorney for relict Martha Dalrymple in Brunswick. (PROB11/932). AWP.
Dalrymple, Martha of Brunswick Co., NC, widow. AWW 12 Dec. 1787 to Elizabeth Dalrymple, widow. (PROB11/1160).
Dandridge, Francis, late of Chelsea, Mddx., but lodging at Mr. Samuel Benwell's near Buckingham Gate, St. George the Martyr, London. Will 21 Feb. 1763. Leg: William Dandridge, son of his late brother Bartholomew Dandridge, now living with William Langborne in York River, VA. Wit: John Claridge of Symond's Inn. Will pr. 19 Nov. 1765 by James and George Mares. PROB11/913).
Daniel, Jenkin of Albany Factory, Hudson's Bay. Will 20 Jan. 1821. Leg: sons and daughters (unnamed). Wit: John Garton and Philip Good. AWW 8 Nov. 1825 to son Griffith Daniel. (PROB11/1705).
Dansey, Frederick of Halifax, NS. Will pr. 28 Nov. 1741. (PROB11/906).
Danson, Barbara of Holborn, Mddx., spinster, who had a plantation on Pascotank River, NC. Will 8 Apr. 1726 pr. 23 Apr. 1726 by affirmation of Daniel Dolley.
Daubuz, Henry James of George Town, SC, mariner. Will pr. 13 May 1777 by relict Christian Daubuz. (PROB11/1031).
Davenport, Addington of Boston, MA, clerk. Will 1 Feb. 1745 AWW 21 Aug. 1747 to Alderman William Baker of London. (PROB11/756). AWP.
Davenport, Addington of Boston, MA, merchant. Will pr. 23 Apr. 1761. (PROB11/864).
Davenport, Thomas of London but late of NY, merchant. Will 22 Feb. 1699 pr. 8 Aug. 1716 by William Horsepool of London, merchant. (PROB11/553). AWP.
Davers, Henry, Lieut. of HMS *Neptune* who died in America, bachelor. Will 13 Jan. 1759 pr. 11 Sep. 1759 by Thomas Bilcliffe, his daughter Elizabeth Bilcliffe and Matthew Thornton. (PROB11/849). AWP.
Davers, Jermyn Esq., formerly of Rushbrooke, Suffolk, and late of VA who died at sea. Will Jul. 1744 pr. 22 Mar. 1751 by mother Lady Margaret Davers. (PROB11/786). AWP.
David, David of Montreal, merchant. Will pr. 11 Mar. 1828.(PROB11/1737).
David, Ezekiel of London, merchant but late of James Town, SC. Will pr. 16 Feb. 1769 by Edward Bruce of London, merchant, with similar powers reserved to Francis Magnus of London, merchant. (PROB11/945). AWP.
Davies, George of Montreal, merchant. Will pr. 28 Jan. 1841. (PROB11/1939).
Davis, John of Deptford, Kent, mariner of HMS *Sea Horse* who died in Boston, MA. Will 10 Feb. 1719 pr. 15 Feb. 1725 by Evan Jones of Deptford, shipwright. (PROB11/601). AWP.
Davis, John of Albany Factory, Hudson's Bay. Will 30 Aug 1820. Leg: wife Nancy Davis; children (unnamed). Execs: brother William Davis and sister Ann Davis, both of London. Wit: Jacob Corrigal and Robert Elliott Byfield. Pr. 8 Nov. 1825 by brother William Davis. (PROB11/1705).

Davis, Lewis, mariner of HMS *Tiger* who died in New England on HMS *Advice*. Will 14 Dec. 1695 pr. 22 Dec. 1702 by relict Hannah Davis. (PROB11/467). AWP.

Davyes, Richard of Peankatank River, VA, planter, late of Shoreditch, Mddx. Will 25 Aug. 1660. Leg: wife Joane Davyes to have whole plantation in Peankatank and stock of tobacco. Pr. 5 Jul. 1661 by relict Joane Davyes. (PROB11/305).

Davies, Richard of St. Louis, MO. AWW 17 Feb. 1853 to John Bryan Sr. (PROB11/2166).

Davis, William of NY, mariner of the ketch *Aldborough* of NY. Will 19 May 1694 appointing his wife Ellen Davis as his attorney and universal legatee. Wit: Mary Chosin, Mary Griffin and Elizabeth Skelton. Pr. 25 Aug. 1694. (PROB11/422). AWP.

Davies, William of King George Co., VA. Will 8 Aug. 1775 pr. 16 Oct. 1775 by John Hopkins of London, druggist. (PROB11/1011). AWP.

Davis, William of RI and native thereof, formerly seaman of HMS *La Constance*. Leg: John Larrick *alias* Lassock . Will 4 Oct. 1809 pr. 29 Sep. 1815 by John Larrick. (PROB11/1572).

Davison, William of QC, Capt. in 52nd Regiment of Foot. Will pr. 1 Jul. 1776. (PROB11/1021).

Dawes, William of Boston, MA, who was wounded near St. Helena, mariner of the *Jeremy*, Capt. Gilbert Bant. Will dated Jamaica 8 Mar. 1698. Leg: John Jowett of London, mariner; brother Thomas Dawes of Boston, bricklayer; friend Hannah Pen of Boston but late of Charles Town, MA. Wit: James Trickey, Ben. Lawrence and Edward Dendy. AWW 1699 [*but no Act in Wills Register*].

Day, James of Paspebiac, Gaspé District, [QC]. Will pr. 20 Feb. 1834. (PROB11/1827).

Dayrell, Paul of Brooklyn, NY. AWW 1 Jun. 1805 to Robert Miller. (PROB11/1427).

De Beaufain, Hector Beringer of Charles Town, SC. Will 17 Oct. 1766 pr. 10 Feb. 1767 by George Schutz. (PROB11/925). AWP.

De Brahm, Mary of Charleston, SC, widow. Will 20 May 1805. Leg: daughters Sarah Jones, Charlotte Jackson, Martha Gadsden and Selina Fenwick; son John Roger Fenwick; granddaughters Mary Edwardina Fenwick(?) and Claudia Tatnall; Frederick William Mulcaster, grandson of late husband; Samuel Wetherill Sr. of Philadelphia. Wit: Emma Gadsden, Daniel Wilson and William Drayton. Pr. 14 Jun. 1806 by Selina Fenwick. (PROB11/1444).

De Butts, Mary of Prince George's Co., MD, widow. Will pr. 23 Jun. 1831. (PROB11/1786).

De Butts, Samuel of Prince George's Co., MD. Will pr. 6 Apr. 1816 by Richard Earl Welby. (PROB11/1579).

De Ceballos, Ciracio, native of the mountains of Santander, now of New Orleans, LA. Leg: father Senor de Ceballos in Mauritius or, if he is dead, brother Don Jose Antonio de Ceballos and his son Don Jose Victor de Ceballos; Don Antonio Ortis, etc.Will pr. 6 Aug. 1819 by Pedro Marin Argote and Thomas Urquhart. (PROB11/1619).

De Huyn, John Christopher of NY. Maj. General in Forces of the Landgrave of Hesse Cassell. AWW 6 Nov. 1784 to daughter Sophie Hauxleden, formerly De Huyn, wife of Frederick Charles Louis De Hauxleden. (PROB11/1123).

Deladicq, Lawrence, citizen and joiner of London, bound for NY by the *Beaver* of London, who died overseas. Will 6 Oct. 1690 pr. 12 Oct. 1691 by brother-in-law Paul Ray. (PROB11/406). AWP.

De Lancey, Elizabeth of St. Mary le Bow, Mddx., widow, whose grandmother Sarah Blakeway and brother Richard Beresford were in Charles Town, SC. Will 4 Jan. 1774 pr. 1 Feb. 1774 by brother Richard Beresford. (PROB11/994). AWP. NGSQ 63/293.

De Lancey, James of Annapolis, NS. Will pr. 30 Apr. 1806. (PROB11/1441).

De Lancey, Oliver of NYC but late of Beverley, Yorks.. Will pr. 9 Jan. 1786 to son Stephen De Lancey. (PROB11/1137).

De Lancey, Stephen of Annapolis, NS. Will pr. 19 Oct. 1809. (PROB11/1504).

De Latre, Philip Chesneau of Niagara, ON. Will pr. 23 Oct. 1849. (PROB11/2100).

De Laune, John of Charles Town, SC, surgeon, late of Stepney, Mddx. Will 16 Sep. 1727 pr. 24 May 1728 by Robert Aubert and Anne de Lannay of Stepney, spinster. (PROB11/622). AWP.

De Lavall, Thomas of NYC. Will 10 Jun. 1682 AWW 7 Feb. 1683 to Thomas Landon. (PROB11/372). AWP.

Del Castillo, Manuel Samaniego Lieut. Col. of Mexican service in New Orleans, LA. Will pr. 9 Jul. 1830. (PROB11/1773).

Delegal, Philip dwelling in St. Peter's Port, Guernsey, whose wife was in SC and son in GA. Will 22 Jan. 1762 pr. 14 Sep. 1764 by Abraham Le Mesurier, attorney for relict Eleanor Delegal and son Philip Delegal in GA. (PROB11/901). AWP.

de Montenach, Charles of Montreal. Will pr. 3 May 1833. (PROB11/1815).

De Neufville, John of Cambridge, MA, merchant. AWW 17 Apr. 1801 to Samuel Williams. (PROB11/1356).

Dennis *alias* **Dinnis, Ann** of Toad's Cove, NL. Will pr. 11 Nov. 1699. (PROB11/453).

Denny, Alexander of Charles Town, SC, mariner who died in Stepney, Mddx. Will 10 May 1728 AWW 4 Aug. 1730 to relict Lucy Denny. (PROB11/639). AWP.

Dent, Elizabeth of Appledore, Kent, late of Manchester Square, Mddx., (widow of Rev. Samuel Dent) who left a bequest to her late husband's sister Anna Travers in Philadelphia. Will 13 Oct. 1808 AWW 20 Mar. 1809 to Sir William Gibbons. (PROB11/1494). NGSQ 63/41.

Derick, Henry of VA. Will pr. 6 Oct. 1677. (PROB11/355).

Derickson, George of Shadwell, Mddx., who died on the ship *Unicorn* in VA, bachelor. Will 18 Oct. 1683. AWW 7 Jun. 1685 to Anne Anderson. (PROB11/380).

Des Barres, Joseph Frederick, of Halifax, NS, late Lieut. Governor of PE. Will pr. 5 Mar. 1825. (PROB11/1696).

Desbrosses, Magdalen of NYC, spinster. AWW 21 Jun. 1796 to William Thwaytes. (PROB11/1276).

Deverall, Benjamin of VA. Will 22 Oct. 1716 pr. 1 Feb. 1720 by Rachel and Jeremiah Deverall. (PROB11/572). AWP.

Dewar, John of Amherstburg, [ON]. Will pr. 20 May 1814. (PROB11/1556).

Dewell, Edward of Warwick Squeak, VA, servant. Admon of Jun. 1637 revoked and will pr. 23 Nov. 1640 by Simon Curnocke. (PROB11/184). ACE.VGE.

Dickenson. *See* **Dickinson.**

Dickey, Andrew. *See* **Johnson.**

Dickinson, Francis of Northam, Devon, mariner bound for VA. Leg: "my wife before God" Elizabeth Moore; Richard, Laurence and Philip Draper; Henry & Rebeckah Petteres and others. Wit: Richard Draper, Johane Draper, Elizabeth More and William Limbre. AWW 24 Sep. 1630 to Richard Draper. (PROB11/158). AWP.

Dickenson, Michael of Altrincham, Cheshire, whose nephew James Talier was in VA. Will 20 Aug. 1695 pr. 17 May 1698 by Michael Colley. (PROB11/445). AWP.

Dickinson, Nathaniel of NB. Will pr. 9 Jul. 1789. (PROB11/1181).

Dicks, Christopher of Beaufet Harbour, NL. Will pr. 10 Nov. 1849. (PROB11/2102).

Dickson. *See* **Dixon.**

Dimmick, Thomas of Boston, New England, shipwright. Will dated 10 Nov. 1724 appoints his wife Elizabeth Dimmick sole executrix and legatee. Witnessed by Francis Groves and Marina Hodgson. Commission issued 20 Dec. 1731 to Arabella Toplady, spinster, principal creditor of the testator, late of Rotherhithe but who died on the merchant ship *Margaret*; the named executrix renouncing. (PROB11/648).

Dison. *See* **Dyson.**

Dixie, Harriet of Stamford, Niagara, [ON]. Will pr. 19 Oct. 1848. (PROB11/2081).

Dixon, Josiah of Aldgate, Mddx., mariner of ship *Preservation* who died in VA. Will 3 Jan 1698 pr. 10 Mar. 1699 by Sarah Yates. (PROB11/449). AWP.

Dickson, Thomas of Boston, MA, surgeon of HMS *Worcester*, *Gibraltar* and *Hawk*. Will 22 Jul. 1748 pr. 12 Jan. 1750 by John Ouchterlony of London, merchant. (PROB11/776). AWP. Further grant in June 1762.

Dixon, Thomas of the Orphan House, Christ Church parish, Philadelphia, but late of St. Botolph Aldgate, London, widower. Will 16 Mar. 1764 AWW 22 Oct. 1773 to sister Ann Adams, widow. (PROB11/991). AWP.

Dobbs, Arthur Esq. of Brunswick, New Hanover Co., Governor of NC. Will 31 Aug. 1763 pr. 9 Jun. 1766 by son Conway Richard Dobbs. (PROB11/919). AWP.

Dobbyn, Richard, formerly of Carrick, Tipperary Co., Ireland, but late of Savannah, GA. Will 19 Sep. 1759 AWW 4 May 1770 to relict Anastatia Dobbyn. (PROB11/957). AWP.

Dobie, James of St. John's, NL, surgeon in Royal Navy. Will pr. 16 Oct. 1826. (PROB11/1717).

Docker, Elizabeth Smith of Commerce, Scott Co., MO. AWW 11 Dec. 1855 to William Wilmot. (PROB11/2223).

Docker, Robert Noble of London District, [ON]. Will pr. 4 Dec. 1848. (PROB11/2084).

Dod, George of Canada. Will pr. 16 Jun. 1847. (PROB11/2057).

Dods, Joseph of Wapping, Mddx, mariner of merchant ship *Mary Ann* bound for VA. Will 20 Apr. 1700. Leg. & exec: Thomas Watson of Wapping, mariner. Wit: Joseph Eardley, Ellinor Knowles and James Fancourt. Pr. 24 Dec. 1700 by Thomas Watson. (Guildhall: Ms 9171/50/169).

Dogett, Benjamin of London, merchant, and late of Kingston, Jamaica, whose mother and brother were in SC. Will 8 Jul. 1703 pr. 29 Mar. 1709 by brother John Dogett. (PROB11/507). AWP.

Dolphin, John of Frederica, GA, bachelor. Will 1 Aug. 1741 pr. 20 Aug. 1745 by niece Martha, wife of Alexander Heron. (PROB11/741). AWP.

Donkester, William of Broadstairs, Kent, mariner of merchant ship *Henrietta* who died in Boston, MA. Will 18 Apr. 1729 pr. 9 Dec. 1730 by aunt Judy Cooke. (PROB11/641). AWP.

Donning, William of Lydney, Glos., whose cousin William Donning was in SC. Will 27 May 1743 pr. 9 Feb. 1744 by relict Joanna Donning. (PROB11/731). AWP. NGSQ 64/136.

Donoyhoe, Anthony of Canada, surgeon in Royal Navy. Will pr. 26 Jun. 1848. (PROB11/2076).

Dorr, Joseph of Boston, MA, merchant. Will 10 Sep. 1828. Leg: brothers John, Samuel Adams and Sullivan Dorr who are to be execs; brothers Ebenezer and William Dorr; sisters Abigail wife of Davis W. Child, Elizabeth Dorr and Lucretia Child wife of Joshua Child. Wit: John Gray, P. Parker and John G. Torrey. Pr. 14 Jul. 1832 by John and Samuel Adams Dorr. (PROB11/1802).

Douglass, John of St. Augustine, E. FL. Will pr. 14 Jul. 1820. (PROB11/1632).

Douglas, Sholto of London, mariner of the *St. George* who died in North America. Will 28 Dec. 1757 AWW 4 Apr. 1759 to Robert Mackoun, attorney for John Dalglish of NY, merchant. (PROB11/845). AWP.

Douglas, Susanna. *See Allman.*

Dover, William of St. Olave, Southwark, Sy., shipwright of merchant ship *Old Neptune* who died in VA, bachelor. Will 20 Dec. 1702 AWW 9 Dec. 1706 to sister Anne Dover. (PROB11/491). AWP.

Downe, Abraham, formerly of MD but died at Broad Oaks, Wimbish, Essex, gent. Will 27 Apr. 1729 pr. 3 Apr. 1734 by relict Elizabeth Downe. (PROB11/664). AWP. NGSQ 62/207.

Downie, George of Lake Champlain, VT, Capt. of HM frigate *Confiance.* Will pr. 15 Nov. 1815. (PROB11/1574).

Downs, Joseph of Albany Fort, Hudson's Bay. Will pr. 3 Apr. 1766. (PROB11/917).

Drew, James of NYC, Capt. of Royal Navy. AWW 7 Aug. 1802 to cr. Stephen Drew. (PROB11/1379).

Drexhagen, formerly Medland, Jane of NYC. AWW 1 Aug. 1856 to Henry Henrichsen. (PROB11/2237).

Driffill, John of Ponpon, SC. AWW 1 Jun. 1797 to Moyer Thomas. (PROB11/1292).

Drummond, Robert of East NJ, Maj. of NJ Volunteers. Will pr. 11 Feb. 1789. (PROB11/1175).

Drumont, James of Stepney, Mddx., mariner, who died in VA. Will pr. 7 Feb. 1667 by Christian Mustard of Stepney. (PROB11/323). AWP.

Dryden, James of London, merchant. Will 30 Jun. 1691 leaves estate including proceeds from 3 plantations in MD purchased from Robert Burman of MD in 1690 to be divided between his wife and children Mary, Elizabeth and Jemima Dryden. Wits William Hiccocks, Nathaniel Palmer and F. Brown. Pr. 13 Aug. 1691 by relict Mary Dryden. (PROB11/403).

Dryden, Mary of St. Martin in the Fields, Mddx., widow, whose son-in-law James Dryden and his wife Eleanor were in Charles Town, SC. Will pr. 9 Jul. 1768 by brother John Skilbeck. (PROB11/940). AWP. NGSQ 62/208.

Drysdale, Hugh, late of Col. Charles Churchill's Regt. of Dragoons, Lieut. Gov. of VA who died there. Will 23 Feb. 1722 pr. 12 Dec. 1726 by relict Hester Drysdale. (PROB11/612). AWP.

Du Bois, Gualtherus *alias* **Walter** of NY, gent. AWW 17 Apr. 1793 to William and Henry Jackson. (PROB11/1231).

Dudgeon, Patrick. *See* **Townsend.**

Duffus, James of Halifax, NS. Will pr. 29 Feb. 1836. (PROB11/1857).

Dulany, Rebecca of Newport, RI, widow. AWW 22 May 1826 to Ann Dulany. (PROB11/1712).

Dumaresq, Perry of Restigouche Co., NB., Lieut. in Royal Navy. Will pr. 19 Jun. 1841. (PROB11/1947).

Dumaresq, Philip of Sydney, Cape Breton Co., NS. Will pr. 7 Jun. 1825. (PROB11/1700).

Dummer, Jeremiah, of Plaistow, Essex, agent of MA and CT. Will pr. 1 Jun. 1739. (PROB11/696). AWP. NGSQ 64/219.

Dumotier, James, merchant living in London whose nephew Gardon was living in Carolina. Will, translated from French, 27 Mar. 1713 pr. 10 Feb. 1715. (PROB11/544). AWP. New grant made in 1722.

Du Moulin, James of MD. Will pr. 15 Jan. 1821 by brother Andrew Joseph Aloysius Du Moulin. (PROB11/1651). .

Dunkan, Robert of Stepney, Mddx., mariner of merchant ship *Society* who died in VA. Will 13 Dec. 1712 pr. 8 Nov. 1714 by Elizabeth Browne. (PROB11/543). AWP.

Duncan, William of Spotsylvania, VA. Will pr. 23 Dec. 1828. (PROB11/1748).

Dunlop, Robert Graham of Colborn, Huron Co. [ON]. Will pr. 19 Sep. 1843. (PROB11/1985).

Dunn, Hon. Henry of Toronto. Will pr. 15 May 1854. (PROB11/2191).

Dunn, Joseph of St. Olave, Southwark, Sy., who died in MD. Will 25 Dec. 1714 pr. 10 Apr. 1718 by relict Elizabeth Dunn. (PROB11/563). AWP.

Dunn, Robert Joseph of Newport, RI, but late of Westmoreland parish, Jamaica. Will 11 Feb. 1776. Leg: wife Amy Dunn; son Robert James Dunn. Wits. John Halliburton, Abraham Redwood Jr. and Ackurs Sisson of Newport. Pr. 30 Sep. 1786 by relict Amy Dunn. (PROB11/1145).

Dunn, Walter of Middlesex Co., VA. AWW 2 May 1820 to father William Dunn. (PROB11/1629).

Dunsford, Rev. James Hartley, clerk of Verulam, Colborne District, [ON]. Will pr. 15 Nov. 1852. (PROB11/2161).

Dunster, Charles of Perth Amboy, NJ, bachelor. Will 25 Apr. 1706 pr. 6 Apr. 1732 by John MacCulloch and John Boughton. (PROB11/651). AWP.

Dunton, John of New England, citizen and stationer of London, late of St. Giles, Cripplegate and of Stepney, Mddx. Will 22 Apr. 1733 pr. 24 Mar. 1733 by Richard Nowland. (PROB11/657). AWP. New grant in Jun. 1744.

Dunton, Thomas of Boston, MA, seaman. AWW 15 Nov. 1707 to James Downing. (PROB11/498).

Dupee, Elias, former carpenter of HMS *Bedford* but late shipwright of the *Adventure* who died at Boston, MA. Will 25 Sep. 1749 pr. 15 Oct. 1753 by Mary Thomas of Whitechapel, Mddx. (PROB11/804).

Dyer, William of Sussex Co., PA, dyer. Will pr. 4 Sep. 1690 by son William Dyer. (PROB11/401).

Dyett, Henry of Gore, Guelph District, [ON], gent. Will pr. 18 Dec. 1800. 6 Jun. 1835. (PROB11/1848).

Dyson, Charles, mariner of HMS *Hastings* whose brothers Philip and Francis Dyson were in VA. Will 8 Jan. 1745, pr. 8 Jan. 1746 by affirmation of cousin John Dyson. (PROB11/744). AWP. NGSQ 64/285.

Dyson, John of St. Ann's parish, Mddx., gent, who made bequests to his cousins Philip and Francis Dison of Norfolk Town, VA. Will 22 Sep. 1747 pr. 7 Nov. 1747 by relict Priscilla Dyson, brother-in-law Joseph Bresse and Silvanus Greville. (PROB11/757). AWP. NGSQ 64/285.

Eades, John of Stepney, Mddx., surgeon's mate who died in New England. Will 17 Jul. 1694 pr. 17 Sep. 1698 by father-in-law George Hallam. (PROB11/447). AWP.
Earle, John of Lance Cove, Great Bell Island, Conception Bay, NL. Will pr. 3 Dec. 1751. (PROB11/791).
Easter, Clement late of Newbolton(?), Norfolk, and late of NY, seaman of HMS *Centurion.* AWW 23 Jul. 1783 to Thomas Pearson. (PROB11/1106).
Eccles, James, Capt., of Fredericton, NB. Will pr. 5 Dec. 1839. (PROB11/1920).
Eckley, John, of Kimbolton, Heref., then of Haverfordwest, [Pembrokeshire] but late of Philadelphia, merchant. Will 17 Jul. 1686 AWW 1 Feb. 1699 to James Lewis, Peregrine Musgrave and Richard Stafford, execs. of relict Sarah Eckley deceased. (PROB11/449). AWP.
Eckley, Sarah of Philadelphia, PA, widow. Will 17 Jun. 1692 pr. 7 Dec. 1698 by James Lewis, Peregrine Musgrave and Richard Stafford. (PROB11/448). AWP.
Eddy, Casper Wistar of NY, physician. AWW 20 Nov. 1838 to Joseph Jackson Lister. (PROB11/1903).
Ede, John of NC who died in Cork, Ireland. AWW 14 Aug. 1760 to pc Paul Henry Robinson; the brother Richard Ede renouncing. (PROB11/858).
Edes, Frances of St. Botolph Bishopsgate, London, widow of Philip Edes of RI, gent. Will 24 Aug. 1691. Leg: niece Jane Vavizor to have 12 acres in Somersham, Hunts; nephews St. John Hubbard and Michael Pearpoint, etc; residue to niece Jane Vavizor and son Thomas Vavizor who are to be execs. Wit: William Hughes, Robert Waple and Richard Welman. Pr. 11 Mar. 1695 by Thomas Vavizor. (Guildhall: Ms 9171/47/49).
Edgar, John of Greenspond, NL, surgeon. Will pr. 20 Jan. 1832. (PROB11/1794).
Edgcumbe, Robert, Clerk of the Cheque to Office of Ordnance of Placentia, NL. Will pr. 31 Jan. 1770. (PROB11/954).
Edge, John of St. Andrew, Holborn, Mddx., gent., who died in Boston, MA. Will 8 Jun. 1717 pr. 17 Feb. 1724 by sister Martha Darby *alias* Comby. (PROB11/595). AWP.
Edmonds, Benjamin Jr. of Boston, MA, mariner. Will 2 May 1735 AWW 3 Jun. 1741 to Albert Dennie, attorney for relict Rebecca, now wife of Moses Penniman, in Braintree, MA. (PROB11/710). AWP.
Edmonds, John of Collingbourne Abbots, Wilts., cutler, who died in VA, bachelor. Will 2 Dec. 1667 pr. 6 Jul. 1672 by uncle George Blanchard. (PROB11/339). AWP.
Edwards, David of Boston, MA, mariner. Will 21 Sep. 1696 AWW 27 Jul. 1698 to Edward Hull, attorney for relict Mary Edwards in Boston. (PROB11/446). AWP.
Edwards, Edward, Lieut. Col. in East India Co.'s service of TX. Will pr. 22 Mar. 1841. (PROB11/1942).
Edwards, Richard of Bradforton, Worcs., gent, late of Edenton, NC. Will 30 Dec. 1755 pr. 8 Dec. 1757 by Henry Murcott of Southam, Warw. (PROB11/354). AWP.
Eeles, William of Kingston, [ON], clerk in Ordnance Department. Will pr. 18 May 1857. (PROB11/2251).
Eilbeck, Jonathan of Norfolk, VA. Will pr. 6 Jul. 1821 by Peter Hodgson. (PROB11/1645).
Elam, Gervas of Newport, but late of Portsmouth, RI, having lands in VA. Leg: brother John Elam of Leeds, Yorks., and his children Samuel and Emanuel Elam of Leeds; Joshua Gervas; Joseph and Mary Storrs, children of William and Hannah Storrs of Hunslet, Yorks; Samuel and Sarah Lapage of Leeds, children of George and Elizabeth Lapage. Affirmation of 13 May 1766 by Emanuel Elam of Leeds, merchant, that this writing was made by Gervas Elam who died on 4 Jun. 1776, and he received it by the merchant ship *Hannah* from his nephew James Elam enclosed with a letter dated NY 20 Mar. 1778. AWW to Joseph Elam 20 May 1778. (PROB11/1042).

Elam, Samuel of Portsmouth, RI, formerly of Leeds, Yorks. AWW 23 Feb. 1815. (PROB11/1565).

Elbridge, John Esq. of Bristol who was born in Pemaquid, ME, as were his sisters Rebecca and Elizabeth. Will 20 Feb. 1739 pr. 27 Mar. 1739 by John Scrope, John Cosens and Samuel Creswick. (PROB11/695). AWP. NGSQ 60/185.

Elliott, Andrew formerly of Senegambia, Africa, but late of Savannah, GA, mariner. Will 28 Sep. 1771 pr. 5 Jan. 1775 by John Holmes, Anthony Ellison and John Green. (PROB11/1004). AWP.

Elliot, George, resident of Whitechapel, Mddx., but bound to VA in the *Accomack*. Will 27 Oct. 1664 pr. 19 Jul 1665 by Elizabeth Corbin. (PROB11/317). AWP.

Eliot, George Augustus of QC, Lieut. Col. and Brigade Major. Will pr. 17 May 1836. (PROB11/1861).

Elliott, Gray formerly of Savannah, GA but late of St. Margaret Westminster, Mddx. Will pr. 9 Jul. 1787 by relict Mary Elliott. (PROB11/1155).

Ellis, John of VA. Will 25 Oct. 1658 pr. 22 Jun 1659 by William Jordan with the consent of the brother Henry Ellis. (PROB11/293). AWP.

Elliott, John of Fort William, St. John's, NL. Will pr. 4 Feb. 1717. (PROB11/550).

Ellis, William Esq. formerly of the West Riding of Yorks. but late of NYC. Will dated NY 6 Aug. 1743 and copy transmitted to London under certification of authenticity and accompanied by supporting depositions. The testator leaves to Ann Clark, daughter of Lieutenant-Governor George Clark Esq. of NY, a sum of £300 when she reaches the age of 21, and a similar sum when he is 21 to William Bromley who was born in 1731 or 1732 to Mary Bromley, sister of Andrew Bromley, and said to be begotten by the testator; to Rev. George Almond, chaplain of HMS *Gosport* and vicar of Mellington £30; to "my man" John Bradshaw £20. The testator asked for his debts to be paid by his cousin and sole executor William Ellis of Great Poultney Street, [London] and, if he were dead, appointed as alternative executors his brother Francis Ellis of Cornhill, woollen draper, or his nephew William Ellis, son of Henry Ellis, late brewer in Wapping, [Mddx.]. Pr. by William Ellis 7 Mar. 1744. (PROB11/732).

Ellis, Rev. William clerk of Windsor, Hampshire Co., NS. Will pr. 6 Aug. 1795. (PROB11/1264).

Ellison, Ellen of NYC, spinster. AWW 7 Nov. 1852 to John Frederick Isaacson. (PROB11/2161).

Ellison, Robert Esq. of Westminster, Mddx., Lieut. Col. of Regt. of Foot who died in Albany, NY. Will 2 Nov. 1754 pr. 28 Jun 1756 by. Hon. Maj. General Cuthbert Ellison. (PROB11/823). AWP.

Ellixon, Jasper of Ratcliffe Highway, Stepney, Mddx., mariner of merchant ship *Preservation* who died in VA. Will 1 Jan 1698 pr. 17 Dec. 1706 by Mary Ellixon. (PROB11/490). AWP.

Elmsley, John, Chief Justice of Lower Canada. Will pr. 19 Nov. 1805. (PROB11/1433).

Elson, Samuel of Black Point, [RI], mariner of HMS *Greyhound*. Will 20 Aug. 1706 pr. 11 Sep. 1707 by Robert Harding of Peterhead, Aberdeenshire, Scotland. (PROB11/496). AWP.

Elston, David of Morris, NJ. Will pr. 5 Oct. 1857 by son David Elston. (PROB11/2258).

Emerson, Mary of Bristol, RI, widow. Will 24 Jul. 1740 pr. 10 Nov. 1748 by affirmation of Richard Partridge of London, merchant. (PROB11/765). AWP

Enderwick *alias* Inderwick, Andrew of Hackensack, Bergen Co., NJ. Will 5 Feb. 1828. Leg: sister Margaret Enderwick; brother John Enderwick; nephew Andrew Enderwick, son of brother Charles. Exec: brother John Enderwick and nephew Andrew Enderwick. Wit: Robert Campbell, Hubert Diwolff and Helen M. Campbell. Pr. 7 Jan. 1834 by Andrew Enderwick. (PROB11/1826).

England, John of Alder Mill, Tamworth, Staffs., gent., who died in MD and had estate in PA and MD. Will 6 Apr. 1730 pr. 28 Mar. 1739 by affirmation of sons John, Allen and Joseph England. (PROB11/695). AWP.

Enton, John of St. Paul, Covent Garden, who died in VA. Will 7 Apr. 1689 AWW 27 Jan 1691 to John Smith. (PROB11/403). AWP.

Esten, James Christie of Toronto, late Chief Justice of Bermudas. Will pr. 12 Jan. 1839. (PROB11/1905).

Evance, Thomas of Hudson's Bay. Will pr. 9 Dec. 1706. (PROB11/491).

Evans, Benjamin of Charlotte Town, PE, merchant. Will pr. 2 Aug. 1826. (PROB11/1715).

Evans, Rev. Evan, vicar of Sutterton, Lincs., who had estate in America and died in MD. Will 2 Nov. 1716 pr. 8 Aug. 1729 by John Brace of London, clothworker.

Evans, Jonathan, formerly of Savannah, GA, surgeon and trader on River Gambia, Africa. Will 10 Aug. 1794. Leg: nephew and niece William M. Evans and Sarah Evans of Savannah who are to be execs. Wit: Francis Tighe and James Anderson [in GA]. Affidavit by Richard Wynne of Savannah of 25 Jul. 1796 as to testator's handwriting. Will pr. 31 Oct. 1796 by Matthew Evans. (PROB11/1280).

Evans, Phineas of London, draper, whose cousin Edward Collins was in VA. Will 7 Sep. 1759 pr. 10 Mar. 1760. (PROB11/854). AWP. NGSQ 64/213.

Eveleigh, Samuel of Bristol but late of Charles Town, SC, merchant. Will 20 Jun. 1764 AWW 30 Oct. 1766 to son Nicholas Eveleigh. (PROB11/922). NGSQ 64/141.

Ewen, James of St. John's, NL. Will pr. 2 Nov. 1686. (PROB11/385.

Ewing, James of St. John, NB. Will pr. 8 Jan. 1829. (PROB11/1750).

Faber, Conrad William of Brooklyn, NY, merchant. Will pr. 22 Aug. 1855 by Thomas Achelis. (PROB11/2217).

Fagg, Francis of Philadelphia. Will pr. 16 Dec. 1829. (PROB11/1763).

Fairchild, John of Durham, Newhaven Co., CT. Will pr. 23 Dec. 1774. (PROB11/1003).

Fairfax, Lady Catherine, Baroness Dowager of Cameron, Scotland, who had lands in VA. Will 21 Apr. 1719 pr. 3 Jun. 1719 by William Cage. (PROB11/569). AWP.

Faldo, Charles of Yateley, Hants., gent. who died in Carolina. Will 1 Mar. 1729 pr. 1 Apr. 1729 by William Palmer of St. Bride's, London. (PROB11/629). AWP.

Falkiner, Thomas of Niagara Garrison, ON, Lieut. of 5th Regiment of Foot. Will 2 Nov. 1795. Leg: brother Frederick Falkiner of Tipperary, Ireland; brother-in-law Thomas Stoney of Co. Tipperary; testator's five children by Margaret Ronan of Tipperary named Daniel, Thomas, Mary, Joanna and Anne, now at Niagara. Wit: Capt. Robert Pratt, Capt. Roger Hale Sheaffe and Lieut. Henry Darling. Affidavit 2 Nov. 1795 by Thomas Ridout of Newark, Upper Canada, [ON] that he witnessed the testator's signature. Will pr. 17 Apr. 1798 by brother Frederick Falkiner. (PROB11/1305).

Fananbrouse, John, mariner of HMS *Pembroke,* bachelor. Will 25 Sep. 1747 AWW 7 May 1750 to Joseph Argent, attorney for Elizabeth Partridge in Boston, MA. (PROB11/779). AWP.

Fane, George, Commander of HMS *Lowestoffe* now in NY Harbour. Will 31 Mar. 1709 pr. 24 Oct. 1709 by brother Charles Fane. (PROB11/510). AWP.

Faneuil, Andrew of Boston, MA, merchant. Will 12 Sep. 1734 pr. 4 Sep. 1738 by nephew Peter Faneuil. (PROB11/691). AWP.

Fanning, Edmund, Dr. of Laws and Army General of PE. Will pr. 21 Apr. 1818. (PROB11/1603).

Fargusion, Robert of Northumberland, mariner of the *Falkland,* dated Tarpaulin Creek, Elizabeth Island, [MA] 21 Jan. 1697, pr. 11 Feb. 1698 by George Wallis. (PROB11/443). AWP.

Farley, Sarah of Savannah, GA, spinster. AWW 20 Oct. 1814 to Robert Cooper. (PROB11/1561).

Farmar, Robert of Mobile, W. FL, Major of 34th Regiment of Foot. Will pr. 3 Aug. 1784. (PROB11/1120).

Farmar, Susan Ravand of NYC, widow. AWW 27 Oct. 1841 to Francis Martin. (PROB11/1952).

Farnham, John of Trinity, NL, carpenter. Will pr. 7 Oct. 1833. (PROB11/1822).

Farquharson, James of Niagara, [ON]. Will pr. 19 Jan. 1815. (PROB11/1564).

Farrant, Henry, formerly of Lanton, Northumberland, but late of Schenectady, Albany Co., NY. Will 22 Mar. 1767 pr. 12 Jul. 1768 by John Steel. (PROB11/940).

Farrant, Thomas of Skaneateles, Onondaga, NY. Will pr. 19 Oct. 1855 by brother William Farrant. (PROB11/2220).

Fary, Joseph of London, merchant, bound to VA by the *Ruth* and who died there on the *James*. Will 2 Feb. 1693 pr. 7 Nov. 1695 by mother Mary Fary, widow. (PROB11/428), AWP.

Fassaker, Richard of Stafford Co., VA, aboard the *Rappahannock Merchant* bound for England. AWW 24 Jul. 1676 to Samuel Phillipps. (PROB11/351). VGE.

Fauquier, Hon. Francis, Lieut. Governor of VA. Will 26 Mar. 1767 pr. 19 Dec. 1771 by son Francis Fauquier. (PROB11/973). AWP.

Fawkner, Elizabeth of Epsom, Sy., widow, whose uncles Edward, Peter and Gersham Bulkley were resident in New England. Will 4 Jun. 1720 pr. 1 Jul. 1720 by Stanley West and Rev. William Harris of London. (PROB11/575). AWP.

Fawsett, Peter of Whitechapel, Mddx., mariner who died on the *Barnaby* bound for VA. Original will 30 Sep. 1680. Leg: brother Charles Fawsett and his daughter Jane Fawsett; wife Hester Fawsett who is to be exex. Wit: Francis Frobisher, John Hewes and George Townrow. Pr. 13 Dec. 1687 by relict Jane Fawsett after sentence for validity of will on same date. (Guildhall: Ms 9172/75).

Fay, Julia Margaret of NYC, spinster. Will pr. 23 Apr. 1843 by Arthur Tracy Jones. (PROB11/1977).

Fellgate, Tobias of Westover, VA. Will pr. 23 Apr. 1635 by relict Sarah Fellgate. (PROB11/167). ACE.GGE.

Fenn, Benjamin of Milford, CT. Will pr. 1 Feb. 1675 by relict Susan Fenn. (PROB11/347).

Fenwick, John Esq., formerly of SC but late of St. George, Hanover Square, Mddx. Will 22 Jul. 1747 pr. 2 Nov. 1747 by son Edward Fenwick. (PROB11/755). AWP.

Fenwick, Robert of Boston, MA, Capt. in Royal Artillery. AWW 18 Mar. 1780 to relict Ann Fenwick. (PROB11/1062).

Fenwick, William of London, merchant who died in Boston, MA. Will 12 Mar. 1738 pr. 13 May 1763 by brother Michael Fenwick. (PROB11/887). AWP.

Ferguson, Adam of Newport, RI, tobacconist. AWW 27 Feb. 1802 to James Cockburn. (PROB11/1369).

Fernald, John of New England, shipwright, now on voyage in *Portsmouth* galley of London. Will 26 Feb. 1701 pr. 21 Oct. 1701 by George Rowe. (PROB11/462). AWP.

Fernsley, John, formerly of ship *Princess Louisa* but late of HMS *Lowestoffe* and HMS *Worcester* who died in Boston Hospital, MA, bachelor. Will 26 Mar 1741 pr. 4 Jan 1749 by sisters Mary Crouchefer, widow, and Sarah Fernsley. (PROB11/767). AWP.

Ferrand, Jacob, clerk of Cornwall, [ON]. Will pr. 10 Jul. 1805. (PROB11/1428).

Ferrers, John of NYC, merchant. AWW 28 Apr. 1815 to James Strachan Glennie. (PROB11/1567).

Ferris, Samuel of MS, surgeon and apothecary. Will pr. 24 Aug. 1841. (PROB11/1950).

Fiander, Samuel of English Harbour, Fortune Bay, NL, planter. Will 7 May 1851. Leg: son Samuel Fiander who is to be exec; second son James Fiander. Wit: Owen Pine and Henry Shepherd. Pr. 30 Jul. 1856 by son Samuel Fiander. (PROB11/2225).

Fidler, James of Stepney, Mddx., mariner, who died on ship *Dispatch* in PA. Will 16 Apr. 1691 AWW 17 Jan. 1700 to pc. Thomas Coutts. (PROB11/454). AWP.

Fidler, Peter, formerly of Bolsover, Derbys., but late surveyor and trader of Hudson's Bay Co. at York Factory. Will 16 Aug. 1821. Leg: library, writings and instruments together with the legacy left him by his uncle Jasper Fidler to the Red River Colony; his children [unnamed except the youngest child Peter Fidler]; his mother Mary Fidler at Hockley, Bolsover, Derbys; brother James Fidler. Execs: Governor of Hudson's Bay Co; Governor of Lord Selkirk's Colony at Red River, and the Secretary of the Hudson's Bay. Co. AWW 22 Oct 1827 to son Thomas Fidler, the named execs. renouncing. (PROB11/1731).

Field, Walter of NL, planter, but late of Christchurch, Hants. Will 6 Mar. 1744. Leg: wife Sarah who is to be exex. Wit: Arthur Blanchard, John Stevens and Thomas Stevens. Pr. 5 Sep. 1727 by relict Sarah Field. (PROB11/790).

Fielding, Ambrose who died in VA. Will 26 Jun. 1673 pr. 1 Jul. 1675 by brother Edward Fielding. (PROB11/348). AWP.

Fielding, Henry of King & Queen Co., VA. Will 26 Oct. 1704 pr. 27 Nov. 1712 by Francis Thompson. (PROB11/529). AWP.

Filmer, Samuel, formerly of East Sutton, Kent, and of VA, but who died in Westminster, Mddx. Will 17 Jul. 1662. AWW 12 Apr. 1671 to Warham Horsmonden, father of cousin Mary Filmer *alias* Horsmonden during her absence in VA. (PROB11/332).

Finnie, William, Lieut. of 61st Company of Marines who died in Boston, MA. Will dated Rubislaw, Scotland, 25 Jul. 1774 AWW 21 Nov. 1775 to cousin George Skene of Rubislaw. (PROB11/1012). AWP.

Fisher, James of Gander Bay, NL. Will pr. 20 Feb. 1769. (PROB11/945).

Fisher, Miers Jr. of Philadelphia, merchant. AWW 15 Feb. 1815 to John Bainbridge Jr. (PROB11/1565).

Fitch, Patrick of NY, mariner of HMS *Launceston*. Will 25 Oct. 1743 AWW 10 Dec. 1751 to John Dupré, attorney for relict Abigail Fitch in NY. (PROB11/791). AWP.

Fitch, Thomas of Boston, MA, merchant. Will 19 Jul. 1735 AWW 5 Sep. 1737 to Thomas Gainsborough, attorney for relict Abiel Fitch and sons-in-law James Allen and Andrew Oliver in Boston. (PROB11/685). AWP.

Fitzgerald, Edward, late of NY but late of Islington, Mddx. Will 8 Aug. 1849. Sole exec: Henry Cromwell. Wit: George Froud of Islington, grocer, Jane wife of Charles Barrett of Great Dodford, Worcs., carpenter. Will pr. 29 Nov. 1849. (PROB11/2102).

Fitzgerald, John of VA, mariner of HM schooner *Sultana*. Will pr. 31 Dec. 1772. (PROB11/983).

Fleckner, William, formerly of Plaquemines, LA, but late of New Orleans, planter, who died in London. Will 24 Dec. 1821, codicil dated London 27 Nov. 1822. Leg: four natural children William Frederick, Susan Maria, Elizabeth and Charles Rivington Fleckner, all under-age; guardians to children, William Rowlett of Carshalton, Surrey, and Gabriel Shaw of London. Execs: Gilbert E. Russell and William Smith Richards of New Orleans. Wit: John Davidson. Affidavit 10 Nov. 1822 by John Hayward Spenceley of London, notary public, that the codicil was given to Mr. Ambrose Lanfar of London, merchant, on his departure for New Orleans on the ship *London* bound for NY. Affidavit 29 Jul. 1823 by William Rowlett of Carshalton that he is attorney for the executors named in the will. AWW 3 Aug. 1824 to Rowlett. (PROB11/1689).

Fleet, William, formerly of Martin Worthy, Hants., and Alderbury, Wilts., but late of Choptank, MD, who died at sea on the *Peach Blossom*, bachelor. Will 6 Apr. 1727 pr. 11 Apr. 1733 by sister Mary, wife of Robert Tanner. (PROB11/658). AWP.

Fleetwood, William of Stepney, Mddx., chandler, late of NJ who died in PA. Will 8 Sep. 1685. Leg: wife Alice Fleetwood who is to be exex. Wit: Thomas Fyge, Jere. Howes and ___?___ Wise. Pr. 22 Aug. 1690 by relict Alice Fleetwood. (Guildhall: Ms 9171/42/276).

Flemming, John of Hudson's Bay, late armourer at Mouse Fort. Will pr. 20 Nov. 1767. (PROB11/933).

Fleming, Rt. Rev. Michael Anthony, Catholic Bishop of NL. Will pr. 7 Jun. 1851. (PROB11/2134).

Fletcher, Reuben of Napoleon, Ripley Co., IN. Will pr. 20 Nov. 1856 by George Fletcher Walker. (PROB11/2241).

Fletcher, Richard of Yarmouth, Annapolis Co., NS, doctor of physic. Will pr. 22 Jan. 1820. (PROB11/1624).

Fletcher, William of Sombra, Lambton, [ON]. Will pr. 10 Nov. 1853. (PROB11/2180).

Flett, George of Red River Settlement, Hudson's Bay, yeoman. Will pr. 14 Nov. 1851. (PROB11/2142).

Flett, William of Red River, Hudson's Bay. Will pr. 9 Jan. 1826. (PROB11/1707).

Flint, Thomas of New England on board HMS *Severn* in Bombay, India, bachelor. Will 19 Jul. 1704 AWW 23 Feb. 1706 to Elizabeth King, widow of William King. (PROB11/486). AWP.

Flood, Walter of St. Botolph Aldgate, London, carpenter. Will 13 Jan. 1636. Leg: John Furnell Jr., son of John Furnell of London, haberdasher, and his daughter Mary Furnell, to have all his goods in VA; Bridget and Margaret Davis; Judith Weane, daughter of William and Joane Weane of Southwark, Sy; Richard Woodhouse of London, carpenter; Francis Warner of VA. Exec: brother-in-law John Furnell. Wit: John Bowden, Thomas Forward, William Weane and Felix Furnell. Pr. 2 Jan. 1636 by John Furnell. (Guildhall: Ms 9051/8/101).

Flower, Daniel, citizen and merchant tailor of London, bound on a voyage to VA. Will 20 Aug. 1663 pr. 18 Jun 1670 by Richard Ellis. (PROB11/333). AWP.

Flower, Elizabeth, widow of Park House near Albion, Edwards Co., IL. AWW 26 Jul. 1847 to Edward Fordham Flower. (PROB11/2059).

Flower, Richard of Park House near Albion, Edwards Co., IL. Will pr. 26 May 1830. (PROB11/1771).

Floyd, Edward of Poplar, Mddx., outward bound for VA in the ship *Augustine*. Will 28 Sep. 1680 appointing Jane Wright of Poplar, spinster, as attorney. Wit: Richard Baxter and John Rayner. AWW 29 Jun. 1681 to [not stated but presumably Jane Wright]. (Guildhall: Ms 9171/37/394v).

Floyd, Thomas of Sandy Hook, [NJ], Lieut. of HMS *Conqueror*. Will 28 Nov. 1777 pr. 22 Jun. 1781 by cousin James Bate of Birchin Lane, London, stationer. Leg: mother Mary Floyd of Shrewsbury, Salop, widow. Wit: Thomas Matsond(?). Deposition 20 Jun. 1781 by Frederick Gardner of Birchin Lane, stationer, that he knew the testator and his handwriting. (PROB11/1079).

Fly, John of Piscataway, NJ, seaman of HMS *Catherine*, widower. Nuncupative will 22 Jun. 1696 AWW 1 Mar. 1698 to William Taverner. (PROB11/444). AWP.

Folger, John of New England, mariner of HMS *Gibraltar*. Will dated 10 Jun. 1744 names Margaret Wood as sole executrix and legatee. Wit: William Chadwick and Charles Cathcart Grant. Pr. 26 Aug. 1745 by Margaret Wood, wife of John Wood. (PROB11/741).

Follet, John, mariner of HMS *Deptford* who died off Cape Henry in VA. Will pr. 22 Jan. 1692 by Richard Mills. (PROB11/408). AWP.

Forbes, George of St. Mary's Co., MD. Will 10 Oct. 1739 AWW 16 Jun. 1742 to William Black, attorney for son-in-law George Gordon and Kenelm Jones in MD. (PROB11/718). AWP.

Forbes, Robert Miller of Peterborough, Colborne District, [ON]. Will pr. 10 Dec. 1847. (PROB11/2066).

Forbes, William Henry of St. John, NB, Capt. in Royal Artillery. Will pr. 13 Feb. 1852. (PROB11/2147).

Forman, William, Commissary and Paymaster of Artillery in North America, late residing in Tower of London who died in NY. Will 3 Aug. 1773 pr. 13 Jun. 1775 by brother Richard Forman. (PROB11/1008). AWP.

Forrester, George of NYC, mariner. Will pr. 14 Feb. 1751 by William Holt of NYC. (PROB11/785). AWP.

Forsyth, Hon. John, Member of Legislative Council of Montreal. Will pr. 10 Mar. 1815. (PROB11/1895).

Foster, Isaac of Spitalfields, Mddx., formerly of Philadelphia, PA. Will 31 Aug. 1779 pr. 23 Mar. 1781 by Simon Bailey. (PROB11/1075). NGSQ 63/39.

Fothergill, Francis of NYC, of Royal Artillery, saddler and collar maker, now bound to London on transport ship *Friendship*. Will pr. 13 Jan. 1769. (PROB11/945).

Fottrell, Edward of Baltimore, widower. Will 17 Feb. 1741 AWW 11 Nov. 1748 to William Black, attorney for cr. William Chapman in MD. (PROB11/765). AWP.

Foulks, Thomas of Princess Anne Co., VA, planter. Will pr. by decree 31 Oct. 1692 by John Vicary. (PROB11/410, 412). GGE.

Fountain, John of Abingdon, Berks., gent., whose brother Roger Fountain died at Lynn Haven, VA. Will 24 Feb. 1711 pr. 16 Feb. 1712 by relict Margaret Fountain. (PROB11/525). AWP.

Fountain, Thomas of Sugar Creek, Walworth Co., WI. Will pr. 7 Aug. 1857 by relict Sarah Fountain. (PRPB11/2256).

Fowler, James of Mile End, Stepney, Mddx., but late of Nansemond Co., VA. Will 27 Apr. 1709 pr. 13 May 1709 by John Goodwin. (PROB11/508). AWP.

Fowler, William of Grace(?) Church, Essex Co., VA, on board *Royal Sovereign* but late of *Winchester*. Will pr 11 Mar. 1745. (PROB11/738).

Fox, John of Camberwell, Sy. who died in Boston, MA, on HMS *Rochester*. Will 28 Oct. 1708 pr. 12 Jan. 1713 by Anne Perry. (PROB11/531). AWP.

Foxcroft, John of Cambridge, MA. AWW 15 Mar. 1804 to John Lovell. (PROB11/1406).

Fogo, Dr. Thomas McMillan of Halifax, NS, serving in the Ordnance Medical Dept. Will pr. 7 Oct. 1850. (PROB11/2120).

Foote, Richard of St. Dunstan in East, London, merchant, who had estate in VA. Will 19 Mar. 1695 pr. 23 Apr. 1697 by relict Hester Foote. (PROB11/437). AWP.

Foy, Lewis of QC City, Captain in Royal Navy on half pay. Will pr. 20 Sep. 1827. (PROB11/1730).

Francis, Anne of Philadelphia, widow. AWW 2 Jun. 1818 to Walter Stirling. (PROB11/1605).

Francis, Eugene *alias* **Owen**, of Bonavista, NL. Will pr. 23 Aug. 1847. (PROB11/2060).

Francis, Turbutt of Philadelphia, reduced Lieut. of 44th Regiment. Will pr. 7 Aug. 1782 by relict Sarah Connelly. (PROB11/1094).

Francois, Charles, Bishop of Capsa, Assistant Bishop of QC, parson of Pointe aux Trembles, QC. Will pr. 13 Feb. 1797. (PROB11/1285).

Francklin, James Boutineau of Halifax, NS. Will pr. 5 Aug. 1841. (PROB11/1950).

Francklin, Susanna of Windsor, NS, widow. Will pr. 27 Aug. 1816. (PROB11/1583).

Frank, Graham of London, merchant, now residing at Ripon, Yorks. Will 24 Nov. 1795. To be buried at Pickhill, [Yorks.] with a gravestone inscribed: "Here lie the remains of Graham Frank, the son of Richard and Ellen Frank, who after residing twenty years in Virginia was a respectable merchant in London." Leg: son Thomas Thorpe Frank; John Eddington of Earle Street, London, merchant; George Browne of Chamberlain's Wharf, London, merchant. Wit: Richard Browne, Na. Harrison and John Cartman. Will pr. 1 Feb 1796 by son Thomas Thorpe Frank. (PROB11/1271).

Fraser, Alexander of Hudson's Bay, mason. Will pr. 22 Feb. 1769). (PROB11/945).

Fraser, Alexander of Savannah, GA, late Lieut. of 71st Regiment of Foot. AWW 17 Dec. 1783 to Robert Waddell. (PROB11/1111).

Fraser, John of Windsor, NS, surgeon. Will pr. 12 Oct. 1819. (PROB11/1621).

Fraser, Thomas formerly of St. Bartholomew's, Charleston, SC, reduced Major of the SC Regiment of Royalists but late of Philadelphia, planter. Leg: wife Ann Loughton Fraser who is to be exex; daughters Eliza Smith Fraser and Jane Winter Fraser. Will 24 May 1817. Codicil dated Philadelphia 20 Sep. 1820. AWW 17 Jul. 1783 to Crawford Davison, attorney for the daughter Eliza Smith Fraser in Philadelphia; the relict Ann Loughton Fraser and the daughter Jane Winter Fraser renouncing. (PROB11/1673).

Fraunces, Edward Esq. formerly of Bere, Jamaica, but late of London, whose cousins Elizabeth, Mary and Martha were in VA. Will pr. 3 Apr. 1741 by brother James Fraunces. (PROB11/708). AWP.

Freame, Thomas Esq. of Philadelphia, Capt. in Gooch's Regiment of Foot. Will 22 Sep. 1740 pr. 4 Sep. 1744 by affirmation of Thomas Penn. (PROB11/735). AWP.

Freeman, Thomas Esq. of St. Clement Danes, Mddx., then of Jamaica but late of NY. Will dated NY 12 Apr. 1729 and copy forwarded to London in 1741. Legacies left to: Mrs. Mary Harris, widow of Edward Harris of Jamaica, gent deceased; Mrs. Ann Wheeler, widow; testator's cousin Cope Freeman; Hannah Bush of Laleham, Mddx., spinster, and others. The testator's property in Jamaica and Great Britain descended to him by will of his father Thomas Freeman deceased and by will of his uncle Edward Freeman deceased. Witnessed by George Coldham, John Seen and Anthony Sanderson. Deposition of 12 Nov. 1741 by Isaac Honnor of Middle Temple, gent, that he received a certified copy of the testator's will from Roger Drake of London, merchant, after it had been brought from Jamaica by a British warship. Pr. 2 Dec. 1742 following a cause brought in London by the sole executor and legatee Sir Thomas Reynell against the testator's relict Grace Murray, formerly Freeman, now wife of Thomas Murray Esq. Sentence was given for the validity of the will. (PROB11/717 & 722).

French, James of Parish Village, Brant Co., [ON], soap & candle maker. Will pr. 17 Jan. 1857. (PROB11/2244).

Freshwater, William of Clerkenwell, Mddx., citizen and haberdasher of London. Will dated VA 9 Mar. 1704 AWW 3 May1706 to sister Elizabeth Freshwater. (PROB11/488). AWP.

Frisby, James of Cecil Co., MD. Will 10 Sep. 1702 pr. 8 Dec. 1703 by son James Frisby. (PROB11/473). AWP.

Frost, Augustine of York Fort, ON. Will pr. 10 Jan. 1759 by James Isham. (PROB11/843). AWP.

Froud, James, seaman of HMS *Africa* in Naval Hospital, Halifax, NS. Will pr. 15 Nov. 1813. (PROB11/1549).

Fry, James Jr. of Southall, Mddx., tanner, late of Nottingham, MD. Will 17 Apr. 1770 pr. 20 Mar. 1771 by William Molleson and Ninian Pinckney of London. (PROB11/965). AWP.

Fry, Susannah. *See* **Tooley.**

Fulham, John of Carolina, sergeant of marines who died on HMS *Oak*. Will 19 Jan. 1703 pr. 1 Sep. 1715 by relict Ursula Fulham. (PROB11/548).

Fuller, James Cannings of Skaneateles, Onondaga, NY. Will pr. 27 Dec. 1851 by solemn affirmation of relict Lydia Fuller. (PROB11/2143).

Fullerton, George of Charleston, SC, merchant. Will 8 Oct. 1708 pr. 8 Sep. 1709 by William Rhett. (PROB11/510). AWP.

Fullerton, James of Halifax, NS, Lieut. Col. of 96th Regiment of Foot. Will pr. 27 Oct. 1834. (PROB11/1837).

Furness, Jacob of Bermondsey, Sy., mariner, who had freeholds in NY. Will 3 Sep. 1723 pr. 11 Feb. 1725 by relict Elizabeth Furnesss. (PROB11/601). AWP.

Futerell, Catherine of Charleston, SC, spinster. AWW 2 May 1832 to William Williams. (PROB11/1799).

Gabourel, Joshua of London, master of the *Maxwell* who died at Cape Fear, NC, bachelor. Will 23 Sep. 1726 pr. 19 Apr. 1737 by brother Amos Gabourel. (PROB11/683). AWP.

Gaddy, James of York Factory, Hudson's Bay. Will pr. 26 Dec. 1834. (PROB11/1840).

Gale, Edward of Symondsbury, Dorset, and late of God Roy River, NL. Will 18 Apr. 1826. Leg: nephew Carter, son of William Carter and his wife Catharine, testator's sister; brothers James and William Gale; sisters Sarah wife of John Hulen, Eleanor wife of James Hulen and Fanny wife of Robert Baker, all of NL. Exec: John Clark of Poole, Dorset, merchant. Wit: J. Waldron, Mary John and John A. Willis. Pr. 15 Dec. 1826 by John Clark. (PROB11/1719).

Gale, Samuel, clerk of Montreal. Will pr. 4 Aug. 1828. PROB11/1744).

Gallie, Francis of Paspebiac, Gaspé District, QC. Will pr. Will pr. 27 Nov. 1833. PROB11/1823).

Gamelin, Peter *alias* **Pierre** of Montreal, Capt. on half pay of Regiment of Canadian Provincials. Will pr. 23 Nov. 1798. (PROB11/1315).

Gange *alias* **Genge, Abraham** of Forteau Bay, Labrador. Will pr. 17 Dec. 1832. (PROB11/1809).

Gapper, Susanna Maria of Bucks Co., PA, widow. Will pr. 29 Sep. 1838 by Richard Van Heythusen. (PROB11/1900).

Garden, John of Philadelphia. Will pr. 23 Jan. 1801 by William Blackburn. (PROB11/1352).

Gardiner, Samuel of Anderson Town, Essex Co., ON. Will pr. 9 Apr. 1856. (PROB11/2230).

Gardiner, Silvester of Newport, RI, doctor of physic. Will pr. 14 Apr. 1787 by Robert Hallowell. (PROB11/1152).

Garland, John of Upper Canada, Lieut. of HMS *Detroite*. Will pr. 16 Jan. 1815. (PROB11/1564).

Garrard, Anne of Up Lambourne, Berks., widow. Will 19 Jun. 1634. Leg: grandchild & exex. Jane Busher; grandchild Anne Busher, now wife of Thomas Hinton, lately gone to VA; grandchildren Philip, Edward, John and Charles Kistell, sons of Philip Kistell. Wit: John Harris and Thomas Deane. Pr. 13 Feb. 1635 by Jane Busher. (PROB11/167). AWP.

Garratt, Robert of Burlington, Otsego Co., NY. AWW 13 Feb. 1832 to Thomas Turton. (PROB11/1795).

Garrett, Amos of Annapolis, MD, merchant. Will 4 Sep. 1714 pr. 22 Dec. 1739 by William Woodward. (PROB11/699). AWP.

Garrick, James of Philadelphia, mate of ship *Lyon*, Capt. John Shaw, in Kingston Harbour, Jamaica. Will 29 May 1781, Wit: John Chambers, Nicholas Willett Chavasse and Robert Bell, ship's nurse, pr. 31 Dec. 1781 by John Shaw. (PROB11/1085).

Garstelle, Frederick of Halifax, NS, bachelor. Will pr. 27 May 1820. (PROB11/1629).

Gate, James of Cordroy River near Cape Ray, NL. Will pr. 13 Sep. 1853. (PROB11/2178).

Gates, Ann of St. Botolph Bishopsgate, London, whose so Thomas Gates was in VA. Will pr. 9 Jan. 1751 by Ann Andrews, spinster. (PROB11/785). APW.

Gates, Thomas of Charleston, SC. AWW 4 Mar. 1853 to James Alexander Simpson. (PROB11/2168).

Gauld, George of FL, Surveyor of FL Coasts. Will dated Pensacola 20 Oct. 1779. Leg: Dr. John Lorimer, Surgeon-General of HM Forces in W. FL and his wife; sister Mabel Gauld; uncle Farquhar Shaw of Banffshire. 22 Jun. 1782. Execs: wife Ann Gauld, Dr. John Lorimer, John Mitchel Esq of Pensacola. Wit: Richard Wegg, John Falconer and Alexander Moore. Pr. by relict 22 Jun. 1782. (PROB11/1091).

Gault, James of Stepney, Mddx., mariner of HMS *Dove* who died in VA. Will 1 Jun. 1695 pr. 1 Sep. 1697 by relict Alice Gault. (PROB11/440). AWP.

Gauvreau, Edward Lieut. in Regiment of NL & recruiting for it in QC City. Will pr. 24 May 1826. (PROB11/1712).

Geary, John of Tring, Herts., yeoman, who had estate in PA. Will 28 Mar. 1696 pr. 9 Dec. 1696 by cousin Henry Geary. (PROB11/435). AWP.

Geere, Dennis of Saugus, MA. AWW 28 Jun. 1642 to Edward Moncke. (PROB11/189). ACE.GGE.

Gely, John *alias* **Jaby, Josia**, of New England, mariner of HMS *Assurance*. Will pr. 15 Sep. 1711. (PROB11/523).

Genge. *See* **Gange.**

Gerrard, Henry of St. Martin Brandon, Charles City Co., VA. AWW 11 Mar. 1693 to Micajah Perry. (PROB11/414). VGE.

Gerarde, John, citizen and barber surgeon of London. Will 11 Dec. 1612. Leg: son-in-law Richard Houlden and his wife Elizabeth, testator's daughter; nieces Agnes, Margaret and Katherine Houlden, the last two to have my adventure of £25 in VA. Wit: William Johnes and Freeman Fox. Pr. 7 Dec. 1622 by the relict Agnes Gerarde. AWW 20 Mar. 1613 by relict. (Guildhall: Ms 9052/30).

Gerrish, Benjamin of Halifax, NS. Will pr. 28 Jun. 1775. (PROB11/1008).

Gerrish, Joseph of Halifax, NS. Will pr. 11 Sep. 1777. (PROB11/1034).

Gibbs, Richard of Bensalem, Bucks Co., PA, yeoman. Will pr. 23 Mar. 1804 by Richard Lowther. (PROB11/1406).

Gibson, Abraham Priest of Boston, MA. Will pr. 11 Dec. 1852 by Thomas Aspinwall. (PROB11/2163).

Gibson, Ann of Charles Town, SC, widow of Daniel Gibson. Will 9 Oct. 1734 pr. 23 Jan. 1736 by Rev. Lawrence Neill. (PROB11/675). AWP.

Gibson, John of HMS *Assurance* who died on James River, VA. Will 4 Dec. 1691 pr. 11 Oct 1692 by Edward Kerby, citizen and merchant tailor of London. (PROB11/411). AWP.

Gibson, John, commander of the *Integrity* of Montreal, QC. Will pr. Will pr. 13 Dec. 1790. (PROB11/1199).

Gibson, Richard of Newport, RI, mariner of HMS *Maidstone*. AWW 16 May 1782 to James Sykes. (PROB11/1090).

Gibson, William of St. Edmund the King, London, haberdasher who had lands in PA. Will 31 Jul. 1683. AWW 9 Jan. 1685 to Jane Barnes. (PROB11/379). AWP.

Gildart, Francis of Washington, MS, Capt. on half pay of Tarleton's Dragoons. AWW 29 Jul. 1816 to James Tidbury. (PROB11/1582).

Gildemaster, Christopher of London, merchant who died in East NJ, bachelor. Will 13 Aug. 1731 pr. 9 Jul. 1736 by brothers John Frederick Gildemaster of Bremen and Daniel Gildemaster of Rotterdam, merchants. (PROB11/678). AWP.

Giles, Jean *alias* **Jane** of Charlestown, SC. AWW 20 Jun. 1797 to James Farquhar. (PROB11/1292).

Giles, John of Charlestown, SC. AWW 10 Nov. 1798 to James Farquhar. (PROB11/1314).

Giles, William of St. Giles in Fields, Mddx., but late of NYC, merchant. Will 9 Sep. 1702 pr. 26 Jan. 1703 by George Giles, Peter Rogers and Charles Rhodes. (PROB11/468). AWP.

Gillespie, George of Bristol Township, Bucks Co., PA, planter. AWW 11 Mar. 1782 to Andrew Drummond. (PROB11/1088).

Gill, William, gent. of London, who inherited lands near Charles Town, SC, by the will of his father Capt. John Gill of Barbados. Will 12 Feb. 1740 pr. 10 Aug. 1743 by sister Frances Gill of London. (PROB11/728). AWP.

Gilliat, Thomas of Richmond, VA, merchant. Will pr. 24 Dec. 1810 by brother John Gilliat. (PROB11/1517).

Gillim. *See* **Guillam.**

Gillyan, Abraham *alias* **Abial** of NY, seaman. Will 30 Mar. 1810 on board HMS *Unicorn* at sea. Leg: brothers Benjamin Gillyan of New Baltimore, NY, and Peter Gillyan of Buttermilk, NY, who are to be execs. Wit: A.N. Kerr and William Baker, First Lieut. AWW 5 May 1833 to Thomas Millett, attorney for named surviving exec. Benjamin Gillyan in North America. (PROB11/1533).

Gladman, George of Eastmain Factory, Hudson's Bay. Will 25 Mar 1820. Leg: Mary Gladman considered to be his lawful wife; his children by her, Elizabeth, William, Robert and Philip Gladman; brother Joseph Gladman. Execs: sons Joseph and George Gladman. Wit: Alexander Christie, chief factor, and Charles McCormick, surgeon. Affidavit by Thomas Vincent of Moose Factory certifying testator's handwriting. Pr. 21 Nov. 1822 by George Gladman. (PROB11/1663).

Glascock, Richard of Richmond Co., VA. AWW 20 Feb. 1812 to William Murdock. (PROB11/1530).

Glasgow, George Mark of QC, Capt. in HM Artillery. Will pr. 22 Nov. 1851. (PROB11/2142).

Gledhill, Joseph, Commander-in-Chief of Garrison of Placentia, NL. Will pr. 15 Dec. 1747. (PROB11/758).

Gledhill, Mary of Isle of Wight, VA, widow. Will 30 Nov. 1712 AWW 23 Jun 1721 to Micajah Perry, attorney for sons James Day and Nathaniel Ridley. (PROB11/580). AWP.

Glencross, William of NY about to depart from London. Will 11 Feb. 1709 pr. 9 Dec. 1713 by Broughton Wright. (PROB11/537). AWP.

Glenny, James of Canada, merchant. Will pr. 20 May 1802. (PROB11/1374).

Glocester *alias* **Warkman, Mark** of St. Katherine by the Tower, citizen and grocer of London. Will 20 Apr. 1670. Leg: wife Elizabeth Glocester; children Mark and Elizabeth Glocester; brothers Edmund, Thomas, Robert and Joseph Glocester; sisters Christian, Anne, Sarah and Mary Glocester; wife and children Mark and Elizabeth to have estate in VA, Irthlingborough, Northants and Staunton, Glos. Wit: William Nevet, Richard Sherwood and Charles Izard. Will pr. 28 Apr. 1670 by relict Elizabeth Glocester *alias* Warkman. (PROB11/332).

Glover, John Robert, of Kingston, [ON], Keeper of Naval Store. Will pr. 17 May 1843. (PROB11/1979).

Glover, Nathaniel of Dorchester, MA, but late of Bermondsey, Sy., tanner. Will 9 Mar. 1726 pr. 21 Mar. 1726 by Jane Davis of Bermondsey. (PROB11/608). AWP.

Gluvias, Hewit of Annapolis Royal, NS, gunsmith. Will pr. 3 Dec. 1762. (PROB11/882).

Goddard, Edmund, citizen and cooper of London who died in VA, bachelor. Will 3 Sep. 1662 pr. 5 Dec. 1680 by sister Hannah Sheffield. (PROB11/368). AWP.

Goddard, William of St. Margaret Moses, London, mariner who died in SC. Will 26 Nov. 1733 pr. 2 May 1740 by aunt Mary Darby, spinster. (PROB11/702). AWP.

Godson, Richard of Ratcliffe, Stepney, Mddx., who died in NY on HMS *Advice*. Will 18 Sep. 1696 AWW 2 Dec. 1702 to pc. Henry Willoughby. (PROB11/467). AWP.

Goldhawk, Mary of Chertsey, Sy., widow, whose cousin Thomas Evance was in SC. Will 22 Oct. 1770 pr. 25 Feb. 1772 by nephew John Hayter. (PROB11/975). AWP.

Goldsborough, William of Talbot Co., MD, gent. Will 15 May 1750 AWW 2 Jan. 1766 to William Anderson, attorney for relict Henrietta Maria Goldsborough in MD. (PROB11/915). AWP.

Goldsmith, Ralph of Barking, Essex, mariner. Will 2 Sep. 1679. Leg: Friends (Quakers) of Meeting Place at Horsley Down, Southwark, Sy; daughter Anne, wife of Thomas Arnall of Bermondsey, Sy., mariner; Clare Sutton, child of testator's son-in-law Henry Sutton of Redriffe, Sy., mariner; daughters Clare, Mary, Elizabeth, Mercy and Sarah Goldsmith; tenement in Middle Street, Galloway, Ireland to his two youngest daughters; estate in Southold, MA, to daughters Elizabeth, Mercy and Sarah. Wit: John Kirke, John Witchell, Robert Bayly and John Saxby. Pr. 10 Oct.1679 by daughters Anne Arnall and Clare Goldsmith. (Guildhall: Ms 9171/36/509).

Goldthwait, Joseph Jr. of NYC, bachelor. AWW 18 Nov. 1780 to son Samuel Goldthwait. (PROB11/1071).

Golightly, Culcheth of St. Andrew's, [Charles Town], Berkeley Co., [SC]. Will 14 Dec. 1749. Leg: wife Mary Golightly; Rebecca Pinckney, youngest daughter of Major William Pinckney, whose uncle Charles Pinckney Esq. is to receive her bequest; daughters Dorothy and Mary Golightly; children of brother Fenwick Golightly in East Indies. Execs: Hon. Edward Fenwicke, Charles Pinckney Esq; George Austin, merchant, and Landgrave Edmund Bellinger. Wit: Lionel Chalmers, John Gibbes and Lucy Ann Edwards. Pr. 18 Mar. 1756 by Charles Pinckney. (PROB11/821). (AWP).

Good, Richard of Moose Factory, Hudson's Bay. Will pr. 29 Jan. 1851. (PROB11/2125).

Goodhue, John of Boston, MA, mariner of HMS *Swiftsure*. Will pr. 25 May 1758. (PROB11/838).

Goodwin, formerly Harwood, Elizabeth of NY, widow. Will pr. 16 Oct. 1851 by Daniel Walker. (PROB11/2140).

Gordon, Ann of Goochland Co., VA, widow. AWW 22 Apr. 1808 to William Murdock. (PROB11/1477).

Gordon, James of Lancaster Co., VA. AWW 27 Apr. 1808 to William Murdock. (PROB11/1477).

Gordon, John of Charles Town, SC, merchant. Will dated Bristol 28 Jul. 1774, Wit: Edward Neufville, Cradock Odford and Samuel Richards. Leg: including lands in East FL conveyed to him by Jesse Fish of St. Augustine with codicil, now of City of Westminster, to: two daughters by first wife, Elizabeth Smith and Sarah Gordon, plantation of 994 acres in Prince William parish, SC, purchased from John William Murray; to sister-in-law Mrs. Margaret Smith lands in GA, SC and East FL.; John Smith Esq. of GA; Thomas Forbes and William Panton of East FL; my children Mary, Adam, Caroline and Jane Drummond Gordon born to his second wife Catherine Shaw. Wits. Thomas Russell, Richard Kirk and A. Chiencultie. Pr. 31 Mar. 1778 by Troy Elliott Esq. of Knightsbridge, Mddx., William Greenwood and William Higginson. (PROB11/1040).

Goring, Lovet of the Inner Temple, Common Cryer and Sergeant at Arms of the City of London. Will 30 Aug. 1695 pr. 29 Dec. 1697 by William Wolley. (PROB11/442). AWP. Further grant 10 Apr. 1710 to Susan Lambe, wife of Joshua Lambe of Roxbury, MA.

Gosse, John of Carbonair, NL. Will pr. 12 Jan. 1835. (PROB11/1841).

Gough, Harry Dorsey of Baltimore. AWW 23 Dec. 1822 to William Hoffman. (PROB11/1664).

Gough, William of Bristol, woollen draper. Will 1 May 1748 pr. 4 Jul. 1750 by nephew Isaac Burgess. (PROB11/781) AWP. In Dec. 1822 grant made to William Hoffman, attorney for James Carroll in North America.

Gould, Francis of Canada, purser of HMS *Prince Regent*. Will pr. 29 Mar. 1817. (PROB11/1590).

Gould, John, Surgeon and Mate of Montreal Hospital. Will pr. 5 Jun. 1801. (PROB11/1359).

Gourley, Jane of Halifax, NS, widow. Will pr. 18 Aug. 1828. (PROB11/1744).

Gover, George of Shadwell, Mddx., cooper who died on the *Ann* bound for Barbados and VA. Will 15 Feb. 1692. Leg: daughter Susannah, wife of George Hooper of Shadwell, who is to be exex. Wit: Ann Sibbells, Thomas Pomeroy and Thomas Porter. Pr. 3 Aug. 1695 by Susannah Hooper. (Guildhall: Ms 9171/47/173v).

Grace, William of St. Katherine by Tower, London, master of the *Owen* who died in Boston, MA. Will 17 Apr. 1744 pr. 30 Sep. 1748 by Catherine Hunter, widow. (PROB11/764). AWP.

Gradwell, James who died on the ship *Preston* on Cooper River, SC. Will dated Charleston, SC 3 Apr. 1699 AWW 25 Oct. 1699 to Edward Hoole. (PROB11/452). AWP. NGSQ 64/139.

Graeme, David Esq. of Charles Town, SC. Will of 12 Jul. 1766 appointing wife Anne Graeme exec. or alternatively Thomas Middleton or James Skirving(?) of SC. Wit: John Moultrie, John K_____ and Mord. McTartan. Declared as valid will at Charles Town 27 Aug. 1766 before wits. Christopher Rolleston and Edward Neufville. Pr. London by Anne Graeme 22 Apr. 1778. (PROB11/1041).

Grafton, Woodbridge, late of Philadelphia, sea captain. Will pr. 17 Oct. 1826 to Francis Barault. (PROB11/1717).

Graham, George of QC, surgeon. Will pr. 18 Dec. 1800. (PROB11/1351).

Graham, John of Wapping, Mddx., mariner of Charles Town, SC, bachelor. Will 9 Jul. 1753 pr. 28 May 1755 by William Littleton of Wapping, Mddx, victualler. (PROB11/815). AWP.

Graham, Lewis of Pelham, Westchester, NY. AWW 19 Dec. 1800 to Effingham Lawrence. (PROB11/1351).

Graham, Philip Percival of Brock, [ON], Commander in Royal Navy. Will pr. 19 Oct. 1849. (PROB11/2101).

Graham, William of QC City, vintner. Will pr. 4 Mar. 1780. (PROB11/1062).

Grant, Alexander of Amherstburg, [ON], Member of the Legislative and Executive Councils. Will pr. 17 Nov. 1830. (PROB11/1778).

Grant, John Esq. of NYC. Leg: son John Burgoyne Grant, Lieut. of Royal Fusiliers under management of execs. James Baillie and Robert Grant Esq.; brother Alexander Grant and his children; sister Hannah Grant; nephew James Fraser Esq; friend Sir James Grant. Wits. John Grant, Benjamin Grosvenor and John McBean. Pr. 5 Dec. 1780 by James Baillie. (PROB11/1072).

Grant, Peter of New Longueil, [QC], trader. Will pr. 4 Dec. 1817. (PROB11/1599).

Grape, James of New Windsor, Berks., gent., whose son Samuel Grape was in SC. Will 22 Apr. 1733 pr. 18 Jul. 1733 by son Richard Grape. (PROB11/660). AWP.

Grave, Anne of St. Botolph Aldgate, London, widow, who had relations George Grave in Hartford, CT, and John Grave in New Haven, CT. Will 10 Feb 1675 pr. 20 Mar 1677 by William Kiffin. (PROB11/353). AWP.

Grave, John of VA. AWW 24 Sep. 1692 to Walter Potter. (PROB11/411). ACE.

Grave, John of Dublin, Ireland, but late in Annapolis, MD. Will 3 Jan. 1743 pr. 18 Jul. 1757 by brother Thomas Grave. (PROB11/831). AWP.

Grave alias Graves, Leonard of Charles Town, SC, planter. AWW 20 Dec. 1799 to nephew Walter Potter. (PROB11/1334).

Graves, Adam of Sorel, William Henry Co., Richlieu District, Montreal., Capt. of Provincial Forces on half pay of Detroit, MI. Will pr. 12 Oct. 1807. (PROB11/1468).

Gravina, formerly Watson, Mrs. De Conty of Halifax, NS. Will pr. 4 May 1754. (PROB11/808).

Gray, Andrew of QC, Capt. in NS Fencibles and Assistant Quartermaster-General of H.M. Forces in North America. Will pr. 27 Feb. 1815. (PROB11/1565).

Gray, Ellis of Boston, MA, merchant. Will pr. 10 Aug. 1782 by Thomas Dolbeare. (PROB11/1094).

Grey, Henry of St. Botolph Aldgate, London, who had estate in VA and died there. Will 8 Aug. 1674 AWW 5 Jun. 1675 to pc. Richard Bankes. (PROB11/348). AWP.

Gray, James of 21st Regiment who died in Philadelphia, surgeon. Will 13 Jun. 1762 pr. 18 Dec. 1771 by father John Gray. (PROB11/973). AWP.

Gray, James of Montreal, Maj. in Regiment of Engineers. Will pr. 27 Sep. 1799. (PROB11/1330).

Gray, Robert of Charlotte Town, PE. Will pr. 14 Oct. 1828. (PROB11/1746).

Gray, Thomas of Boston, MA, merchant. Will pr. 10 Aug. 1782 by Thomas Dolbeare. (PROB11/1094).

Greves, Adam of Charles Town, SC, who died on HMS *Rose*, bachelor. Will 27 Jun. 1737 AWW 13 Apr. 1738 to Edward Jasper, attorney for Edward Stephens in SC. (PROB11/688). AWP.

Greaves, William of Halifax, NS, surgeon in Royal Navy. Will pr. 18 Jun. 1811. PROB11/1523).

Green, Edward of VA, grocer. Will pr. 9 Aug. 1698 by brother Robert Green. (PROB11/447). GGE.

Green, Matthew of NYC. AWW 5 Jun. 1852 to relict Jane Green. (PROB11/2154).

Green, Thomas of Christchurch, Hants, late residing in Greenspond, NL, planter. Leg: son Thomas Green and his wife Mary; Robert, Edward, William and George, sons of said John and Mary Green; granddaughters Susan and Jane Green. Exec: Thomas Woolley. Wit: Nathaniel Smith, James Crain and Thomas Reed Jr. AWW 20 Mar. 1830 to Thomas Woolley. (PROB11/1768).

Green, William of Trinity, NL, bachelor. Will pr. 15 Nov. 1754. (PROB11/811).

Greene, Winifred of Kingsbury, Mddx., widow, whose son John Greene went to VA. Will 1 Feb. 1641. Leg: siblings John and Francis Finch, Joane Coomes, Ann Fegon, widow; niece Mary Finch. Wit: Richard Rochdale, scrivener, and Henry Firebrace. Pr. 5 Oct. 1641 by brother John Finch. (PROB11/187). AWP. NGSQ 69/117.

Greenfield, Thomas, seaman of HMS *Milan* in Naval Hospital at Halifax, NS. Will pr. 23 Sep. 1814. (PROB11/1560).

Greive, James, mariner bound in the *Sarah* to VA. Will 28 Jan. 1729 pr. 9 Dec. 1732 by Catherine Scott, widow. (PROB11/655). AWP.

Grendon, Thomas of Westover, Charles City Co., VA, gent. Will pr. by Arthur North 4 Apr. 1685. (PROB11/379). ACE. GGE.

Greves, Adam of Charles Town, SC, mariner. Will 27 Jun. 1737 AWW 13 Apr. 1738 to Edward Jasper. (PROB11/688). AWP.

Grey. *See* **Gray.**

Grierson, James of Augusta, GA, Colonel of the Loyal Militia Regiment, who died in St. Paul's, GA, merchant. Will pr. 11 Feb. 1789 by the son Thomas Grierson. (PROB11/1175). ALC.

Grierson, John of Tarbolton, Ottawa River, [ON], Lieut. in Royal Navy. Will pr. 26 Nov. 1851. (PROB11/2142).

Griffin, Humphrey of Limehouse, Mddx., mariner of the *Griffin* bound for VA. Will 28 Mar. 1674. Leg: wife Lucy Griffin to have his house during her lifetime and to be exex; son George Griffin. Wit: Margaret Cooper, George Alder and Henry Sergent. Pr. 13 May 1691 by relict. (Guildhall: Ms 9171/43/178v).

Griffin, James of Oxford, Worcester Co., MA. Will 2 Jul. 1768 AWW 24 Sep. 1773 to Thomas Kast, attorney for William Watson of Oxford and relict Prudence Griffin. (PROB11/991). AWP.

Griffin, Jean of Highnockeet River, Anseminac, VA. Will pr. 15 Apr. 1661 by George Griffin. (PROB11/304).

Griffith, Edward of Charles Town, SC, but late of City of Chester, planter. Will 28 May 1778. Leg: wife Martha Griffith to retain her two plantations she has in her own right near Salt Kertcher, SC, purchased by her late father Thomas Miles and the other from her late grandfather Mr. Mather, as well as a quarter share of a plantation at Horse Savannah; children Edward, Hannah and Mary Griffith to have property inherited from their late grandfather Thomas Miles; daughter Jane Griffith; brothers Thomas, John and Joseph Griffith; three sisters Alice wife of John Walley, Ann wife of Edward Maddock and Margaret Griffith. Wit: James Backarn, Stephen Hickson and John Dennil, all of Chester. Pr. Chester 6 Apr. 1764 and at PCC London 12 Oct. 1785 by William Greenwood and William Higginson. (PROB11/1134).

Griffiths, James, Landgrave of Port Royal, SC. Will 6 Jan. 1709 pr 12 Feb. 1709 by father John Griffiths. (PROB11/506). AWP.

Griffiths, John of NYC, merchant. AWW 7 Dec. 1799 to daughter Cornelia, Baroness de Diemar. (PROB11/1334).

Griggs, Michael of Lancaster Co., VA, gent. Will pr. 10 Sep. 1688 by relict Ann, now wife of Richard Bray. (PROB11/392). GGE.

Grinaway *alias* **Grinway, John** of Croke Harbour, NL, planter. Will pr. 23 Dec. 1774. (PROB11/1003).

Grindall, Christopher of MD, mariner. Will pr. 24 Nov. 1748. (PROB11/765).

Grove, Samuel of St. Helena, Granville Co., SC, merchant. AWW 15 May 1777 to relict Jane Grove. (PROB11/1031).

Grover, Joseph *alias* **Jotham** of merchant ship *Providence*, bachelor, whose grandmother was in Boston, MA. Nuncupative will 4 May 1710 AWW 27 May 1710 to William Lanchester. (PROB11/516). AWP.

Grover, William Esq. of Reading, Berks., late Chief Justice of E. FL who died at sea. Will 7 Jan. 1766 pr. 23 Jan 1768 by son John Grover of King's College, Cambridge. (PROB11/935). AWP.

Groves, Elizabeth of Charleston, SC, spinster. Will pr. 1 Jun. 1810 by sister Susannah Hawkins. (PROB11/1512).

Grubb, John of Charlottetown, PE. Will 28 Sep 1844. Leg: wife Sarah Anne Grubb; sons Robert Samuel and Edward Walter Grubb to have house in Charlottetown called Holland Grove; James St. George Burke; John Eustace Grubb. Wit: R. Hodgson and Joseph Hensley of Charlottetown. Pr. 5 Mar. 1847 by son Robert Samuel Grubb. (PROB11/2052).

Gruet, Peggy of Newark, NJ, widow. AWW 16 Jan. 1838 to Thomas Trevor Tatham and Henry Tatham. (PROB11/1889).

Gruthy, Thomas of St. John's, NL. Will pr. 27 Nov. 1716. (PROB11/554).

Guest, John of Inner Temple, London, but late of Philadelphia, widower. Will 28 Aug. 1697 pr. 22 Apr. 1708 by cousin Capt. John Geast, citizen and haberdasher of London. (PROB11/500). AWP.

Guillam *alias* **Gillim, Michael** of Channel Island, Cape Ray, NL. Will pr. 31 Dec. 1850. (PROB11/2123).

Guillum, Peter, master of the brig *Jane & Margaret* who died in VA, bachelor. Will 22 Feb. 1700 AWW 23 Feb. 1702 to father John Guillum. (PROB11/464). AWP.

Gunnell, Edward of Shadwell, Mddx., mariner, who bequeathed estate in VA to his sons George and Edward Gunnell. AWW 22 Jan. 1666 to his legatees and executors John Witney and John Osborne. (PROB11/319).

Gushue, George of Brigus, Conception Bay, NL, planter. Will pr. 28 Feb. 1837. (PROB11/1872).

Gushue, James of Brigus, Conception Bay, NL, master of the merchant schooner *Success* at sea. Will pr. 29 Jan. 1813. (PROB11/1540)

Gwinn, James of Nantucket, MA, mariner. Will pr. 15 Jun. 1818 by relict Mary Gwinn. (PROB11/1605).

Gwin, John of James City, VA, merchant. AWW 25 Nov. 1684 to Henry Jenkins. (PROB11/378). VGE.

Gwinnett, Ann formerly of Wolverhampton, Staffs., but late of GA, widow. AWW 4 May 1785 to Peter Belin, husband and adr. of the daughter Elizabeth Belin, formerly Gwinnett, deceased. (PROB11/1129).

Hacker, John, formerly of VA, planter, and late of Limehouse, Mddx. Will 7 Jan. 1654. Leg: William Rookeing of VA, planter, to have a horse and the fowling piece which was his father's, Allan James, now resident in VA; wife Elizabeth Hacker to have lease of cottage in Fretherne, Glos. for life, then to son John Hacker; kinsman Ralph Hacker, son of brother Thomas Hacker of Penzance, Corn. Execs: wife Elizabeth and son John. Wit: Thomas Cutlett and John Minterne. Pr. 8 Jun. 1654 by relict. (PROB11/233).

Hackett, John of PA, bachelor. Will 27 Mar. 1721 AWW 25 Feb. 1731 to brother Thomas Hackett. (PROB11/642). AWP.

Hackett, Robert of NYC, bachelor, mariner of HMS *Garland*. Will dated 24 May 1757 witnessed by James Carter, Thomas Pettit and Ebenezer Franklin. AWW 31 Mar. 1768 to William Depeyster, attorney for Richard Pettit residing in NY. (PROB11/937).

Haddocke, William, undertaking a voyage to VA. Will 4 Oct. 1648. Leg: brother Richard Haddocke, girdler; who is to be exec; Ellen Hay. Wit: Thomas Hayer, Mathew Burchfield and James Windus. Appointment of Arthur Purnell as attorney revoked. Pr. 27 Aug. 1649 by brother Richard Haddocke. (PROB11/209).

Hagen, George of Ferrisburgh, Addison Co., VT, miller and gardener. Will 16 May 1852. Leg: nephew George Miles of Ferrisburgh to be excused repayment of money owed for purchase of farm acquired by testator from Mary Barton and to have estate purchased from Benjamin Field; sister Ann Brown in England; nephew Henry Miles to have 60 acres at back of Gibbeon Fuller's. Execs: Rufus Hazard, Frances Seales and Andrew Holmes. Wit: Aaron B. Webb and Cyrus Wener. AWW 23 Feb. 1854 by his solemn affirmation to Alfred Brown, attorney for Rufus Hazard and Andrew Holmes in VT. (PROB11/2186).

Hale, Charles of Gore District, [ON]. Will pr. 26 Jun. 1855. (PROB11/2214).

Hale, Elizabeth. *See* Cole.

Hale, Hon. John, of QC, Receiver-General for Lower Canada. Will pr. 6 Apr. 1839. (PROB11/1909)

Haliburton, Susanna of Windsor, NS, widow. Will pr. 23 Jan. 1851. (PROB11/2125).

Halkett, Frederick of Toronto, Lieut. & Capt. in Coldstream Guards. Will pr. 12 Jun 1841. (PROB11/1947).

Hall, Charles, citizen and fishmonger of London and late of MD who died in VA, bachelor. Will 28 Feb. 1698 pr. 12 Jun. 1699. (PROB11/451). AWP.

Hall, Henry Long of Amherstburg, [ON], brewer. Will pr. 7 Jun. 1833. (PROB11/1817).

Hall, Robert of Marlborough, Prince George's Co., MD, gent. Will 4 Dec. 1719 pr. 18 May 1720 by James Douglass of London. (PROB11/574). AWP.

Hall, Sir Robert of Kingston, [ON], late Acting Commissioner of Royal Navy at QC. Will pr. 6 Aug. 1818. (PROB11/1607).

Hallett, Samuel, of St. John City, NB, Capt in De Lancey's 2nd Battalion of Provincials. Will pr. 9 May 1800. (PROB11/1342).

Halley, Francis of All Hallows Staining, London, who died in VA. Will 28 Jun. 1698 pr. 28 Sep. 1702 by cousin Edmond Halley and father Richard Pyke. (PROB11/466). AWP.

Halsey *alias* **Holsay, Esay** of Suffolk, MA, mariner, bachelor. Bequeaths clothing in Old England and wages due to him for service on the *Morning Star* to his brother William Halsey who is named as executor. Will 14 Jul. 1677 witnessed by John Bryne, John Scobett and Andrew Norton, pr. 14 Sep. 1677 by William Halsey. (PROB11/354).

Ham, Matthew, mariner, formerly of New England but late of St. Olave, Southwark, Sy. Will 10 Mar. 1698 pr. 3 Jan. 1704 by Alice Pomery. (PROB11/474). AWP.

Haman, Richard of St. Olave, Southwark, Sy., mariner, who died on merchant ship *New York* in NY. Will 20 Feb. 1715 pr. 1 Feb. 1717 by relict Anne Haman. (PROB11/556). AWP.

Hambelton, John, seaman of HMS *Canterbury*, bachelor. Will 10 Sep. 1748 AWW 1 Mar. 1750 to Owen Gray, attorney for William Gale in NY. (PROB11/777). AWP.

Hamerton, Pinchback of London who died in VA, bachelor., son of Edmond Hamerton who died in VA. Will 6 Jan. 1721 pr. 29 Dec. 1729 by sister Hannah Cloke. (PROB11/634). AWP.

Hamilton, Andrew Esq. of Philadelphia. Will 31 Jul. 1741 AWW 8 Dec. 1742 to Ferdinando John Paris, attorney for William Allen and sons James and Andrew Hamilton in PA.. (PROB11/722). AWP. NGSQ 60/181 and 61/4.

Hamilton, George Lewis of QC. Will pr. Major in Royal Artillery Regiment. Will pr. 31 Aug. 1801. (PROB11/1361).

Hamilton, John of Norfolk, VA., HM Consul to VA. Will pr. 15 Jan. 1817. (PROB11/1588).

Hamilton, Mary of Philadelphia, widow. AWW 20 Dec. 1794 to Lady Ann Hamilton. (PROB11/1253).

Hamilton, William of Louisburg, NS, Lieut. of 22nd Regiment of Foot who died at sea. Will dated 14 Mar. 1759 witnessed by Thomas Townsend, John Burke and Humphrey Jones, all of the 22nd Regiment. AWW 18 Nov. 1763 to Margaret McCaslan, spinster, niece and legatee, the named executors John Wallace of Dublin, Ireland, merchant, and James Clegg of Liverpool, attorney, having renounced. (PROB11/893).

Hammerton, Elizabeth of Charles Town, SC, widow who died at sea. Will 27 Oct. 1738 AWW 18 Jan. 1750 to brother Nathaniel Hollier of Lynn, Norf., schoolmaster. (PROB11/776). AWP.

Hammond, Charles of Haldin, Newcastle District, [ON], Royal Navy. Will pr. 24 Jun. 1854. (PROB11/2193).

Hammond, William of Ratcliffe, Mddx., gent., whose uncle was William Clopton of VA. Will 9 Jul. 1732 pr. 17 Jul. 1732 by Samuel Skinner and Josiah Cole. (PROB11/652). AWP. NGSQ 60/260).

Hampton, John of Somerset Co., MD, minister of the gospel. Will 28 Oct. 1719, limited probate 8 Aug. 1722 to the brother Robert Hampton. (PROB11/586). AWP.

Hamson, Daniel of Stepney, Mddx., mariner of HMS *Mermaid* who died on merchant ship *Hamilton*, bachelor. Will 26 Sep. 1712 AWW 27 Jan. 1715 to Thomas Newby, attorney for John Newby in New England. (PROB11/546). AWP.

Handy, Charles of Newport, RI, merchant. Will pr. 24 Mar. 1796 to sons John and Thomas Handy and Stephen Deblois. (PROB11/1272).

Hannington, William of Shediac, Westmoreland Co., NB. Will pr. 29 Dec. 1841. (PROB11/1955).

Hans *alias* Hance, Peter of the merchant ship *Providence* who died in VA. Will 11 Jan 1698 pr. 11 Dec. 1708 by relict Sarah Hans with similar powers reserved to Robert Townsend. (PROB11/505). AWP.

Harding, Ichabod *[Schabod in database]* of Chichester, Sussex, whose cousin Archibald Bailey went from Cork, Ireland, to Swanzey, MA, in 1768 and had descendants. Will 29 Aug. 1779. "Whereas my cousin Archibald [Bailey] settled in America some years ago and has not late been heard of and may be dead; in that case I wish that, if he can have issue" £600 shall be divided between his children. "Whether he is dead or alive I hereby deem him as dead." Will pr. 26 Jan. 1780 by Thomas Grant Sr., and John Gooch. (PROB11/1060). NGSQ 66/222.

Harding, William of Rotherhithe, Sy., who died in VA, bachelor. Will 13 Nov. 1732 pr. Nov. 1742 by Adriana Dunn *alias* Oakley. (PROB11/730). AWP. TNA: C12/1767/39. NGSQ 64/288.

Hardy, Edward of St. John's, NL. Will pr. 3 Jan. 1761. (PROB11/862).

Hare, Margaret of Philadelphia, PA, widow. AWW Dec. 1819 to Walter Stirling, attorney for Robert Hare and John Hare Powel in Philadelphia; the other executor Charles Willing Hare having been cited but not appearing. (PROB11/1623).

Harman, John of Bermondsey, Sy., mariner who died on merchant ship *Forward* in VA. Will 12 Feb. 1711 pr. 23 Dec. 1728 by relict Mary Harman. (PROB11/626). AWP.

Harmer, George of Albermarle Co., [VA]. AWW 20 Apr. 1799 to John Lambert. (PROB11/1322).

Harnett, John of St. Lawrence in Isle of Thanet, Kent, but late of Newport, RI, mariner. Will 16 Oct. 1778. Leg: brother Peter Harnett; sisters Dorothy, Thomasine and Ann Harnett. Pr. by James Stock of Ramsgate, Kent, and brother-in-law John Maxted of Norwood, Kent. Wit: J. Watts, John Taylor and P. Gold. Pr. 18 May 1785 by James Stock. (PROB11/1120).

Harris, Edward of Burlington, NJ, gent. AWW 23 Aug. 1827 to son Edward Harris. (PROB11/1729).

Harris, George of Westover, Charles Co., VA. AWW 20 Aug. 1674 to relict Sarah Greendon *alias* Harris. (PROB11/345). VGE.

Harris, John of Goatacre, Hillmarton, Wilts., clothier, who had lands in PA. Will 1 Apr. 1693 pr. 9 Jun 1693 by relict Jane and son Samuel Harris. (PROB11/415). AWP.

Harris, Samuel of Charlestown, MA, mariner of merchant ship *Martha and Hannah*. Will 20 Nov. 1720 pr. 4 Jan. 1721 by brother Amos Harris. (PROB11/578). AWP.

Harrold, Alfred of Philadelphia, merchant. Will pr. 22 May 1845 by brother Frederick William Harrold and Arthur Ryland. (PROB11/2018).

Hart, Andrew of Wapping, Mddx., mariner who died on the *Amity* in VA. Will 8 Feb. 1717 pr. 18 Nov. 1723 by John Wilson. (PROB11/594). AWP.

Hart, Esther. *See* **Hudson.**

Hart, George of Esgood, Dalhousie District, [ON]. Will pr. 12 Jul. 1852. (PROB11/2156).

Heart, James, mariner of HMS *Africa* in Chesapeake Bay. Will 7 Feb. 1795. Leg: sole exec. James King at King's Arms, Southampton, Hants. Wit: Capt. Rod. Home, William Henryson, First Lieut. Pr. 13 Apr. 1796. (PROB11/1273).

Hart, Samuel of New Orleans, LA, merchant. AWW 15 Mar. 1834 to John Hodgson. (PROB11/1829).

Hart, Thomas of NYC, mariner. Will 25 Aug. 1761 pr. 11 Jan. 1774 by relict Ester Hart. (PROB11/994). AWP.

Hastings, John of London, mariner, but late of Prestonpans, Scotland, master of ship *James* who died in VA. Will 15 Jul. 1701 AWW 27 Sep. 1707 to sister Janette Hastings in Prestonpans. (PROB11/496). AWP.

Hearn, Anthony of Penn Township, PA. Will pr. 1 Apr. 1818 by Redmond Byrne, John Carroll and Joseph Smyde. (PROB11/1603).

Heart. *See* **Hart**

Harrison, Hendrick, mariner of ship *Barnardiston* who died in VA. Will 28 Oct. 1689 pr. 2 Mar. 1694 by Ann Thomson *alias* Hollyday. (PROB11/419). AWP.

Harrison, John of St. Mary, New Orleans, LA, planter. AWW 11 Mar. 1806 to John Bannatyne. (PROB11/1440).

Harrison, Nicholas of VA, planter, but who died in St. Sepulchre, London. Nuncupative will of about Oct. 1652. Leg: mother Dorothy Harrison to have all estate. Wit: J. Parsons and Elizabeth Lewis. AWW 28 Sep. 1653 to said mother. (PROB11/229).

Harvie, John of Anticosti Island, QC, Lieutenant in Royal Navy. Will pr. 11 Dec. 1838. (PROB11/1904).

Harwar, Thomas of Essex Co., VA, widower. AWW to the son Thomas Harwar of Essex Co., VA. Litigation papers at TNA:PROB 32/46/15 & 17. (Nov. 1704).

Harwood, Elizabeth. *See* **Goodwin.**

Harwood, Thomas of Streatley, Berks., who had plantations in MD. Will 22 Apr. 1704 pr. 14 Mar 1713 by son Rev. Thomas Harwood. (PROB11/532). AWP.

Haslewood, William, Lieut. of Royal American Regt. who died in North America, bachelor. Will 5 Apr. 1756 AWW 4 May 1759 by father Edward Haslewood of Bridgnorth, Salop., mercer. (PROB11/846). AWP.

Hatch, Matthew of St. Leonard Eastcheap, London, who died in GA, bachelor. AWW 12 Mar. 1765 to Leonard Gorst. (PROB11/907). AWP.

Hatton, John of London, salter, who died in VA. Will 14 Dec 1654 pr 22 Jul. 1663 by brother Thomas Hatton. (PROB11/311). AWP.

Hawkes, George Wright, born in England and late of NY but about to embark for England leaving his family in America. Will 5 Jun. 1807. Leg: wife and exec. Ann Lawrence Hawkes to have his entire estate in America which is then to pass to his children Adelaide and Wooton. Execs: Mr. J. Lawrence, Robert Troup, William Henderson, Peter Goslet of NYC and Rev. David Grossett. Wit: John Cox and Thomas Vanderpool. Will pr. 8 Oct. 1821 by Thomas Hawkes, Roger Wright Hawkes and Ann Lawrence Hawkes. (PROB11/1648).

Hawkes, Priscilla. *See* **Stockdale.**

Hawkins, John of Queen Anne Co., MD. Will 23 Apr. 1717, pr. 12 Nov. 1719 by son Ernault Hawkins. (PROB11/571). AWP.

Hawkins, John of NY, Commissary and Paymaster to Royal Artillery. Will dated 6 Aug. 1763 leaves bequests to his uncle George Hawkins and aunt Ann Hawkins and to his sister Arabella Gaillard. Deposition of 5 Jan. 1764 by Elizabeth Neal of St. Margaret Westminster, Mddx., widow, that she knows the testator's handwriting and that the will is his. Pr. 5 Jan. 1764 by George Hawkins. (PROB11/895).

Hawkins, John of Limehouse, Mddx., mariner of HMS *Essex* and late of HMS *Juno* who died in NY Hospital. Will 13 Sep. 1746 pr. 30 Jun. 1767 by relict Sarah Hawkins. (PROB11/929). AWP.

Hawkins, Mary of St. Margaret Westminster, Mddx., widow, who died in Boston, MA. Will 30 May 1715 pr. 17 Feb. 1721 by brother Randolph Hopley Jr.

Hawkins, Thomas of St. John's NL, planter. Will pr. 23 Dec. 1724. (PROB11/600).

Hawkins, William of Kingston upon Thames, Surrey, barber-surgeon, but late of Boston, MA. Will drawn up and witnessed in Boston, 27 Feb. 1667 pr. 27 Jul. 1686 by sister Rachel Wade. (PROB11/384). This will declared invalid and later will of 1 Aug. 1684 introduced and pr. 2 Apr. 1702 by relict Dorothy Hawkins. (PROB11/464). AWP. NGSQ 66/219.

Hay, Peter of Petty Harbour, NL, boat keeper. Will pr. 23 Mar. 1771. (PROB11/965).

Hayes, Joseph of Ware, Gloucester Co., VA. Will pr. by decree 8 Jun. 1678 by Anne Hayes. (PROB11/357).

Haynes, George of St. George, Southwark, Sy., gent., whose wife's former husband Thomas Adams resided in New England. Will 12 Jan. 1763 pr. 26 Jan. 1763 by brother William Haynes and Charles Ryder. (PROB11/883). AWP.

Haynes, Herbert of Abingdon, Gloucester Co., VA, who died in St. Peter Cornhill, London. Will 20 Jan. 1737 AWW 15 Dec. 1737 to Job Wilkes, attorney for relict Sarah Haynes and father Thomas Haynes in VA. (PROB11/686). AWP.

Haynes, Thomas of Warwick Co., VA. Will 1 Sep. 1742 AWW 27 Sep. 1746 to James Wilkes, attorney for son Andrew Haynes in VA. (PROB11/749). AWP. NGSQ 64/286.

Hayward, George of D'Loupe River, QC, gent. Will pr. 24 Aug. 1842. (PROB11/966).

Hazen, William Jr. of Fredericton, NB. Will pr. 5 Oct. 1816. (PROB11/1584).

Heacock, Peter of Middletown Township, DE Co., PA, widower. AWW 30 Jun. 1837 to daughter Elizabeth Bottomley by her solemn affirmation. (PROB11/1880).

Heale, George of Lancaster City, Rappahannock, VA. AWW 10 Mar. 1709 to Arthur Bayly. (PROB11/507). VGE.

Heart. *See* **Hart.**

Heath, Joseph Thomas of Steilcoom, OR. Will pr. 3 Feb. 1851 by brother Thomas Mason Heath. (PROB11/2127).

Heath, William of Gore District, [ON], yeoman. Will pr. 23 Feb. 1848. (PROB11/2069).

Heighington, Conway of Harbour Grace, Conception Bay, NL, merchant, Justice of Peace and Lieutenant in Royal Navy. Will pr. 16 Nov. 1696. (PROB11/1281).

Helden, Mary of Egham, Sy., whose kinswoman Mrs. Elizabeth Bruce was in Carolina. Will 23 Sep. 1752 pr. 16 Jan. 1753 by daughter Mary Foster. (PROB11/799). AWP.

Hemard, Peter of Spitalfields, Mddx., weaver, who died in VA. Will 14 Sep. 1713 pr. 17 Mar. 1719 by relict Elizabeth Hemard. (PROB11/567). AWP.

Hemphill, Edward of Halifax Naval Hospital, NS, seaman of HMS *Penelope*. Will pr. 14 Jul. 1792. (PROB11/1221).

Henderson, Harry near York River, Kent Co., VA, planter. Will pr. 3 Nov. 1674. (PROB11/346). VGE.

Henderson, James of NYC. Will 7 Oct. 1743 pr. 28 Feb. 1760 by relict Tessia Henderson and daughter Margaret Haviland. (PROB11/853). AWP.

Henderson, Joseph of Montreal, Lieut. of Royal Marines. Will pr. 3 Mar. 1834. (PROB11/1829).

Hendricks, John of NY, carpenter. Will dated 11 Nov. 1757 witnessed by Francis Peacock, Joseph Young and Sam Strickland. All his wages due from a voyage made as carpenter's mate aboard the *Britannia* from London to the East Indies to his executor Elliott Allchurch of Deptford, Kent. Pr. 21 Oct. 1760. (PROB11/859).

Henley, Robert of Abbotts Wootton, Dorset, whose nephew John Henley resided in NC. Will 25 Mar. 1757 pr. 11 Dec. 1760. (PROB11/861). NGSQ 63/133/

Henry, John of Richmond, VA. Will pr. 13 Dec. 1809 by brother James Henry. (PROB11/1506).

Heron, Benjamin Esq. of New Hanover, NC. Will 4 Sep. 1768 pr. 4 Jul. 1770 by relict Alice Heron. (PROB11/959). AWP.

Heron, Francis, chief trader of Red River Settlement, Rupertsland, Hudson's Bay. Will 7 Aug. 1835 and codicil of 4 Jan. 1841. Leg: wife Isabella Heron; children Edward, Jane Mary, Francis, Eleanor, Frances and Jemima Heron. Execs: George Simpson Esq., Governor of Rupertsland; William Smith Esq., Secretary of Hudson's Bay Co; Rev. David Thomas Jones; Rev. William Cockran; Duncan Finlayson Esq., chief factor of Hudson's Bay Co; testator's brother James Heron of Lower Canada. Wit: William Todd, John Lloyd and John McAllam. Pr. 4 Jan. 1841 by George Simpson. (PROB11/1939).

Herring, James of New Rochelle, Westchester Co., NY. Will pr. 5 Aug. 1830 by relict Mary Herring. (PROB11/1775).

Hewitt, William of Charles Town, SC, surgeon, Ensign in 28th Regiment of Foot. Will 16 Feb. 1763 AWW 22 Dec. 1766 to John Cole, attorney for brother Thomas Hewitt in Cork, Ireland. (PROB11/924). AWP.

Hewson, Mary of PA, widow. Will pr. 15 Apr. 1796 by James Blunt. (PROB11/1273).

Hext, Edward gent. of Charles Town, SC. Will 6 Oct. 1739 pr. 30 Dec. 1742 by brother David Hext and John McCall. (PROB11/722). AWP.

Hiatt, James of Point Township, Northumberland Co., PA, purser in the Royal Navy and hairdresser. AWW 18 Feb. 1814 to James Park, attorney for James Hepburn in Northumberland Co. (PROB11/1552).

Hickman, Jonathan of Grand Bank, Fortune Bay, NL, planter. Will pr. 26 Jun. 1850. (PROB11/2114).

Hicks, Richard, citizen and armourer of London bound to VA in the *Planter.* Leg: John Cox, citizen and haberdasher of London who is to be exec. Wit: Joseph Hitcham and Thomas Moone. Pr. 29 May 1648 by John Cox. (PROB11/204).

Higgins, Nathaniel of Cape Cod, MA, mariner on HMS *Torbay,* but late of HMS *Hornet,* bachelor. Will 23 Nov. 1743 AWW 4 Dec. 1746 to Sarah Browne of Hackney, Mddx.. (PROB11/751). AWP. NGSQ 64/290.

Hill, Adam of Talbot Co., MD, mariner. Will 2 Mar. 1767 pr. 14 Mar. 1768 by William Campbell of London. (PROB11/937). AWP.

Hill, Charles of Halifax, NS, Member of HM Council. Will pr. 28 May 1827. (PROB11/1725).

Hill, Isabella of Halifax, NS, widow. Will pr. 20 Apr. 1844. (PROB11/1997).

Hill, Richard, now bound to New England, son of William Hill of Cookham, Berks., husbandman deceased. Leg: siblings George, Mary, Alice and Elizabeth Hill; cousin and exec. Nicholas Greene of Cookham, tailor. Wit: Thomas Pennant, scrivener, Andrew Griffith and Thomas Greene. Pr. 21 Sep. 1635 by Nicholas Greene. (PROB11/169). AWP.

Hill, Richard of Evans, Erie Co., NY, widower. Will 9 Jul. 1844. Leg: eldest son George Hill & youngest son Thomas Hill; daughters Mary, Martha and Anne Hill. Execs: Samuel Freeman and William Lucust of Evans Town. Will pr. 27 Sep. 1854 by daughter Mary Hill. (PROB11/2197).

Hill, Samuel of London who died in VA, bachelor. Will 21 Oct 1693 pr. 2 Oct. 1695 by father Edward Hill. (PROB11/427). AWP.

Hill, Willoughby of St. Andrew, Holborn, London, marine of *India King* who died in VA. Will 21 Aug. 1697 pr. 21 May 1703 by relict Joan Hill. (PROB11/471). AWP.

Hilton, Benjamin of NYC, widower. AWW 1 Mar. 1834 to James Tidbury. (PROB11/1829).

Hilton, Robert of Dukes Place, Mddx., merchant, formerly of New England but late of London. Will 15 Feb. 1717 pr. 13 Mar. 1717 by Samuel Lilly. (PROB11/557). AWP. NGSQ 69/196.

Hinchman, John of Evesham, Burlington Co., NJ. AWW 2 Jun. 1890 to James Bell. (PROB11/1193).

Hinton, Elizabeth of Chelsea, Mddx., widow, whose half-brother Peter Francis de Prefontaine was an inhabitant of Philadelphia. Will 29 May 1763 pr. 14 Dec. 1775 by Marianna Chauvin and Margaret Allderton. (PROB11/1014). AWP. NGSQ 62/211.

Hintze, Christopher of PA, of 20th Regiment of Foot. Will pr. 17 Nov. 1783. (PROB11/1110).

Hitchock, Henry of Old Pellican Harbour, Trinity Bay, NL. Will pr. 15 Aug. 1831. (PROB11/1782).

Hobbs, Thomas of St. Clement Danes, Mddx., whose sister Elizabeth was wife of Francis Weekes of Middlesex Co., VA. Will 13 Oct. 1697 pr. 20 Oct 1697 by John Hawles, John Lilly and relict Catherina Hobbs. (PROB11/447). AWP.

Hockley, Thomas of Philadelphia, merchant. Will pr. 5 Dec. 1781 by Samuel Smith. (PROB11/1085).

Hodges, Frederick Downer of Pearl Street, NYC, gent. Will pr. 29 Nov. 1845 by relict Elizabeth Hodges. (PROB11/2026).

Hodges, Peter, late of East West Jersey, America, planter, late of Bermondsey, Sy. Will 21 Jul. 1697. Leg: Elizabeth Willis of Bermondsey, spinster, testator's intended wife, to have all his lands and other estate in NJ. Wit: Joann Pryor Sr., Mary Pryor, Joann Pryor Jr., Hannah Richeson and John Parry Sr. Pr. 21 Dec. 1697 by Elizabeth Willis. (PROB11/442).

Hodgson *alias* **Wilson, Mark**, of St. John, NB, Paymaster of 8th or King's Regiment. Will pr. 2 Mar. 1822. (PROB11/1654).

Hogarth, George of Montreal, Brevet Lieut. Col. in 26th Regiment of Foot. Will pr. 26 Oct. 1854. (PROB11/2198).

Holbrook, George Papps, Surveyor-General of St. Johns, NL. Will pr. 29 Aug. 1834. (PROB11/1835).

Holding, Edward, mariner of the *Sandwich* and late master of the *Friends' Goodwill* who died in Boston, MA, bachelor. Will 6 Mar. 1746 pr. 27 Feb. 1751 by Mary Pomfrett of St. George's Mddx., widow. (PROB11/785). AWP.

Holdritch, James of Crowland, Lincoln Co., Niagara, [ON], yeoman. Will pr. 4 Jul. 1843. (PROB11/1982).

Holiday, William of Goose Creek, SC, planter. AWW 26 May 1810 to William Lee. (PROB11/1511).

Hollamby, James of NYC, coachmaker. AWW 8 Apr. 1780 to Alexander Goudge. (PROB11/1063).

Holland, Joshua of Shadwell, Mddx., mariner, whose son John Holland was in America and daughter Elizabeth Holland was in PA. Will 17 May 1690 pr. 26 May 1690 by son Thanks Holland. (PROB11/399). AWP.

Holloway, William Cuthbert Elphinstone of Montreal, Col. in Royal Engineers Regiment. Will pr. 13 Nov. 1850. (PROB11/2122).

Holsay, Esay of Suffolk, MA, mariner. *See* **Halsey**.

Holt, James of VA, planter. Will 8 Dec. 1629. Leg: son James Holt to have all his estate and servants in VA; his servant William Blond to be forgiven one year of his service. Execs: Nathaniel Flood, Henry King and Theophilus Berrestone, planters. Wit: Theophilus Berrestone and Peter Perkins. AWW 12 May 1631 to son James Holt. (Guildhall: Ms 9171/26/159).

Holwell, James Zephaniah of St. Joseph de Chambly, Montreal, QC. Will pr. 8 Apr. 1856. (PROB11/2230).

Holwell *alias* **Holwill, Samuel** of St. John's, NL. Will pr. 5 Sep. 1836. (PROB11/1867).

Home, Charles of NYC, gent. Will 15 Sep. 1740 pr. 12 Feb. 1748 by William Home of Bastonrig, Scotland. (PROB11/760). AWP.

Hooker, Col. Edward of St. Mary at Hill, London, tallow chandler, whose sister Mary Hooker was in New England. Will pr. 16 Jul. 1651 by son Cornelius Hooker; the relict Elizabeth Hooker renouncing. (PROB11/217). GGE.

Hope, Henry, Lieut. Governor of QC, Col. in 44th Regiment of Foot. Will pr. 31 Jul. 1789. (PROB11/1181).

Hopes, John of Limehouse, Stepney, Mddx., shipwright bound for VA on the *Augustin* of London. Will 20 Sep. 1669. Leg: wife Ann Hopes who is to be sole exex. Pr. 16 Jun. 1676 by relict Ann Hopes. (Guildhall: Ms 9171/35/462).

Hopkins, John of Philadelphia. Will pr. 24 Aug. 1850 by Samuel Fatin. (PROB11/2118).

Hopton *alias* **Hopeton, Alexander Waldeon** of Burford, Brock District, [ON]. Will pr. 2 Apr. 1749. (PROB11/2091).

Hopton, John formerly of Charleston, SC but late of Islington, Mddx., merchant. Will 17 Aug. 1821 pr. 14 Jun. 1832 by John Hopton Russell Chichester. (PROB11/1801). NGSQ 65/135.

Hopton, William of Charles Town, SC. AWW 11 Aug. 1788 to John Hopton. (PROB11/1169).

Hornbe, Robert of St. Botolph Aldgate, London, bound overseas by *Benjamin* and died in VA. Will 27 Jan. 1702 pr. 25 Aug 1704 by relict Elizabeth Hornbe. (PROB11/477). AWP.

Horsmanden, Daniel, Chief Justice of NYC. Will pr. 8 Apr. 1786 by Miles Sherbrooke. (PROB11/1141).

Horwood, Joel of Boston, MA, mariner of HMS *Sheerness*. Will 22 Jun. 1697 pr. 12 Aug. 1697 by brother Henry Horwood. (PROB11/439). AWP.

Hosenburg, Andrew of New Orleans, LA, seaman who died having no relations. Will dated Charity Hospital, New Orleans 27 Jan. 1843. Leg: William Roberts to have all his estate in the hands of Dan. Bennett and Son. Pr. 4 Dec. 1843 by named exec. (PROB11/1989).

Hoskins, Richard of PA and having lands there, merchant resident in parish of St. Stephen, Coleman Street, London. Will 4 May 1700 pr. 20 Mar 1701 by Theodore Eccleston. (PROB11/459). AWP.

Houghton, John of Charles Town, SC, merchant. Will 1743 pr. 27 Apr. 1751 by John Owen of London, merchant. (PROB11/787). AWP.

Howard, Michael of Talbot Co., MD, gent. Will of 1 Feb. 1735 pr. 23 Mar. 1738 by brother Francis Howard. (PROB11/688). AWP. New grant in 1757.

How, Edward of Annapolis Royal, NS. Will pr. 6 Feb. 1752. (PROB11/792).

Howe, Viscount George Augustus of St. James Westminster, Mddx., but late of Ticonderoga, [NY], bachelor. Will dated 22 Feb. 1746, witnessed by George Gray, Thomas Page and W. Hall, appoints Richard, Lord Howe as sole executor. AWW 2 Mar. 1759 to Richard, Lord Howe. (PROB11/844).

Howell, John of Philadelphia, PA, mariner of HMS *Woolwich*. Will dated 24 Nov. 1757, witnessed by P. Parker and Edward Hawkins, appoints John Grimes of HMS *Woolwich* sole executor and legatee. Pr. by John Grimes 23 Jul. 1759. (PROB11/847).

Howett, John of Elizabeth City, VA, planter. Will pr. 28 Jul. 1659 by Thomas Howett. (PROB11/294). VGE.

Howson, Thomas of MD. Will pr. 10 Jun. 1718 by mother Mary Howson. (PROB11/564). AWP.

Hoyles, Newman Wright of St. John's, NL, merchant. Will pr. 25 Aug. 1855. (PROB11/2218).

Huckstep, Samuel of Ewhurst, Sx., and King & Queen Co., VA. Will 9 Aug. 1693 pr. 3 Jan 1696 by relict Jane Huckstep. (PROB11/433). AWP.

Hudson, formerly Hart, Esther of Halifax, NS. Will pr. 24 Nov. 1836. (PROB11/1869).

Hudson, John of Boston, MA, mariner of ship *Paget*. Will 20 Aug. 1700 pr. 3 Jul. 1702 by Jane Jenkinson. (PROB11/465). AWP.

Hudson, John (1766). *See* Hughson.

Hudson, William of Halifax, NS, Master in Royal Navy. Will pr. 9 Jun. 1836. (PROB11/1863).

Huger, Daniel of Berkeley Co., SC. Will 16 Nov. 1754 AWW 7 Jan. 1756 to Thomas Corbett, attorney for Francis Lejean Sr. and Jr. in SC. (PROB11/820). AWP.

Hughes, Edward of West Chester City, [PA], mariner bound to sea. Will 23 Sep. 1702 pr. 17 Dec. 1703 by Elizabeth Clayton, widow. (PROB11/473). AWP.

Hughes, John of Fort Albany, servant to Hudson's Bay Co. Will pr. 21 Nov. 1726 by brother William Hughes. (PROB11/612).

Hughes, John Stokes of New Orleans, LA. Will pr. 13 Oct. 1856 by sister Elizabeth Moule. (PROB11/2240).

Hughes, Robert of Wapping, Mddx., mariner of HMS *Tartar* who died in VA. Will 12 Feb. 1708 pr. 30 May 1727 by relict Mary Hughes. (PROB11/615). AWP.

Hughson *alias* Hudson, John of Adam's Cave, Conception Bay, NL. Will pr. 3 Jan. 1766. (PROB11/915).

Huisman, Abraham of NYC, merchant. Will 4 May 1748 pr. 29 Dec. 1748 by Joseph Mico of London, merchant. (PROB11/766). AWP.

Humble, George of Fort Albany, Hudson's Bay. Will pr. 16 Feb. 1775. (PROB11/1005).

Humphreys, William of Marblehead, MA, seaman. Will pr. 9 Jul. 1784. (PROB11/1119).

Hunt, Betty of NYC, spinster. AWW 30 Jan. 1847 to Edward Leam. (PROB11/2048).

Hunt, John of Newport, RI, mariner. AWW 5 Sep. 1763 to Joseph Sherwood. (PROB11/891).

Hunt, Samuel of Fort St. John, [BC], supernumerary in HMS *Canceaux*. Will pr. 8 Jun. 1782. (PROB11/1091).

Hunt, Thomas of Chalfont St. Giles, Bucks., yeoman who died in Carolina, bachelor. Will 7 Dec. 1689 AWW 14 Aug 1699 to brother Andrew Hunt. (PROB11/452). AWP.

Hunter, John of Norfolk, VA, merchant, who died in NYC. Will pr. 10 Apr. 1783 by Thomas McCulloch. (PROB11/1102). ALC.

Huntington, Thomas of New Rochelle, Westchester Co., NY. Will pr. 30 Jul. 1801 by Peter Shute and Newberry Davenport. (PROB11/1360).

Hunton, Nathaniel of East Ham, Essex, gent, whose sister Elizabeth March and nephew Matthew Hunton were resident in Charlestown, MA. Will 3 Aug. 1705 pr. 21 Aug. 1706. (PROB11/489). AWP. NGSQ 68/115.

Hurry, Samuel of Philadelphia, merchant. Will pr. 14 May 1824 by relict Elizabeth Ann Hurry. (PROB11/1685).

Hurst, Joseph Fowler of Cobourg, Northumberland & Durham Cos., [ON], merchant. Will pr. 28 Dec. 1852. (PROB11/2163).

Huston, John of Cornwallis, King's Co., NS. Will pr. 2 Nov. 1802. (PROB11/1383).

Hutchings, Richard of Charles Town, SC, schoolmaster. Will 22 Sep. 1788 pr. 10 Feb. 1791 by nephew William Hutchings. (PROB11/1201). NGSQ 63/203

Hutchinson, Abigail of Halifax, NS, spinster. Will pr. 19 Dec. 1843. (PROB11/1990).

Hutchinson, Grizelda of Halifax, NS, spinster. Will pr. 6 Jun. 1823. (PROB11/1672).

Hutchinson, Henry of St. Mildred Poultry, citizen of London. Will dated Warwicksquick, VA, 10 Nov. 1674. Leg: wife Anne Hutchinson who is to be exex. Overseers: Mr. Richard Bennett and Mr. Richard Death who are to recover the cargo and receive with the help of his daughter Bridget Hutchinson the tobacco he brought in by agreement with Capt. [Tobias] Felgate. Wit: Robert Galins, Nathaniel Hooke, Thomas Coachman and Anne Averie. Pr. 20 Aug. 1735 by relict Anne Hutchinson. (Guildhall: Ms 9171/27/95v).

Hutchinson, Thomas of Port Stanley, London District, [ON]. Will pr. 28 Sep. 1855. (PROB11/2219).

Hutton, William of St. John's, NL, master of the barque *Speculation*. Will pr. 1 Oct. 1800. (PROB11/1348).

Huxtable, Elizabeth of Chatham, Lake of Two Mountains District, [QC]. Will pr. 25 Oct. 1841. (PROB11/1953).

Impett *alias* **Inpett, Thomas** of Cape Barracks, QC, Capt. in 32nd Regiment. Will pr. 19 Nov. 1833. (PROB11/1824).

Impey, Michael of QC, Major in 6th Regiment of Foot. Will pr. 5 Dec. 1801. (PROB11/1367).

Inderwick *See* **Enderwick**

Ingate, Ann of London, at present in NYC, widow. Will 2 Feb. 1846.Leg: son Charles Colville Ingate to inherit house in St. George in the East, London; son James Wright Ingate to have another house in London and to be exec. AWW 1 Jun. 1847 to George Lawrence, attorney for named exec. (PROB11/2057).

Ingersoll, Jared of Newhaven, CT. AWW 8 Feb. 1783 to Dennis de Berds. (PROB11/1100).

Inglis, Hon. & Rt. Rev. Charles, Bishop of NS and NB. Will pr. 1 Mar. 1823. (PROB11/1667).

Inglis, Rt. Rev. John of Halifax, Bishop of NS. Will pr. 15 Nov. 1850. (PROB11/2122).

Ingraham, George of York, MA, seaman of HMS *Grafton* but late of HMS *Newcastle*. Will 9 Oct. 1761 pr. 28 Jun. 1764 by Robert Smith. (PROB11/899). AWP.

Ingram, George of Medonte Town, Simcoe, ON, yeoman. Will pr. 21 Dec. 1853. (PROB11/2182).

Ingram, Isaac of Garton, Sussex, yeoman, bound for PA aboard the *Welcome*, Mr. Robert Greenway. Leg: sister Merriam Short; Jane Batchelor; Thomas Fitzwater; David Ogden; poor Quakers. Wit: Richard Angelo, Richard Whitpaine and George Thompson. AWW 12 Jul. 1684 to proctor on behalf of execs. John Songhurst and Thomas Wynne. (Guildhall: Ms 9171/39/13).

Inkster, James of Red River Settlement, [Hudson's Bay], husbandman. Will pr. 31 Oct. 1855. (PROB11/2220).

Inman, Mary, formerly of Chesterfield, Derbys., and late of Wapping, Mddx., spinster, who died in SC. Will 16 Aug 1764 pr. 23 Nov. 1769 by Thomas Pike of Wapping, timber measurer. (PROB11/952). AWP.

Irbye, Walter of Albemarle, Northampton Co., VA, planter. Will pr. 30 Jul. 1652 by mother Olive Irby *alias* Cooper. (PROB11/222). VGE.

Irvin *alias* **Irvine** *alias* **Irving, John** of Picton, NS, yeoman. Will pr. 8 Dec. 1842. (PROB11/1972).

Irving, Paulus Emilius of Halifax, NS, Brevet Major & Capt. in 62nd Regiment of Foot. Will pr. 3 Mar. 1817. (PROB11/1590).

Isham, Charles Thomas of York Factory, Hudson's Bay, but late of Stepney, Mddx. Will 17 Feb. 1809. Leg: natural son Thomas Isham in Hudson's Bay; natural son James Isham; natural daughter Mary Isham. Exec: Alexander Lean. Wit: Thomas Haddan and John France. Pr. 3 Jan. 1815 by named exec. (PROB11/1564).

Isham, Henry of Henrico Co., VA. Will pr. by William Randolph 5 Jun. 1680. (PROB11/363). GGE.VGE.

Isham, James of Hudson's Bay, late Governor of York Fort. Will pr. 4 Feb. 1763. (PROB11/884).

Ivamey, John of New Bonaventura, NL, planter. Will pr. 14 Nov. 1834. (PROB11/1838).

Ivamy, William of New Bonaventura, Trinity, NL. Will pr. 21 Aug. 1815. (PROB11/1572).

Izard, Mary wife of Ralph of Berkeley Co., SC. Will pr. 26 Jul. 1700 by husband Ralph Izard. (PROB11/456). AWP.

Izard, Ralph of Berkeley Co., SC. Will 13 Sep. 1757 AWW 18 May 1763 to son Ralph Izard, attorney for brother-in-law Daniel Blake, Henry Middleton and Benjamin Smith in SC. (PROB11/887). AWP.

Jaby, Josia. *See* **Gely, John.**

Jackman, Joseph John of Surry Co., VA, who died in Deal, Kent, gent. Will 22 Apr. 1714 pr. 22 May 1714 by relict Mary Jackman. (PROB11/540). AWP.

Jackson, Arthur of Bristol, Glos., surgeon, who died in VA, bachelor. Will 18 Jun. 1702 AWW 18 Nov. 1713 to sisters Elizabeth and Rachel Jackson. (PROB11/537).

Jackson, Christopher of London, mariner of merchant ship *Port Neilson*, who died in Hudson's Bay, bachelor. Will 30 May 1711. Execs: Anthony and Margaret Holmes. Wit: John Earle, Mungo Greems and Richard Symonds. Pr. 4 Jun. 1717 by Anthony Holmes after sentence for validity of will. (PROB11/558 & 561).

Jackson, Edward of Boston, MA, gent. Will 8 Jun. 1757 AWW 7 May 1763 to Nathaniel Paice, attorney for Daniel Marsh, Samuel Sewall and Thomas Cushing in Boston. (PROB11/887). AWP.

Jackson, Samuel of New England, mariner of HMS *Windsor Castle*. Will pr. 9 Feb. 1693 by Anthony Dowrich. (PROB11/413). AWP.

Jackson, James of Montreal, gent. Will pr. 23 Oct. 1833. (PROB11/1822).

Jacob, Henry of St. Andrew Hubbard, London. Will 5 Oct. 1620. Leg: wife Sarah Jacob; his children in VA. Wit: James Page and George Crouch. Pr. 5 May 1624 by relict Sarah Jacob. (PROB11/143). AWP.

Jago, John, negro cook of HMS *Mediterranean* who died on merchant ship *Humphrey* in VA, bachelor. Will 30 Oct. 1731 pr. 6 Dec. 1739 by John Coldham. (PROB11/699). AWP.

Jaques, William of Beauport, [QC]. Will pr. 28 Jan. 1828. (PROB11/1735).

James, Henry of Bristol, merchant tailor who had lands in PA. Will 20 Apr. 1724 pr. 1 Oct. 1728 by daughter Hannah James. (PROB11/625). AWP.

James, John of Philadelphia but at present in London, late mariner of HMS *Dreadnought* and now of the *Assistance* of Philadelphia. Will dated 3 Dec. 1760, witnessed by Thomas Parry and Daniel Alexander Jr., clerk to Thomas Bland of Tower Hill, London, leaves his estate to be divided between his brother James James of Philadelphia and his sister Hannah James. Pr. 16 Feb. 1762 by Thomas Bland of London, merchant. (PROB11/873).

James, Peter Paumier of Halifax, NS, Commander in Royal Navy on half pay. Will pr. 23 May 1844. (PROB11/1998).

James, Thomas of Philadelphia who died in London, bachelor. Will 22 Jul. 1706 AWW 11 Feb. 1712 to John Askew, attorney for Edward Shippen and Samuel Preston of Philadelphia, merchants. (PROB11/525). AWP.

James, William, Clerk of the Cheque, Ordnance Office, QC. Will pr. Will pr. 11 Mar. 1795. (PROB11/1257).

Janson, Mary of Newland, Exhall, Warw., whose son George Janson married without his father's consent, failed in his trade as an apothecary and fled to VA in 1693 to escape his creditors. (PROB11/420). AWP. NGSQ 67/290.

Jardine, Robert S. of Madison Co., VA. AWW 13 Dec. 1815 to James Ross. (PROB11/1575).

Jarmain, Edward of Stanlow, Welland Co., [ON], yeoman. Will pr. 13 Aug. 1855. (PROB11/2218).

Jarvis, Edward, former chief factor and late superintendent of Albany Fort, Hudson's Bay. Will 17 Jun., codicil 18 Jun.1796. Leg: Alexander Lean, Secretary to Hudson's Bay Co; Thomas Searle of Banbury, Oxon., surgeon; putative son Edward Jarvis, apprentice to Mr. Welshman, surgeon at Hinton, Warw; brother John Jarvis in Philadelphia. Execs: Alexander Lean and Thomas Searle. Wit: David Geddes, H.J. More and Richard Good. Pr. 30 Aug. 1789 by Alexander Lean. (PROB11/1311).

Jarvis, Elizabeth of Enfield, Mddx., whose sister Ann Torbut resided in Frederick Co., MD. Will 1802 pr. 24 Mar. 1843. (PROB11/1388). NGSQ 63/200.

Jarvis, Thomas, formerly of VA but late of St. Olave, Old Jewry, London, merchant. Will 6 Apr. 1684 pr. 18 Apr. 1684 by relict Elizabeth Jarvis, brother Edmond Foster and George Richards. (PROB11/375). AWP.

Jauncey, William of NYC. Will pr. 11 Jul. 1829 by Thomas Barclay and John Rutherford. (PROB11/1758).

Jay, Peter of Rumbout Precinct. Dutchess Co., NY. AWW 27 May 1785 to James Daltera. (PROB11/1129).

Jeanes, Morgan of Forteaux Bay, Labrador. Will pr. 21 Sep. 1830. (PROB11/1776).

Jeffreys, Peter, mariner of HMS *Kinsale* who died in MD on merchant ship *Prosperous Ann*, bachelor. Will 20 May 1731 pr.22 Jan 1733 by brother Robert Jeffreys. (PROB11/656). AWP.

Jeffreys, William of St. James Westminster, Mddx., mariner of merchant ship *Mary & Francis* who died in VA, bachelor. Will 7 Sep. 1711 pr. 9 Jan. 1715 by uncle John Jeffreys. (PROB11/544). AWP.

Jenkins, Rev. George of Montreal, Chaplain to H.M. Forces. Will pr. 12 Nov. 1821. (PROB11/1650).

Jenkins, John of Renewse, NL. Will pr. 1 Dec. 1737. (PROB11/686).

Jenkins, John of Kingsclear, York Co., NB. Will pr. 20 May 1805. (PROB11/1302).

Jenkins, John of Trinity, NL, gent. Will pr. 31 Dec. 1816. (PROB11/1587).

Jennings, Edmund of Yorkshire who had relatives in MD and VA. Will 10 Mar. 1756 pr. 24 Mar. 1756 by son Edmund Jennings. (PROB11/821). AWP.

Jenys, Thomas of Charles Town, SC, merchant. Will 19 Oct. 1745 pr. 26 Oct. 1750 by Stephen Bedon Jr. (PROB11/783). AWP.

Jephson, William of Halifax, NS, Deputy Barrackmaster-General. Will pr. 15 Mar. 1815. (PROB11/1566).

Jerningham, Henry Esq. of St. Mary's Co., MD. Will 19 Nov. 1772 pr. 5 May 1775 by daughter Frances Henrietta Jerningham. (PROB11/1007). AWP.

Jesson, Robert of Philadelphia, PA, merchant & widower. Will 3 Apr 1732 pr. 18 Jun. 1740 by Rebecca, wife of Solomon Goade of Philadelphia, mariner. (PROB11/703). AWP.

Jimenez, Jose. *See* **Ximenez.**

Jobson, Samuel Sr. of Bermondsey, Sy., woolstapler, who had lands in PA and whose son Michael Jobson was in Philadelphia. Will 29 Jul. 1706 pr. 9 Nov. 1708 by affirmation of Thomas Mayleigh and grandson Samuel Jobson. (PROB11/505). AWP.

Johns, John of St. Botolph Bishopsgate, citizen and clothworker of London who died in Carolina. Will 22 Aug. 1698 pr. 17 Jan. 1700 by relict Frances Johns. (PROB11/454). AWP.

Johns, William of Sorel [QC], sergeant and conductor of stones. Will pr. 15 Apr. 1784. (PROB11/1116).

Johnson, Andrew of Woodford, Essex, mariner of merchant ship *Essex*, who died in VA, bachelor. Will 14 Aug. 1705 pr. 28 Apr. 1708 by Martha Tilbury *alias* Splitt. (PROB11/501). AWP.

Johnson *alias* **Dickey, Andrew**, gunner of Albany Fort, Hudson's Bay. Will pr. 19 Dec. 1713. (PROB11/537).

Johnson, Charles Christopher of Montreal, formerly Colonel in Army. Will pr. 26 Oct. 1854. PROB11/2199).

Johnson, Daniel of Lynn, MA, trumpeter of HMS *Advice*. Will 22 Jun. 1695 pr. 6 Apr. 1696 by Patrick Hayes. (PROB11/431). AWP.

Johnson, John of Lubeck, [Germany] but late of Wapping, Mddx., mariner who died in VA, bachelor. Will 26 Oct 1680 pr. 27 Jul 1682 by Joane Cheny. (PROB11/370). AWP.

Johnson, John of Dunn, Niagara, ON, in service of East India Co. Will pr. 20 Oct. 1846. (PROB11/2043).

Johnson, Sir John of Montreal. Will pr. 27 Sep. 1751. (PROB11/2139).

Johnson, Luke of VA, planter. Will pr. 1 Aug. 1659 by John Turton and James Cary. (PROB11/294). ACE.VGE.

Johnson *alias* **Bowes, Maria** of Montreal City, widow. Will pr. 15 Jul. 1850. (PROB11/2116).

Johnson, Peter of Shadwell, Mddx., mariner of ship *Anne* who died in VA, bachelor. Will 13 Nov. 1691 pr. 8 Aug. 1693 by Gabriel Whithorne. (PROB11/415). AWP.

Johnson, Robert Esq., Governor of SC. Will 25 Dec. 1734 AWW 9 Aug. 1735 to son Robert Johnson Esq. (PROB11/672). AWP.

Johnson, Samuel of MD, mariner. Will pr. 15 Dec. 1741. (PROB11/714).

Johnson, Sarah of Charleston, SC, widow. AWW 7 Jul. 1838 to Thomas Crowder. (PROB11/1898).

Johnson, Simon of NYC, gent. AWW 23 May 1823 to Gabriel Shaw. (PROB11/1670).

Johnson, Uzal of Newark, NJ, surgeon of NJ Volunteers on half pay. AWW 3 Apr. 1728 to James Tidbury. (PROB11/1739).

Johnson, Sir William of Johnson Hall, Tryon Co., NY. AWW 9 Feb. 1776 to Samuel Baker. (PROB11/1016).

Johnson, William of Renews, NL. Will pr. 24 Jan. 1833. (PROB11/1810).

Johnson, William of Georgina, York, [ON], Lieut. in Royal Navy. Will pr. 23 Jun. 1852. (PROB11/2154).

Johnson, William Stratford of Upper Canada, Lieut. in 83rd Regiment of Foot. Will pr. 10 May 1839. (PROB11/1911).

Johnston, Gabriel, of Edenhouse, NC, Governor of N.C. AWW 31 Aug. 1791 to Alexander Anderson. (PROB11/1208).

Johnston, John of Halifax, NS, barrister at law. Will pr. 6 Jul. 1839. (PROB11/1913).

Johnstone, John of Fort Vancouver, Columbia City, [WA]. Will pr. 4 Jun. 1856 by Isabella Miller *alias* Moar. (PROB11/2234).

Johnston, Robert of VA, merchant. Will pr. 5 Apr. 1766 by James Russell. (PROB11/917). VGE.

Jones, Allen of Bourbon, VA. AWW 2 Oct. 1792 to William Murdock. (PROB11/1224).

Jones, Arthur Johnston of Toronto, Lieutenant on half pay. Will pr. 18 Jun. 1835. (PROB11/1848).

Jones, Evan of Charles Town, SC, merchant. Will dated 11 Jun. 1772 witnessed by Joseph Creighton, Abraham Michau Jr. and Christopher Rogers. Leg: his sister and executrix in Bow Street, Bloomsbury Square, London; Mr. Richard Downes of Charles Town, merchant; Theodore Gaillard Jr. of the same, merchant; uncle John Jones on the testator's farm near Bala, Merionethshire; the sisters of his deceased father Robert Jones. Pr. 4 May 1774 by Margaret Jones. (PROB11/998).

Jones, George of Philadelphia but who died in Worcester, yeoman. Will 22 Sep. 1743 AWW 14 Feb. 1752 to sister Elizabeth Clay, widow. (PROB11/792). AWP.

Jones, Henry of Charleston, SC, merchant. AWW 20 Jun. 1815 to Thomas Crokatt and Charles Alderman. (PROB11/1569).

Jones, Rev. Hugh of Christchurch, Calvert Co., MD. Will 3 Jan. 1702 AWW. 15 Jun. 1704 to Barbara Jones. (PROB11/477). AWP.

Jones, Jacob of Halifax, NS, clerk of HM sloop *Zebra*. Will pr. 11 Feb. 1779. (PROB11/1050).

Jones, John of Philadelphia, merchant. Will 17 Jan. 1723 pr.11 Dec. 1723 by the relict Joanne Jones. (PROB11/594). AWP.

Jones, John Coffin of Boston, MA. Will pr. 17 Sep. 1838 by Ebenezer Chadwick. (PROB11/1900).

Jones, Jonathan of Baddock, Cape Breton Island [NS], yeoman. Will pr. 18 Jun. 1812. (PROB11/1534).

Jones, Lewis of St. Helena, Granville Co., SC, clerk. Will 10 Feb. 1744 pr. 4 Oct. 1748 by brother John Jones. (PROB11/765). AWP.

Jones, Livellet *alias* **Elipilor** of Fairfield, CT, mariner on HMS *Suffolk*. Will 18 May 1709 AWW 29 Mar. 1710 to Mary Collins. (PROB11/514). AWP.

Jones, Owen of NY, mariner of HMS *Richmond*. Will 6 Jun. 1697 AWW 27 Oct. 1698 to George Farewell, attorney for relict Elizabeth Jones in NY. (PROB11/447).

Jones, Samuel of Gloucester, MA, mariner of HMS *Warspight* who died in Southwark, Surrey. Will 20 Mar. 1673 pr. 1 Oct 1673 by sister Susanna, wife of Richard Smith. (PROB11/343). AWP.

Jones, Samuel of London, mariner who was bound to VA in the ship *Jacob* but died on the *York*, bachelor. Will 30 Oct. 1690 pr. 30 May 1693 by brother John Jones, citizen and pewterer of London. (PROB11/414). AWP.

Jones, Thomas, mariner of HMS *Pembroke* who died on Hog Island, VA. Will 16 Aug. 1697 pr. 7 Oct. 1698 by Dyer Wade. (PROB11/447). AWP.

Jones, Thomas of NY, Judge of Supreme Court. Will pr. 18 Aug. 1792 to relict Ann Jones. (PROB11/1222).

Jones, William of Rotherhithe, Sy., who died in Bethnal Green, Mddx., merchant whose son-in-law Mann Page had a plantation in New Kent Co., VA.. Will 4 Nov. 1714 pr. 2 Jan. 1719 by son John Page. (PROB11/567). AWP.

Jones, William of NYC, purser of HMS *Coventry*. Will 6 Nov. 1764 pr. 18 Jul. 1765 by relict Rachel Jones. (PROB11/910). AWP.

Jones, William, armourer of HMS *Rattler* in Naval Hospital of Halifax, NS. Will pr. 14 Jul. 1813. (PROB11/1546).

Jordan, John Morton of Annapolis, MD, merchant. Will pr. 31 Jul. 1772. (PROB11/979).

Joslin, John of Tilbury Hall near Clare, Essex, yeoman, whose son William Joslin was residing in America. Will 10 Jul. 1830 pr. 20 Jan. 1831 by sons Peter and Hezekiah Joslin and William Purkis. (PROB11/1780).

Jukes, Edward of Charles Town, SC. Will 4 Oct. 1710 pr. 14 Nov. 1715 by relict Dorothy Jukes. (PROB11/549). AWP.

Julin, Carls of Wapping, Mddx., mariner of *Charles Town Packet*, bachelor. Will 17 Mar. 1759 pr. 12 Aug. 1760 by Johannes Scheelhase. (PROB11/858). AWP.

Julyan, Robert of Gamean's Cottage, Beauport Road, near City of QC, Commander in Royal Navy. Will pr. 24 May 1856. (PROB11/2232).

Kane, John Sr. of NYC. AWW 23 Nov. 1822 to Gabriel Shaw. (PROB11/1663).

Kavanagh, Joseph of St. John's, NL, hairdresser and barber. Will pr. 10 Mar. 1817. (PROB11/1590).

Kearny, Philip of Perth Amboy, NJ, who inherited lands in Philadelphia from his grandmother Elizabeth Brittain. Leg: wife Isabella Kearny; sons Michael, Philip, Ravaud and Francis Kearny; daughters Susanna, wife of Richard Stevens, Elizabeth Skinner, Sarah, Isabella and Joanna Kearny; grandson Philip Kearny Skinner. Wit: William Stevenson, John Johnston and Edward Wilson.Will 25 Apr. 1770 AWW 31 Mar. 1783 to John Abraham Denormandie. (PROB11/1101)

Kearsley, Margaret of Philadelphia, widow. AWW 2 Aug. 1779 to Phineas Bond. (PROB11/1056).

Keating, Edward of Kingston, Midland District, [ON], physician. Will pr. 5 Jun. 1822. (PROB11/1658).

Keddel *alias* **Kiddel, John** of Little Bay, NL. Will pr. 8 Oct. 1841. (PROB11/1952).

Keech, Simon of Stepney, Mddx., bachelor, who died in Accomack Co., VA. Nuncupative will 13 Feb 1688 AWW 2 Aug 1688 to Ellis Kelly, attorney for sisters Mary and Joanna Keech, Elizabeth Woodnett, widow, and Sarah Tilly, widow. (PROB11/392). AWP.

Keech, Thomas, surgeon of merchant ship *Goodwill*, who died in MD. Will 2 Mar. 1716 pr. 29 Nov. 1717 by George Fisher, citizen and surgeon of London. (PROB11/561). AWP.

Keen, John of NS, soldier on board HMS *Centurion* in River St. Lawrence. Will pr. 9 Apr. 1760. (PROB11/855).

Keen, William of St. John's, NL, merchant. Will pr. 9 Jan. 1755. (PROB11/813).

Keir, Patrick of VA, surgeon of HMS *Shoreham*. Will pr. 4 Feb. 1702. (PROB11/463).

Kelland, William, formerly of Sally's Cove, Trinity Bay, but late of St. John's, NL, planter. Will 25 May 1823. Leg: brother John Kelland and sisters (unnamed); nephews William Kelland, John Kelland and Robert R. Oakey. Exec: brother John Kelland. Wit: Thomas Taylor, John Savell and James Quints. AWW 28 Aug. 1824 to John Ridout, attorney for brother John Kelland at St. John's, NL. (PROB11/1689).

Kellett *alias* **Kelly, Roger** of Canada, Lieut. in 44th Regiment of Foot. Will pr. 7 Jan. 1780. (PROB11/1060).

Kelly, Mary of Halifax, NS, widow. Will pr. 14 Jan. 1854. (PROB11/2184).

Kelly, Roger. *See* **Kellett.**

Kempe, Richard of Kick Neck, VA. Will pr. 6 Dec. 1656 by relict Elizabeth Lunford *alias* Kempe. (PROB11/260). ACE.

Kennan, Henry of Josephtown, GA, gent, who died at St. Dunstan in the East, London. Will dated 30 Apr. 1763 leaving instructions for sale of his 400 acres at Mill Island, St. Matthew's parish, with bequests to his wife Susannah Kennan and children Henry, James, Elizabeth and Marianne. Deposition of 9 Mar. 1767 by John Kennan of St. Andrew Undershaft, London, gent, brother of the testator, that the handwriting on the will is his brother's. Pr. 9 Mar. 1767 by the relict Susannah Kennan with similar powers reserved to Patrick Mackay and George Cuthbert of Christchurch parish, GA. (PROB11/1293).

Kennedy, Adam of St. Michael, Crooked Lane, London, merchant intending for NY but who died in Antigua. Will 14 Sep. 1697 pr. 18 Aug. 1698 by William Gordon. (PROB11/447). AWP.

Kenedy, James, Corporal in 1st Battalion of Royal Scots of QC. Will pr. Will pr. 31 Jul. 1815. (PROB11/1570).

Kennedy, John of Halifax, NS, of HMS *Mercury*. Will pr. 7 Apr. 1777. (PROB11/1030).

Kent, Luke of Malahide, Middlesex, London District, [ON], yeoman. 26 Apr. 1852. (PROB11/2151).

Kenyan, Abraham of Warfield, Berks, clerk, who had estate in VA. Will 15 Apr. 1693 pr. 28 Jan. 1704 by son Jabez Kenyan. (PROB11/474). AWP.

Kenyon, Samuel, formerly of Manchester, Lancs., but late of Boston, MA, mariner. Copy of will pr. Jan. 1710 in Boston, MA. TNA: PROB20/2952.

Kerby, James of Halifax, NS. Will pr. 22 Nov. 1837. (PROB11/1886).

Kerr, Thomas of Portsmouth, Hants., Stepney, Mddx., mariner of HMS *Chatham* who died in NY. Will 28 Feb. 1716 pr. 13 Apr. 1730 by relict Jane Kerr. (PROB11/636). AWP.

Keynell, George of St. Katherine by the Tower, London. Memorandum of goods sent by him to VA by the *James*, Mr. Tobias Felgate, in 1622. Leg: his wife Frances Keynell; John Harrison of the *James*. AWW to relict Frances Keynell. (PROB11/144). AWP.

Kibble, Stephen of NY, merchant. Will 7 Aug. 1779. Leg: mother Martha Kibble of the City of London; sister-in-law Mrs. Jane Wallace; niece Dorothy Wallace; house in Wall Street, NY, occupied by Thomas Leonard, to wife Catherine Kibble and daughter Catherine Kibble. Execs: wife, William Butler Esq., James Doyle and Benjamin James. Wit: Richard Bayley, surgeon, John L.C. Roome, notary, and Thomas Wright. Certified in NY 14 Dec. 1779. AWW 19 Jan. 1782 William Butler Esq. (PROB11/1086).

Kiddel. *See* **Keddel.**

Kidgell, Nicholas of Stepney, Mddx., but late of Charles Town, SC. Will 5 Aug. 1726 AWW 22 Jul. 1727 to relict Sarah Kidgell. (PROB11/616). AWP.

Kilvert, Roger of London, mariner who had debts owed him in VA. Will 15 Sep. 1661. Leg: sister Sarah Marston to have his share in ship *Concord*; brother Thomas Marston; uncle Sir John Watts of Herts. Wit: Richard Edlin, Edward Whiteing; Stanhope Mill, John Dixon and Joseph Staveley. Pr. 16 Jul. 1663 by sister Sarah Kilvert *alias* Marston. (PROB11/311)

Kincaid, George of Christ Church parish, GA. Will pr. 7 Oct. 1791. (PROB11/1209).

King, Eusebius of Bristol, Prince George Co., VA. Will 9 Feb. 1709 AWW 17 Sep. 1711 to Isham Randolph, attorney for William Randolph Sr. of Henrico Co., VA. (PROB11/523). AWP.

King, John of Halifax, NS, mason of HM Careening Yard. Will pr. 17 Feb. 1813. (PROB11/1541).

King, John Curle of Hampton, VA, mariner who died in St. Martin in Fields, Mddx. Will 5 Nov. 1763 pr. 15 Nov. 1763 by William Boyd. (PROB11/893). AWP.

King, Nathaniel of Boston, MA, mariner of HMS *York*. Will 31 Dec. 1741 AWW 27 Nov. 1747 to Thomas Newman, attorney for relict Mary King in Boston. (PROB11/757). AWP.

Kinsey, Ralph of St. Botolph Aldersgate, London, yeoman, who had lands in PA. Will 23 Jun 1682 pr. 29 Jun. 1682 by brothers William Kinsey and Robert Browne, tailors. (PROB11/370). AWP.

Kneller, Henry of QC City, gent. Will pr. 16 Apr. 1776. (PROB11/1018).

Knight, Henry of St. Martin in Fields, Mddx., who died in MD, mariner. Will 25 Nov. 1672 pr. 12 Jan 1675 by uncle Robert Day. (PROB11/347). AWP.

Knight, Stephen of St. John's, NL. Will pr. 2 Dec. 1814. (PROB11/1563).

Knight, Thomas of Eastmain, Hudson's Bay, surgeon. Will pr. 12 Dec. 1797. (PROB11/1299).

Knight, William of Williamsburg, VA, widower, residing at Roade, Northants. Will 3 Jul. 1768 pr. 2 Jan. 1771 by brother Robert Knight. (PROB11/963). AWP.

Knipe, William of Portsmouth, NH, sailor of HMS *America*. Will 5 Oct. 1749 pr. 27 Nov. 1750 by Dr. Robert Ratsey. (PROB11/783). AWP.

Knolles, John of Bath, Somerset, apothecary, late surgeon's mate of W. FL Hospital. Will 10 Dec. 1761 pr. 2 Sep. 1767 by William Street of Bath, apothecary. (PROB11/932). AWP.

Koux, Wilhelmina Jacoba of Middleburgh, [NY]. Will pr. 6 Jun. 1749. (PROB11/770).

Lachoe, Andrew of NS, Lieut. in Regiment of Foot. Will pr. 28 Jun. 1822. (PROB11/1658).

Lacy, Patrick of HMS *Restoration* and *Essex* who died in VA, bachelor. Will 9 Jul. 1700 pr. 5 Aug. 1700 by uncle Thomas Connaway. (PROB11/456). AWP.

Ladlie, James. *See* Ludlow.

Lake, Charles, Rector of St. James's parish , Anne Arundel Co., MD. Will 2 Nov. 1763 AWW 3 Apr. 1765 to Dr. Messenger Monsey, attorney for Rev. Samuel Keene. (PROB11/908). AWP.

Lake, John of Fortune Bay, NL. Will pr. 31 Dec. 1841. (PROB11/1955).

Lamb, Hugh of Edmonton, Mddx., yeoman. Leg: wife Sarah Lamb; Henry Haly of London, gent; Elizabeth Twyford; Hannah, daughter of Stephen Hubbersly; Joseph Lamb of Oxford and his children; brother Daniel Lamb of Oxford to have testator's real estate in PA and NJ. Wit: Henry Arnold, Elizabeth Waller and John Wells. Will pr. 20 Oct. 1686 by brother Daniel Lamb. (Guildhall: Ms 9171/40/245).

Lamb, William of Montreal, merchant. Will pr. 31 Aug. 1847. (PROB11/2061).

Lambert, Robert of QC, in the service of Capt. Lewis Kirke. Will pr. 4 Nov. 1631. (PROB11/160).

Lambert, Vincent of MD who died a prisoner in France. Will 2 Feb. 1703 pr. 30 Jul. 1703 by father Edward Lambert. (PROB11/470). AWP.

Lambert, William of Boston, MA. Will 15 Apr. 1748 AWW 6 Mar. 1750 to Thomas Lane, attorney for nephew William Lambert of Boston, sugar refiner. (PROB11/777). AWP.

Lamer, Richard of Halifax, NS, Lieut. in Maj. General Richard O'Farell's Regiment of Foot. Will pr. 25 Aug. 1758. (PROB11/840).

Lane, Hon. Ambrose, Lieut. Col. of Militia and Town Major of Charlotte Town, PE. Will pr. 7 Sep. 1854. (PROB11/2197).

Lane, Martha of Blandford, Dorset, spinster who died in NC. Will 19 Dec. 1754 pr. 15 Dec. 1756 by nephew Thomas Fitzherbert. (PROB11/826). AWP.

Langaller *alias* Langally *alias* Langlee, Nicholas of Petty Harbour, NL, planter. Will pr. 1 Mar. 1717. (PROB11/551).

Langhorne *alias* Ingoldsby, Mary of Holborn, Mddx., who died at Staughton, Hunts., and whose brother John Oxenbridge had one child in Jamaica and one in New England. Will 24 Nov. 1686 pr. 15 Dec. 1686 by the son Sir William Langhorne. (PROB11/385). AWP.

Langley, John of St. Saviour, Southwark, Sy., physician, whose daughter Margaret Day was in MD. Will 9 Feb. 1698 pr. 15 Feb. 1699 by relict Thomazine Langley. (PROB11/449). AWP.

Langworthy, John of St. John's, NL, sailor. Will pr. 22 Mar. 1785. (PROB11/1127).

Lanman, William of Boston, MA, gent. Will 11 Jul. 1724 or. 8 Sep. 1725 by son William Lanman of London. (PROB11/611). AWP.

Larabee, John of New England. Will pr. 19 Jun. 1694 by Elizabeth Crawford. (PROB11/420).

Larner, Richard of St. Martin in Fields, Mddx., Lieut. in 22nd Regiment who died in Albany, NY. Will dated Halifax, NS, 1 Aug. 1757 pr. 25 Aug. 1758 Ann, wife of Thomas Lynes. (PROB11/840). AWP.

Lash, Robert, seaman of HMS *Beaulieu* in NS Naval Hospital. Will pr. 13 Jun. 1795. (PROB11/1262).

Laugher, Elizabeth. *See* **Worthington.**

Laurens, James, native of Charles Town, SC. Will dated Vigan, Salvador, 6 Sep. 1782 pr. 21 May 1784 by relict Mary Laurens and nephew Henry Laurens with similar powers reserved to brother Henry Laurens.(PROB11/1117).

Lavington, Stephen Esq. of St. Celement Danes, Mddx., and late of Antigua but about to depart for North America. AWW 8 Dec. 1759 to Edward Codrington, attorney for John Lightfoot, Samuel Redhead and Dr. James Athill in Antigua. (PROB11/851). AWP.

Law, John, mariner of HMS *Pembroke*, bachelor. Will 31 Oct. 1747 AWW 7 May 1750 to Joseph Argent, attorney for Elizabeth Partridge in Boston, MA. (PROB11/779). AWP.

Lawrence, Richard, residing at Boston, MA, mariner of HMS *Squirrel* who died overseas. Will 17 Aug. 1739 AWW 22 Jan. 1742 to Peter Warren, attorney for relict Mary Lawrence in Boston. (PROB11/715). AWP.

Lawry, GAWWn, late Governor of East Jersey who died in Elizabeth Town, NJ. Will 12 Aug. 1687 AWW 7 Oct. 1697 to Obediah Haige, grandson by daughter Mary Haige. (PROB11/440). AWP.

Lawton, Joseph of Charleston, SC, merchant. AWW 22 Aug. 1855 to Francis Frederick Whitehead and John Dicken Whitehead. (PROB11/2218).

Lay, Benjamin of Colchester, Essex, glover late of Abington, PA. Will Mar. 1732 AWW 2 Jul. 1760 by affirmation to Samuel Cook of South Halstead, Essex, weaver. (PROB11/857). AWP.

Leake, John of Hermitage, NYC, gent. Leg: brother-in-law Robert Burrage to have estate at Thurlton, Norfolk; Thomas Carpenter and Thomas Thomas to have farm at Westchester; Martha Clinton, daughter of Governor of NY; daughters of late nephew Robert Burrage; niece Martha Norton; John Leake Norton. Wit: Henry Roome, Susanna Degroot and Alexander Thompson. Will pr. 1 Mar. 1815 by John Leake Norton. (PROB11/1566).

Leask, Isaac of Orkney Island now of the Prince of Wales Fort, [Manitoba]. Will dated 13 Sep. 1765 witnessed by Moses Norton and Josh Richards. Leg: half his estate to his mother Ellison Leask and half to his sisters Barbary Long and Ann Leask of Rotherhithe. Pr. 8 Oct. 1774 by Ellison Leask. (PROB11/1002).

Leaver, John of Halifax, NS. Will pr. 26 Apr. 1847. (PROB11/2054).

Le Cocq, Peter of Boston, MA. Will pr. 5 Mar. 1799 by relict Elizabeth Le Cocq. (PROB11/1321).

Lee, Charles of Berkeley Co., VA, Maj. General. AWW 18 Jun. 1785 to Sir Robert and Charles Kerries. (PROB11/1131).

Lee, Isaac of Rappahannock River, VA, mariner, but late of Stepney, Mddx. Will 18 Nov. 1726 pr. 3 Nov. 1727 by William Dawkings of London. (PROB11/618). AWP.

Lee, John of Charlestown, MA, carpenter. AWW 11 Jun. 1692 to Giles Titfield. (PROB11/410).

Lee, John of Boston, MA. Will pr. 30 Nov. 1840 by son John Francis Lee. (PROB11/1936).

Lee, Joseph of Cambridge, MA. AWW 16 Apr. 1803 to Thomas Dickason Jr. (PROB11/1390).

Lee, Martha of Whitechapel, Mddx., widow, whose daughter Martha married William Fitzhugh of Cople, VA, and daughter Lettice married John Corbin of Essex Co., VA. Will 26 Apr. 1725 pr. 5 May 1725 by Tobias Silk and Williams Wareham. (PROB11/603). AWP. NGSQ 63/131.

Lee, Sarah of Boston, MA. Will pr. 31 Oct. 1850 to brother John Francis Lee. (PROB11/2121).

Leeming, Peter of Harbour Grace, NL. Will pr. 18 Mar. 1822. (PROB11/1655).

Lees, Thomas of Philadelphia, seaman in merchant service. Will pr. 20 Jun. 1853. (PROB11/2174).

Leeth, Thomas of Stepney, Mddx., mariner of merchant ship *Anne & Mary* who died in VA. Will 24 Oct. 1693 pr. 1 May 1711 by sister Jane Holmes. (PROB11/521). AWP.

Leman, Hickford of London, gent, late of Piscatua, MD, bachelor. Will 14 Aug. 1703 pr. 30 Aug. 1732 by brother Daniel Cooper. (PROB11/653). AWP.

Lenfestey, Peter of QC, shoemaker and merchant. Will pr. 10 Mar. 1815. (PROB11/1566).

Lenom, William of Newport, RI, mariner of HMS *Somerset.* Memorandum of 11 Feb. 1778. Leg: Daniel Fraizer and George Brindle. Wit: Thomas Higgens, Thomas Shea, James Enbet and John Halliburton, surgeon of RI Hospital. AWW to Daniel Frazier 21 Jan. 1780. (PROB11/1061).

Lenthall, Philip of London, mariner who died in Philadelphia. Will 20 Jan. 1714 pr. 15 Jan. 1724 by brother John Lenthall of St. Dunstan in West, London, stationer.

L'Escott, Frances of Charles Town, SC, widow of advanced age. Will 24 Aug. 1752 AWW 26 Sep. 1753 to George Chardin, attorney for Isaac Mazyck and Zachariah Villepontoux. (PROB11/804). AWP.

Le Serurier, James of Charleston, SC, but formerly of St. Quentin, Normandy. Will dated 21 May 1698. To his wife Mrs. Elizabeth Leger his whole estate and she is to be sole exex. and love all their children without distinction. If either he or she should die on their voyage, the executor is to be the testator's son James Le Serurier of London, merchant. £5 to the poor of the French church of Charleston. Witnessed by Crouill and George Harris, Lewis de St. Julien, P. Lasall and John Mead. Pr. 4 Oct. 1706 by Elizabeth Leger *alias* Le Serurier. (PROB11/490).

Leslie, John of St. Augustine, E. FL, merchant, second son of Alexander Leslie of Bainagreth, Moray, Scotland, now about to embark for Great Britain. Will dated Charleston, SC, 6 Aug. 1798. Leg: Elizabeth Wain, daughter of Rebecca Paigret(?) of E. FL, who lived as testator's wife for 7 years and by whom he had 3 children but whom he repudiated in May 1797 because of her bad habits; younger brothers Alexander and Archibald Leslie; older brother William Leslie; partner William Panton at present of Pensacola; Thomas Forbes of Nassau, New Providence and his son John Forbes; John Forrester of St. Augustine; Edwin Gardner of Charleston, SC, merchant. Will pr. 16 Jul. 1804 by William Forbes. (PROB11/1411).

Letchworth, Thomas, younger son of Thomas Letchworth, citizen and fishmonger of London, intending a voyage to VA and who died overseas. Will 8 Dec. 1654 pr. 13 Mar 1657 by said father. (PROB11/263). AWP.

Levermore, Barbara of VA. Will pr. 25 Sep. 1716 by Thomas Richardson. (PROB11/554). VGE.

Levett, Elizabeth of Prince George's Co., MD, widow. Will 22 Sep. 1725 pr. 5 Dec. 1730 by James Maddock and Margaret Clarke *alias* Buchanan now wife of George Buchanan. (PROB11/641). AWP.

Lewis, John of Charles Town, SC, cordwainer who died in St. Thomas's Hospital, Southwark, Sy. Will 25 Jun. 1753 pr 6 Jul. 1753 by John Taylor and Thomas Hardwick. (PROB11/803). AWP.

Lewis, William Henry of Kingston, [ON], Quartermaster of 8th or King's Regiment of Foot. Will pr. 22 Apr. 1831. (PROB11/1784).

Ley, Humphrey on board the *Phoenix* bound for James River, VA, who died overseas. Will 20 Sep 1658 AWW 9 Mar. 1663 to sister Judith Skinn *alias* Leigh. (PROB11/310). AWP.

Liddell, Archibald of St. George, Mddx., commander of galley *Elliott* who died in Charles Town, SC. Will 4 May 1747 pr 7 Jun. 1748 by Archibald Elliott of London, merchant. (PROB11/762). AWP.

Lidgett, Charles, formerly of Boston, MA, but late of St. Bride's, London. Will 9 Apr. 1698 AWW 16 May 1698 to brother-in-law John Hester. (PROB11/445). AWP.

Ligertwood, Alexander of Halifax, NS, Deputy Quartermaster of HM Forces. Will pr. 21 Mar. 1817. (PROB11/1590).

Light, Mrs. Jane of Canada. Will pr. 16 Apr. 1857. (PROB11/2250).

Lightfoot, Frances of Newport, RI, spinster. Will pr. 29 Nov. 1800 by Rev. William Lloyd Baker. (PROB11/1350).

Lillie, John of Stepney, Mddx., mariner of ship *John* who died in VA. Will 6 Dec. 1692. Leg: wife Isabel Lillie who is to be exex. Wit: James Newton, John Dennis and Nathaniel Hake. Pr. 4 Sep. 1692 by relict Isabel Lillie. (Guildhall: Ms 9171/48/450).

Linacre, John of RI, private of 65th Marine Company aboard HMS *Asia*. Will 31 Dec. 1776, Wit: John Laver, sergeant of Marines, and Thomas Carter. Pr. 3 Jul. 1777 by sole exex. daughter Ann Linacre. (PROB11/1033).

Lincoln, Robert of Limehouse, Mddx., mariner of the *Loving Friendship* bound for VA. Will 21 Sep. 1691. Leg: cousins Mary and Elizabeth Grantham; Sarah Bowman, widow of John Bowman, etc. Sole exec: John Marshall. Wit: John Davidson, Robert Watson and Thomas Quilter. Pr. 2 Sep. 1692 by John Marshall. (Guildhall: Ms 8171/44/398).

Linn *alias* Linns, John formerly of MD but late of Bristol, mariner. Will 17 Nov. 1750 pr. 1 Jan. 1751 by Sarah, wife of John Humphreys of Bristol. (PROB11/785). AWP. NGSQ 63/130.

Linzee, John of Milton, MA, former Capt. in Royal Navy. AWW 16 Apr. 1799 to William Burgess. (PROB11/1322).

Lithgow, William of City of London, merchant, but late of Wilmington, NC. Will pr. 9 Mar. 1748 by Nathaniel Fletcher. (PROB11/760). AWP. Further grant July 1754).

Littlepage, Edmund, formerly of York River, VA, but late of London who died in Enfield, Mddx., bachelor. Will 6 May 1712 pr. 8 Aug. 1712 by nephew Joseph Littlepage. (PROB11/528). AWP.

Livingston, Gilbert Robert of Schenectady, NY, reduced Capt. of Cavalry in American Legion. Will pr. 23 Jan. 1817. (PROB11/1588).

Livingston, John of New London, CT, late in London and who died in St. James Westminster, Mddx.. Will 17 Feb. 1720 pr. 12 May 1720 by James Douglass. (PROB11/574). AWP.

Livingston, Mortimer of NYC. Will pr. 8 Jan. 1858 by Charles William Foster and William Sydney Drayton. (PROB11/2263).

Lluellin, Daniel of VA, planter, late of Colchester, Essex. Will 5 Feb. 1664. Leg: wife Anne Lluellin to have lands in Charles Co., VA, during her life and then they are to pass to son Daniel Lluellin; daughters Martha Jones and Margaret Cruse; Mary Elsing and Mary Derrington, widow, both of Colchester. Execs: Thomas Vervell of Roxwell, Essex, James Jauncey of London and William Walker of Colchester, shopkeeper. Pr. 11 Mar. 1664 by William Walker and Giles Sussex. (PROB11/313).

Llewellin, William of Swansea, Wales, who died in NY, late master of brigantine *Artemisia*. Will pr. 21 Aug. 1782 by Morgan Lewis and William Franklyn. (PROB11/1094).

Lloyd, Arthur of Bessborough, Marché Township, Carleton, [QC]. Will pr. 9 Jul. 1853. (PROB11/2175).

Lloyd, Edward of Whitechapel, Mddx., but late of MD, planter. Will 7 Mar. 1696 pr. 14 Jul 1696 by relict Grace Lloyd. (PROB11/432). AWP.

Lloyd, Elizabeth of Elizabeth River, Lower Norfolk, VA, widow. Pr. 15 Jun. 1657 by brother-in-law Thomas Eavans. (PROB11/265). ACE.VGE.

Lloyd, Henry of Boston, MA. Will pr. 30 Apr. 1796 by Katharine Lloyd. (PROB11/1274).

Lloyd, James of Boston, MA, merchant. Will pr. 5 Apr. 1696 by Francis Brinley and John Nelson. (PROB11/431). GGE.

Lloyd, John of Sarphley, Goose Creek, SC. Will 27 Jul. 1733 AWW 7 Jun. 1746 to John Nickelson. (PROB11/747). AWP.

Lloyd, John Barnaby or Orleans Island, QC. Will pr. Will pr. 26 Nov. 1836. (PROB11/1869).

Lloyd, Sarah. *See* **Waring.**

Lloyd, Simon of VA, mariner. Will 25 Dec. 1655 pr. 30 Jul. 1657 by Robert Conway, citizen and joiner of London. (PROB11/266). AWP.

Lloyd, Thomas, Capt. of H.M. Independent Company of NL. Will pr. 25 Nov. 1710. (PROB11/518).

Lloyd, Thomas of QC, doctor of medicine. Will pr. 14 Dec. 1836. (PROB11/1870).

Lloyd, Thomas Waring of Fort George, [ON], Lieut. in 8th or King's Regiment of Foot. Will pr. 19 May 1817. (PROB11/1592).

Lluellin. *See* **Llewellin.**

Lockley, William of Prince George Co., VA, merchant. Will pr. 8 Jun. 1745 by relict Margaret Frances Lockley. (PROB11/740). VGE.

Lodge, Catharine of Cobourg, Newcastle District, [ON]. Will pr. 22 Mar. 1853. (PROB11/2169).

Lodge, Mary of Cobourg, Newcastle District, [ON], spinster. Will pr. 23 Mar. 1853. (PROB11/2169).

Lomas, John, formerly of Annapolis, MD, and late of Glasgow, Scotland, gent. Will 22 Oct. 1754 AWW 22 Nov. 1757 to John Mill, attorney for James Johnson in VA. (PROB11/834). AWP.

Long, Augustine, citizen and wheelwright of London, whose granddaughter Elizabeth Rise was living in VA. Will 8 Feb. 1726 pr. 14 Apr. 1726 by relict Alice Long. (PROB11/608). AWP.

Long, William of St. John's, NL, ordnance mason. Will pr. 22 Feb. 1760. (PROB11/853).

Longley, Robert Benjamin of Boston, MA, outward bound on Imperial ship *St. Joseph.* Will 19 Jan. 1787. Leg: & exec. father Robert Longley, apothecary of Old Broad Street, London. Wit: Thomas Lawrence of Drapers' Hall, Titus Owen and John Edward Longley. Pr. 20 Dec. 1792 by cr. Francis Henry Cleriston. (PROB11/1226).

Longmore, George of QC, doctor of physic. Will pr. 7 Sep. 1812. (PROB11/1537).

Loring, Joshua Esq. of Roxbury, Suffolk, MA. Will 4 Oct. 1774 pr. 2 Nov. 1781 by relict Mary Loring Leg: house in Roxbury to wife; eldest son Joshua Loring; children Joshua, Joseph Royal, Benjamin, John and Hannah Loring. Wit: E. Goldthwait, Peter Hughes and W. Sherburne. (PROB11/1084).

Loring, Robert Roberts of Toronto, late Lieut. Col. in Army. 2 Mar. 1850. (PROB11/2110).

Loughman, James of St. Botolph Aldgate, citizen and saddler whose sons William and Daniel Loughman were in MD. Will 8 Jul. 1665 AWW 2 Nov. 1665 to relict Jane Loughman. (Guildhall: Ms 9052/15).

Loughnan, Clementina. *See* **Beckwith.**

Loveless, Thamar of NY, gent. Will pr. 7 Jan. 1856 by John Marles. (PROB11/2225).

Lowder, John of Royal Sappers and Miners in Royal Hospital, Halifax, NS. Will pr. 24 Jul. 1834. (PROB11/1834).

Lowe, Henry Sr. of St. Mary's Co., MD, gent. Will 25 Oct. 1717 pr. 1 Jun 1731 by daughters Elizabeth Darnall and Dorothy Hall. (PROB11/646). AWP.

Lowe, John of Hingham near Boston, MA, mariner of HMS *Triton,* bachelor. Will 9 Jul. 1707 AWW 12 Nov. 1708 to Adam Bird. (PROB11/505). AWP.

Lowe, Micajah of Charles City Co., VA, but late of Carshalton, Sy., merchant. Will 20 Jan. 1703 pr. 17 Mar. 1703 by Micajah Perry. (PROB11/469). AWP.

Lowe, Nicholas of St. Mary's Co., MD, gent. Will pr. 8 Sep. 1731. (PROB11/646).

Lucas, Charles of Shadwell, Mddx., mariner of the *Hopewell* who died in MD. Will 5 Nov. 1718 pr. 20 Jun. 1722 by sister Elizabeth Poulter. (PROB11/585). AWP.

Lucas, James Pengelly master's mate of HMS *Sylph.* Will pr. 6 Sep. 1815. (PROB11/1573).

Ludlow, Christopher of NY, surgeon of Garrison Hospital. Leg: father Daniel Ludlow of Ledbury, Glos., or, if dead, testator's six brothers (named). Wits; Joshua H. Smith, William Henderson and Abram Emmans. Will pr. 26 Feb. 1784 by father Daniel Ludlow. (PROB11/1113).

Ludlow, Gabriel Gabriel, President and Commander-in-Chief of St. John, NB. AWW 19 Aug. 1809 to Isaac Minet. (PROB11/1502).

Ludlow, Gabriel Verplanck of NY, Ensign on half pay of De Lancey's Brigade. Will 1 Feb. 1818. Leg: wife Elizabeth to have house in Broadway; lawful daughters (unnamed except for Elizabeth); siblings Gulian, Mary and Frances; brother-in-law John Hunter and his wife to be guardians of testator's children. Exec: brother Gulian Ludlow. Wit: Samuel Van Wyck, J.L. Pell and T. Pointz Jr. Codicil 20 May 1828 relieves brother Gulian of executorship. AWW 20 May 1828 to James Tidbury, attorney for relict Elizabeth Ludlow. (PROB11/1740).

Ludlow, George of York, VA. AWW 1 Aug. 1656 to Roger Ludlow. (PROB11/256). ACE.GGE.VGE.

Ludlow, Gulian of NYC. AWW 24 Mar. 1848 to John Stride. (PROB11/2071).

Ludlow *alias* Ladlie, James of Placentia, NL, bachelor. Will pr. 1 Dec. 1752. (PROB11/798).

Luony, Dennis of St. John's, NL. Will pr. 18 Jan. 1679. (PROB11/356).

Lymburner, John of QC. Will pr. Will pr. 19 Dec. 1772. (PROB11/983).

Lynch, Dominick formerly of Paris. Will pr. 10 Dec. 1840 by Nicholas Luguer and daughter Jane Pringle. (PROB11/1938).

Lyon, John, formerly of New England but late of frigate *Elizabeth* in State service. AWW 30 Oct. 1658 to sole leg. Alice Linsey. (PROB11/282). AWP.

Lyon *alias* Lyons, John of Philadelphia, botanist and gardener. AWW 23 Oct. 1816 to James Lee. (PROB11/1585).

Lyon, John of Charleston, SC, mariner. AWW 12 May 1802 to Robert Naylor. (PROB11/1375).

Lyon, Robert of Halifax, NS, gent. Will pr. 4 Jan. 1821. (PROB11/1638).

Lyte. Thomas Maximilian of Twillingate, NL, merchant. Will pr. 15 Jul. 1852. (PROB11/2156).

Mabey, Micajah of Montreal, Surgeon to HM Forces on half pay. Will pr. 14 Aug. 1835. (PROB11/1851).

Macaire, Francis, native of Pont en Royan, France, merchant of Lyons, Captain of 71st Regiment who died in Charles Town, SC. Will 2 Nov. 1687 pr. 6 Apr. 1691 by Cephas Tutet. (PROB11/403). AWP.

Madge, Catherine of Peterborough, [ON], widow. Will pr. 7 May 1856. (PROB11/2233).

Macy, James of Labrador, planter. Will pr. 13 Apr. 1797. (PROB11/1289).

Macy, Robert of Square Island, Labrador, planter. Will pr. 1 Oct. 1805. (PROB11/1432).

Maguire, John of Kingston, [ON]. Sergeant of 1st Battalion of Royal Artillery. Will pr. 2 Aug. 1851. (PROB11/2138).

Mahier, Richard of New England but late of London, mariner, who died in Rotherhithe, Sy. Will 4 Mar. 1721 pr. 4 Jul. 1721 by John Lloyd. (PROB11/580). AWP.

Mallortie, David of London, mariner , commander of the *Susannah* bound to Africa, Carolina and other parts of America, who died in Port Royal, SC, bachelor. Will 2 Jul. 1735 pr. 6 Oct. 1736 by father James Mallortie of London, merchant. (PROB11/679). AWP.

Mallory, Florisbella of St. John's parish, King William Co., VA. Will 26 Nov. 1758 pr. 11 Sep. 1769 by brother William Mallory and nephew Thomas Avera. (PROB11/951). AWP.

Mallory. John, citizen and leatherseller of London whose brother William Mallory resided near James Town, VA. Will 23 May 1747 pr. 16 Dec. 1752 by relict Mary Mallory. (PROB11/798). AWP.

Mallory, William of Elizabeth City, NC. Will 26 Mar. 1750 AWW 11 Sep. 1769 to the son William Mallory; the relict Mary Mallory having died before executing. (PROB11/951). AWP.

Maltby, George of Halifax, NS, Lieut. of Marines on HMS *Defiance*. Will pr. 17 Nov. 1763. (PROB11/893).

Manson, John of Halifax, NS. Will pr. 23 Feb. 1758. (PROB11/835).

Mapson, Thomas of Bethnal Green, Mddx., whose eldest son Thomas Mapson was supposed lost on a voyage to New England. Will23 Oct. 1656 pr. 17 Jul. 1660 by relict Joane Mapson. (PROB11/299). AWP.

Markin, Thomas of Stepney, Mddx., who died in MD, master of the *Sarah & Hannah*. Will 13 Nov. 1711 pr. by the relict Sarah Markin. (PROB11/531). AWP.

Marks, John James formerly of Portland, MA, but late of Bristol, master mariner. Will pr. 16 May 1816 Pr. by Frederick Charles Husenbeth (PROB11/1580). Inventory of 1817.

Marlar, John Thomas, late of Baltimore, MD, but late residing in London. Will 4 Feb. 1802. Leg: Richard Down of London, banker, trustee for Richard Douch and Stephen Gillum; sister Amelia Ann, wife of Edward Stewart of Aldermanbury, London. Wit: Chr. Norris, Henry Teton and William Grainger. Will pr. 2 Dec. 1804 by Edward Stewart. (PROB11/1418).

Marr, Andrew of Charles Town, SC, merchant. Will pr. 27 Sep. 1786 to James Carsan. (PROB11/1146).

Marriott, William Esq. of Gray's Inn, Mddx, whose sister (Dorothy) Waters died in VA leaving three sons. Will 2 Aug. 1717 pr. 9 Sep. 1719 by William Cooper. (PROB11/570). AWP. NGSQ 62/199.

Marsh, Joseph, marine of Portsmouth Division who died in Boston, MA. Will 6 May 1767 pr. 7 Dec. 1770 by Thomas Marston of Portsmouth, Hants. (PROB11/962). AWP.

Marsh, Thomas of Queen Anne Co., MD, gent. AWW 22 Apr. 1784 to Joseph Reed. (PROB11/1116).

Marsh, William of Charlestown, MA, now residing in Stepney, Mddx., who died on ship *Mary*. Will 29 Oct. 1695 pr. 13 Dec. 1695 by Richard Robison. (PROB11/429). AWP.

Marshall, Elias of Halifax, NS. Will pr. 3 Nov. 1806. PROB11/1452).

Marshall, George of Shadwell, Mddx., mariner of the merchant ship *Bayly* who died in VA, bachelor. Will 11 Apr 1719 pr. 18 Jun. 1720 by Ann Coggins. (PROB11/575). AWP.

Marshall, John of Shadwell, Mddx., mariner of merchant ship *Resolution* who died in MD. Will pr. 3 Dec 1717 by relict Sarah Marshall. (PROB11/561). AWP.

Marshall, John of St. John's, NL. Will pr. 18 Mar. 1718. (PROB11/563).

Marshall, Ricketts. *See* **Ricketts, Henry.**

Marshall, William of Baton Rouge, [LA], planter. Will 14 Dec. 1803. Leg: Charles Profit; George Ross of New Orleans; brother George Marshall of Dundee, Scotland; sister Isabella Marshall of Dundee. Execs: brother George Marshall, James Profit and Philip Hicky of Baton Rouge, and Charles Norwood of New Orleans. Wit: James Mather, Charles Patton, Thomas Urquhart, James Martin, John Joy, Andrew Burke and James Copland. Certificate by Narcissus Brontin of New Orleans that the will has been faithfully copied. Pr. 28 Apr. 1804 by brother George Marshall. (PROB11/1407).

Marston, Thomas of NYC, gent. Will pr. 21 Nov. 1814 by Francis Bayard Winthrop. (PROB11/1562).

Marten, Henry of Petty Harbour, NL. Will pr. 19 Apr. 1758. (PROB11/837).

Martin, James of Stepney, Mddx. Will 11 Aug. 1690. Leg: mother Martha Martin *alias* Grinnell to have all estate in England; brothers Thomas and John Martin; sister Mary Grigson; Thomas Fry; the Friends' Meeting at Ratcliffe, Mddx., to have all estate in East Jersey and PA. Wit: John Astry, John Crane and Thomas Lawrence. Pr. 20 Jan. 1691 by mother Martha Martin *alias* Grinnell and brother John Martin. (Guildhall: 9171/44/27).

Martin, John of New England, bachelor on board *Jersey*, bachelor. AWW 5 Feb. 1674 to James Babson. (PROB11/344).

Martin, Joseph of Albany Factory, Hudson's Bay. Will [*contents largely illegible*] pr. 24 Oct. 1826. (PROB11/1717).

Martyn, Michael of London and late of Boston, MA, mariner. Will 1 Feb. 1698 pr. 1 Mar. 1701 by relict Sarah Martyn. (PROB11/459). AWP.

Martin, Richard of Bristol, merchant who died in VA. Will 30 Sep. 1719 pr 1 Jun. 1721. (PROB11/580). AWP.

Martin, Samuel of Far Rockaway, Hempstead, Long Island, NY, physician. Will pr. 12 Jul. 1806 by brother William Martin. (PROB11/1446).

Mason, Thomas of Cecil Co., MD, merchant who died in Philadelphia. Will 4 Nov. 1731 AWW 6 Jun. 1732 to Andrew Duchee. (PROB11/652). AWP.

Massenburgh, John of Elizabeth City Co., VA, mariner. Will pr. 6 Jul. 1749 by Thomas Turner. (PROB11/772). VGE.

Massey, formerly McGinnis, Mary, widow of Montreal. Will pr. 10 Jul. 1839. (PROB11/1913).

Masson, Francis of QC, H.M. Botanical Collector. Will pr. 13 Sep. 1806. (PROB11/1449).

Mather, Richard Esq. of Pittsburgh, PA, late Capt. of Royal Americans who died in Pittsburgh. Will 28 Jun. 1758 AWW 18 Apr. 1763 to brother Thomas Mather. (PROB11/886).

Mather, Samuel of Milton, Norfolk Co., MA. AWW 22 Mar. 1816 to John Bainbridge. (PROB11/1578).

Mather, Thomas of London, mariner bound to NYC and West Indies by the *Thomas and Anne* but who died at sea. Will pr. 7 Mar 1687 by sister Martha Coppocke. (PROB11/386). AWP.

Mathers, Joseph of NYC, merchant. Will pr. 26 Jan. 1843 by Charles Denston. (PROB11/1973).

Matthew, Thomas of Cherry Point, Bow Tracy, Northumberland Co., VA. Will pr. 28 Feb. 1707. (PROB11/492). VGE.

Matthews, Elizabeth of St. Mary Woolnoth, London, widow, who died in New England. Will 2 Jun. 1686 pr. 17 Nov. 1690 by mother Susanna Lonsdale. (PROB11/402). AWP.

Matthews, Capt. John of Royal Navy and late of the city of Chester whose cousin John Bosell was of Kingston, Jamaica, and kinswomen Ann Bosell was born in Antigua, and Eliza Bosell in NY. Probate to John Legh, John Webster and Rev. William Nelson. (Jun. 1798).

Matthews, Thomas, mariner of HMS *Eltham* who died in Boston, MA. Will 26 Nov. 1746 pr. 3 Dec. 1746 by Richard Crafts of Deptford, Kent. (PROB11/751). AWP.

Mauroumet, John, midshipman of privateer *Boyne* of Dublin and late Lieut. of NY Provincials who died in the Havannah. Will 15 Apr. 1757 from SC records AWW 4 Jan. 1775 to James McKenzie, now husband of relict Anne in SC. (PROB11/1004). AWP.

May, John of Coldash, Thatcham, Berks., bucket maker who had land in PA. Will 5 Jul. 1720 pr. 18 Jun. 1722 by affirmation of relict Mary May. (PROB11/585). AWP.

May, Thomas. *See* **Best.**

Maybank, David of Christ Church, Berkeley Co., SC, carpenter. Will 27 Apr. 1713 AWW 27 Feb. 1725 to Samuel Wragg, attorney for daughter Susanna Bond and Thomas Barton in SC. (PROB11/601). AWP.

Maybank, Susanna of Christ Church, Berkeley Co., SC, widow. Will 14 Jun. 1716 AWW 27 Feb. 1725 to Samuel Wragg, attorney for Susanna Bond and Thomas Barton in SC. (PROB11/601). AWP.

Maynard, Henry of Dublin, Ireland, merchant, who died in VA. Will 21 Dec. 1719 pr. 13 Oct. 1727 by relict Henrietta Maynard. (PROB11/617). AWP.

Maynard, Thomas of Halifax, NS, Capt. in Royal Navy. Will pr. 8 Jun. 1857. (PROB11/2253).

Maynard, William, Lieut. in 2nd Regiment of NYC Foot Guards. AWW 23 Jun. 1781 to brother Henry Maynard. (PROB11/1979).

Mayne, John, surgeon of Harbor Grace, NL. Will pr. 20 Jan. 1817. (PROB11/1588).

Mayo, John of Bayford, Herts., whose daughter Mary was wife of Col. Henry Sclater, Gov. of NY. Will 15 Mar. 1675 pr. 6 May 1691 by son Israel Mayo. (PROB11/404). AWP,

Mayo, Mary. *See* **Slater.**

McAllester, John. *See* **McCallester.**

McAllum, Robert of Halifax, NS, corporal in Capt. Rolle's Company. Will pr. 3 Nov. 1764. (PROB11/903).

McCall, Catharine Flood of Clydeside, Essex Co., and Richmond, VA., but late resident at Georgetown, [Washington], D.C. Will 29 Feb. 1828. Leg: uncle George McCall's sons James, Archibald and John McCall to have my money in the hands of Robert Hunter and James Dunlop of London; Mrs. Reas and Mrs. Mary Fisher of Philadelphia; Mrs. Isabella Brown of Richmond [and other small bequests]; Lawrence Muse to have lands near Farnham in

Richmond Co and lots in Tappahannock. Exec: Walter Jones. Wit: Martha Peter, Mary Peter and Mary C. Smith. AWW 28 April 1831 to Archibald McCall. (PROB11/1784).

McCallester *alias* **McAllester, John** of NYC, mariner. Will 5 Jun. 1778 pr. 13 Feb. 1783 by brother and sole legatee David McCutcheson. (PROB11/1100).

Macallum, Rev. John of Red River Settlement, [Hudson's Bay], clerk. Will pr. 25 Oct. 1850. (PROB11/2121).

Macarmick, William, Lieut. Governor of Cape Breton Island, [NS]. Will pr. 12 Dec. 1815. (PROB11/1575).

Macaulay, James of York, [ON]. Will pr. 16 Aug. 1822. (PROB11/1660).

McClellan, John of Hythe Farm, Newcastle, [ON]. Will pr. 4 Dec. 1838. (PROB11/1904).

McClure, Alexander of Charlestown, SC. Will pr. 17 Dec. 1812 by uncle Cochrane McClure. (PROB11/1539).

McCord, Henrietta Maria of Montreal. Will pr. 25 Feb. 1812. (PROB11/1530).

McCrackan, John of Old Glenluce, Galloway, Scotland, who died in New Haven, CT. Will 16 Jul. 1763 pr. 9 Feb. 1769 by uncle James McDoul of London. (PROB11/946). AWP.

McCullen, Eleanor of Rockland, Baltimore. Will pr. 20 Nov. 1840. (PROB11/1936).

McDonald, Archibald of St. Andrew Seigniory, Argenteuil District, Montreal, retired Chief Factor of Hudson's Bay Co. Will pr. 14 Jun. 1854. (PROB11/2193).

McDonell, Charles, of Grove, NL, Capt. in Col. Frasier's Highland Regiment, bachelor. Will pr. 24 Nov. 1763. (PROB11/893).

McDonnell, John of St. Andrew Seigniory, Argenteuil District, Montreal, employee of Hudson's Bay Co. Will pr. 22 Jul. 1835. (PROB11/1849).

McEvers, James of NYC, merchant. AWW 1 Jul. 1811 to daughter Dame Elizabeth Myers. (PROB11/1524).

McEvers *alias* **McIvers, James** of NYC, merchant. AWW 7 Jun. 1823 to Margaret Baynard. (PROB11/1672).

McFaden, Lachlin of NYC, mariner of HMS *Deal Castle.* Will 10 May 1766 witnessed by Daniel Niven, Robert Scott and Alexander McIntosh. AWW by his solemn affirmation to Isaac Lascelles Winn, attorney for the named executrix Rachel Scott, wife of Robert Scott, widow of John McFaden. (PROB11/985).

McGilconell, Donald of Halifax, NS, sergeant in Capt. Hugh McKenzie's Company. Will pr. 3 Nov. 1764. (PROB11/903).

McGill, Hon. James of Montreal. Will pr. 25 Aug. 1814. (PROB11/1559).

McGillivray, Joseph of the Indian Territories in British North America, Fort Good Hope, Mackenzies River, [North West Territories], Chief Trader of the Hudson's Bay Co. Will 22 Jun. 1830. Leg: Mme. Frances Bouché of Riviere du Chêne, Montreal; Mme. Jourdaine of Berthier, (QC); Hector McGillivray at Columbia River; Alfred McGillivray of Montreal; brother Simon McGillivray. Wit: Edward Smith, M. McPherson and John M. McLeod. Pr. 12 Apr. 1833 by Joseph Felix La Rocque. (PROB11/1814).

McGillivray, Simon of Vaudreuil, [QC], chief trader of Hudson's Bay Co. 13 Nov. 1840. (PROB11/1936).

McGinnis, Mary. *See* **Massey.**

McGuiry, Laughlin, mariner who died on ship *Monmouth* in NY, bachelor. Will 21 Dec. 1749 pr. 28 Jun. 1750 by Thomas Packer. (PROB11/780). AWP.

McIver, John of NYC but formerly of GA, gent. AWW 20 Nov. 1821 to Charles Everett. (PROB11/1650).

McIvers, James. *See* **McEvers.**

Mackenzie, Duncan of St. Martin in Fields, Mddx., gunsmith, about to undertake a long voyage and who died in NY, bachelor. Will 26 Apr. 1728 pr. 1 Apr. 1736 by brother Alexander Mackenzie. (PROB11/676). AWP.

Mackenzie, Robert, corporal of 77th Regiment who died in Amboy Barracks, NJ. Will 15 Sep. 1762 AWW 23 May 1764 to Donald Mackenzie. (PROB11/898). AWP.

Mackintosh, Charles of NYC but late of St. Martin in Fields, Mddx., who died at sea. Will Feb. 1747 AWW 3 Feb. 1750 to John Fell, now husband and attorney of relict Susanna Fell in NYC. (PROB11/777). AWP

Mackintosh, Duncan of QC City, Lieut. Col. in 60th Regiment of Foot. Will pr. 20 Jul. 1815. (PROB11/1570).

McIntosh, James of Chickashaw Nation, [OK], planter. Will pr. 30 Apr. 1787. (PROB11/1152).

McIntosh, John of Guildford, [NC], late private in 71st Regiment of Foot who was killed at the Battle of Guildford in Mar. 1778 and having a wife in Charles Town, SC. AWW 22 Jul. 1783 to relict Elizabeth, now wife of Alexander Buchanan. (PROB11/1106).

Mackintosh, Lachlan of Charleston, SC, gent. Will pr. 12 Oct. 1789 by Simon Mackintosh. (PROB11/1184).

Mackintosh, William of Lachine, [QC]. Will pr. 18 Aug. 1842. (PROB11/1967).

McKay, Alexander, postmaster of Rupertsland, Hudson's Bay. Will pr. 11 Nov. 1842. (PROB11/1971).

McKay, John of Albany Factory, Hudson's Bay. Will pr. 6 Mar. 1813. (PROB11/1542).

Mackay, John of Windsor, Hampshire Co., NS. Will pr. 10 Sep. 1827. (PROB11/1730).

McKenzie, Alexander of Montreal. Will pr. 23 Apr. 1831. (PROB11/1784).

McKenzie, James of Kingston, [ON], Master in Royal Navy. Will pr. 18 Jun. 1836. (PROB11/1863).

McKenzie, Roderick of Port Neuf, [QC], Chief Trader of Hudson's Bay Co. Will pr. 11 Jan. 1831. (PROB11/1780).

McKie, Peter, Surgeon of H.M. Customs of St. John's, NL. Will pr. 3 Jan. 1837. (PROB11/1871).

McKie, Rachael of St. John's, NL, widow. Will pr. 13 Jan. 1845. (PROB11/2011).

McKinnon, Ranald of Argyle, NS. Will pr. 8 Jun. 1810. (PROB11/1512).

McKinstry, Rev. William of Concord, Merrimack Co., NH. AWW 5 Mar. 1824 to William Pulsford. (PROB11/1683).

McLean, Francis of Halifax, NS, Col. of 82nd Regiment. Will pr. 9 Mar. 1785. (PROB11/1127).

McLean, John of Elmsley, Johnstown, [ON], surgeon of Royal Navy on half pay. Will pr. 24 Oct. 1842. (PROB11/1969).

McLeod, Alexander Roderick of Montreal, servant of Hudson's Bay Co. Will pr. 3 Jan. 1842. (PROB11/1956).

McLeod, William of Elizabeth Town, NJ, Capt. of Royal Regiment of Artillery. Will 28 Sep. 1778. Leg: children William McLeod, Lieut. of 59th Regiment, Hannah, Susanna and Alexander McLeod. Execs: Anthony Forman of Ordnance Office, Tower of London, John H. Hart and George Ross of Elizabeth Town. Wit: Matthias Williamson, John Williamson and George Ross. AWW10 Mar. 1784 to Anthony Forman. (PROB11/1114).

McLeod, William of Greenwich, King's Co., NB, Lieut. in Royal Navy. Will pr. 15 Mar. 1856. (PROB11/2229).

McMaster, Samuel James of St. Andrew's, Charlotte, NB. Will pr. 10 Apr. 1851. (PROB11/2131).

McMaster, Thomas Edwin of NB. Will pr. 24 Mar. 1845. (PROB11/2014).

McMaster, William of Augusta, Kennebee Co., MA, yeoman. AWW 24 Jul. 1815 to Samuel Williams. (PROB11/1570).

McMullin *alias* **McMellin, Neal** of NY, sailor. Will 16 Aug. 1778. Wit: John Evans and Thomas Thornton. Leg: Dugall McNaught of NY, tailor AWW 12 Feb. 1784 to Dugall McNaught. (PROB11/1113).

McNab, Duncan of E. Hawkesbury, Prescott Co., Ottawa. Will pr. 3 May 1851. (PROB11/2133).

McNab, John of Baldoon, Kent Co., [ON]. Will pr. 16 Jan. 1824. (PROB11/1680).

McNab, Rymer. *See* **Rymer, Duncan.**

McNeal, Neil of Charleston, SC, mariner. AWW 22 Mar. 1824 to John Bainbridge. (PROB11/1683).

McNear, James of 42nd Regiment of Foot in North America. Memorandum by testator dated Elizabeth Town, [NJ], 16 Sep. 1763 empowering James McNear of 35th Regiment to receive his pay. AWW granted 27 Mar. 1766 to the said James McNear. (PROB11/917).

Macpherson, Donald of Pittsburgh, PA, Lieut. Col. in 10th Royal Veteran Battalion. Will pr. 5 Jun. 1830. (PROB11/1772).

McTavish, John George of Two Mountains Lake, Montreal, Chief Factor of Hudson's Bay Co. Will pr. 26 Oct. 1847. (PROB11/2063).

McTavish, Alexander, chief trader of Hudson's Bay Co., of Nepigon, [ON]. Will in the form of a letter of 27 Jan. 1830. AWW to mother Isabel McTavish, widow. (PROB11/558).

McTavish, Simon of Montreal. Will pr. 17 Oct. 1804. (PROB11/1416).

Maitland, Hon. Richard of NYC, Deputy Adjutant-General to HM Forces. Will 16 Feb. 1771 AWW 20 Jul. 1773 to James Syme, attorney for brother Col. Alexander Maitland, William McAdam, merchant, and Rev. John Ogilvie, all of NYC. (PROB11/990). AWP.

Mandes, Isaac of Pensacola, W. FL. Will pr. 21 Jul. 1769. (PROB11/950).

Manigault, Gabriel of Charles Town, SC, merchant. Will pr. 27 Oct. 1784 by grandson Joseph Manigault. (PROB11/1122).

Mann, Nicholas of Boston, MA. Will pr. 9 May 1749. (PROB11/770).

Manning, Jacob of Salem, MA, mariner of HMS *Romney*. Will 28 Dec. 1708 pr. 5 Jan. 1709 by Warwick Palfray of Salem. mariner. (PROB11/506). AWP.

Manstidge, Robert of Taunton, Som.., who died overseas, son of Thomas Manstidge deceased. Will 6 Jan. 1625. Leg: uncle and exec. Richard Longe of Taunton to have proceeds from sale of his goods in VA from *James* of London, Mr. Tobias Felgate; sister Jone Manstidge; brothers William, Isaac and Emanuel Manstidge. Wit: John Sparkes, Robert Dennes, Richard Brewster and William Greene. Pr. 9 Feb. 1630 by Richard Longe. (PROB11/157). AWP.

Mather, Richard of Pittsburgh, PA, Capt. of Royal Americans. Will 28 Jun. 1758 AWW 18 Apr. 1763 to brother Thomas Mather. (PROB11/886).

Mathewes, Thomas of Merchants Hope, VA, surgeon. Nuncupative will 16 Jun. 1645 given at William Baker's house in Wapping, Mddx. in the presence of Alexander Eaton, apothecary, and Rebecca Pope, widow, both of Wapping. Leg: Mr. Abraham Redman; brother Knowles; sister Redman; John Carey of Ratcliffe; Mr. Pidgeon, Rev. Richard Jones. The testator wishes his will made in VA to stand. AWW 3 Jul. 1645 to cr. Thomas Wilson. (Guildhall: Ms 9171/30/50).

Meadows *alias* **Medhurst, William,** mariner of HMS *Nonsuch* in North America. Will appointing his father William Meadows of Chatham, [Kent], exec. & leg. to receive his pension from the Royal Artillery and wages for sea service. Wits. Wat Griffith, Silas Hiscutt and Richard Willis, boatswain. AWW 21 Jan. 1780 to Robert Medhurst, son and adr. of the father William Medhurst deceased. (PROB11/1060).

Medhurst, William. *See* **Meadows**.

Medland, Jane. *See* **Drexhagen**.

Meekes, John of Shadwell, Mddx., surgeon, who had plantations near Potomac River, MD. Will 1692. (Guildhall: Ms 9171/ 27/19).

Meese, Henry, of St. Katherine Creechurch, citizen and draper of London who had lands in VA. Will 12 Jan. 1681 cites articles of 16 Apr. 1675 with Frances Pert of Mountnessing,, Essex, widow of Henry Pert, relating to testator's marriage to their daughter Ann. Leg: wife Ann Meese; children Henry, John, Anne and Frances Meese who are to inherit plantations in VA and MD. Wit: Ben. Mosse, Thomas Birchall and Thomas Johnson. Pr. 5 Apr 1682 by relict Anne Meese. (PROB11/369). AWP.

Meier, Rachel of Clermont, Columbia Co., NY, widow. AWW 20 Dec. 1820 to Edward Ellice. (PROB11/1637).

Mendes, Isaac of Pensacola, W. FL. Will 8 Mar. 1767 pr. 21 Jul. 1769 by William Barrow. (PROB11/950). AWP.

Menefie, George of Buckland, VA. Will pr. 26 Feb. 1747. (PROB11/199). ACE.VGE.

Menzies, Robert of Halifax, NS, sergeant in Capt. Hugh McKenzie's Company. Will pr. 3 Nov. 1764. (PROB11/903).

Mercer, James, late of Gen. Webb's Regt. of Foot who died in Albany, NY, bachelor. Will 6 Apr. 1648 pr. 14 Feb. 1759 by uncle Richard Fenton in London. (PROB11/844). AWP.

Mercer, late Nevile, Mrs. Mary of VA. Will pr. 8 Jun. 1768. (PROB11/940).

Mercer, Richard of Charleston, merchant. Will pr. 18 Apr. 1788 by relict Grace Mercer. (PROB11/1165).

Merrefield, Edward of German Town, Philadelphia, innholder. Will 3 Nov. 1766 pr. 4 Jul. 1768 by son Vernon Merrefield. (PROB11/941). AWP.

Merry, David of Philadelphia, seaman on ship *Ocean* in service of East India Co. Will pr. 21 Nov. 1795. (PROB11/1267).

Merryfield *alias* **Merifield, William**, of Torbay, NL. Will pr. 14 Oct. 1788. (PROB11/1171).

Messenger, James of Goochland Co., VA, carpenter and builder of Waller Mines. Will pr. 9 Jan. 1857 by relict Maria Messenger. (PROB11/2244).

Metcalfe, John of King & Queen Co., VA, merchant. Will 10 Jul. 1760 pr. 11 Mar. 1762 by Thomas Metcalfe in VA. (PROB11/874). AWP.

Metcalfe, Simon of Prattsburgh, Charlotte Co., NY. AWW 20 Dec. 1800 to Alexander Ellice. (PROB11/1286).

Mew, Noell of Newport, RI, and intending for Old England. Will 3 Aug. 1691 AWW 4 Apr. 1700 to Thomas Zachary, attorney for relict Mary Mew in Newport, RI. (PROB11/455). AWP.

Mew, Samuel of St. Mildred Poultry, citizem and salter of London whose brother Ellis Mew and sister Sarah Cowper were in New England. Will 6 May 1671 pr. 17 May 1671 by Edward Bilton and Thomas Lamb. (PROB11/336). AWP.

Middleton, Arthur of St. James Goose Creek, Berkeley Co., SC. Will 7 Jun. 1740 AWW 5 Aug. 1740 to son William Middleton, attorney for relict Sarah Middleton. (PROB11/704). AWP.

Middleton, Robert of VA, bachelor. AWW 18 Jul. 1627 to son Benjamin Middleton. (PROB11/152). GGE.

Middleton, Thomas of London, Esq., who had estate in Barbados, Antigua and New England. Will 5 Dec. 1672 pr. 16 Dec. 1672 by son Benjamin Middleton. (PROB11/340). AWP.

Middleton, Thomas of Charles Town, SC. AWW 2 Mar. 1799 to John Shoolbred. (PROB11/1321).

Mill, Matthew of Philadelphia, mariner. Will pr. 20 May 1830 by sister Sarah Mill. (PROB11/1171).

Miller, Joseph of New Bonaventure, NL. Will pr. 25 Jul. 1856. (PROB11/2236).

Miller, Thomas of New Bonaventure, NL. Will pr. 28 Sep. 1835. (PROB11/1852).

Milligan, William of Charleston, SC, merchant. Will pr. 1 Jun. 1811 by Alexander Anderson. (PROB11/1523).

Mills, Andrew, purser of HMS *Greyhound* who died in NY. Will 12 Dec. 1743 pr. 5 Feb. 1750 by relict Eleanor Mills. (PROB11/777). AWP.

Mills, Thomas of Exeter, Devon, vintner, whose only child William Mills he supposed to be in VA. Will 18 Mar 1653 pr. 26 Sep 1653 by relict Honor Mills. (PROB11/228). AWP.

Milne, William of Ancaster, [ON], Lieut. in Royal Navy. Will pr. 6 Feb. 1826. (PROB11/1708).

Milnes, Rev. James of Edinburgh, NB. Will pr. 25 Sep. 1816. (PROB11/1584).

Milton, Henry of Alexandria, DC, seaman of HMS *Princess Charlotte*. Will 2 Nov. 1805. Leg: Nancy Hulls of Alexandria to have wages due for testator's service on several ships. Wit: Thomas Woodhouse and Philip Poyer. AWW 2 Aug. 1821 to Nancy Hulls, spinster. (PROB11/1647).

Minnick, Christian of Bristol, Bucks Co., PA. Will pr. 7 Jul. 1786 by Joseph Plant. (PROB11/1144).

Mitchell, Dame Mary of Halifax, NS, widow. Will pr. 17 Feb. 1826. (PROB11/1709).

Mitchell, Robert of Savannah, GA. AWW 17 Oct. 1746 to brother John Mitchell. (PROB11/2043).

Mitchelson, John of VA, merchant. Will pr. 19 Aug. 1756 by brother James Mitchelson. (PROB11/824). VGE.

Moe, Cheesman of Peterborough, [ON], Lieut. in Royal Navy on half pay. Will pr. 18 Jul. 1839. (PROB11/1913).

Molson, Hon. John of Montreal. Will pr. 20 Sep. 1854. (PROB11/2197).

Molyneux, Anthony Lancaster, HM Consul for GA. AWW 7 Jun. 1852 to brother William Hargraves Molyneux. (PROB11/2155).

Monier, John, Surgeon of H.M. Garrison of St. John's, NL. Will pr. 3 May 1762. (PROB11/876).

Monk, John of Charleston, SC, house carpenter. Will pr. 2 Oct. 1789 by William Monk and James Horsnell. (PROB11/1184).

Monk, John Benning of Carleton, [QC]. Will pr. 18 Jun. 1855. (PROB11/2214).

Montagu, Lord Charles Greville of Halifax, NS. Will pr. 7 Jun. 1784. (PROB11/1118).

Montgomery, George of QC, apothecary to H.M. Forces. Will pr. 25 Mar. 1831. (PROB11/1783).

Montgomery, James of VA, late surgeon of HMS *St. Albans*. Will pr. 24 Dec. 1697. (PROB11/442).

Montgomrey, Malcolm of Syracuse, Onondaga Co., NY. Will pr. 19 Jul. 1856 by relict Anna Rosina Montgomrey. (PROB11/2236).

Moody, James of Sissiboo, Digby, NS. Will pr. 2 Jul. 1812. PROB11/1535).

Moone, George of Frimington, Devon, mariner, who died in James Town, VA. Will pr. 3 Jul. 1680 by relict Alice Moone. (PROB11/364). NGSQ 69/199).

Moore, Catharine Charles of Holmesburg, PA, widow. AWW 23 Dec. 1837 to Alfred Alexander Julius. (PROB11/1888).

Moore, Sir Henry of Jamaica, Governor of NY Province. Will 1 Apr. 1769 pr. 7 Jun 1770 by relict Catharina Maria Moore. (PROB11/958). AWP

Moore, Jane of Holmesburg near Philadephia, spinster. AWW 15 Dec. 1846 to Alfred Alexander Julius. (PROB11/2047).

Moore, Lambert of Brooklyn, NY. AWW 7 May 1808 to John Mackenzie. (PROB11/1479).

Moore, Robert of Kingston, [ON], on naval establishment. Will pr. 11 Jan. 1839. (PROB11/1905).

Morden, James of Halifax, NS, Storekeeper of H.M. Ordnance. Will pr. 8 Aug. 1794. (PROB11/1236).

More, David of Inglis, FL, mariner of HMS *Portland*. Will pr. 28 Sep. 1709. (PROB11/511).

Morecroft, Edmund of VA. Will pr. 20 Jun. 1639 by sister Elizabeth Morecroft. (PROB11/180). ACE.VGE.

Morgan, Christopher of Bromley by Bow, Mddx., bachelor, who had estate in VA. AWW 22 Feb. 1706 to brother John Morgan. (PROB11/487). AWP.

Morgan, Francis of New London, CT. AWW 20 Nov. 1849 to James Francis Morgan. (PROB11/2103),

Morgan, George who died at sea or in VA, bachelor. Will pr. 15 Apr. 1669 by Richard Knewstubb. (PROB11/329).

Morley, Katherine of Great Stanmore, Mddx., widow whose eldest son John Morley was resident in New England. Will 3 Jul. 1645 pr. (Guildhall: Ms 9171/30/58).).

Morrey, Richard of Philadelphia, gent. Will 30 Aug. 1753 AWW 12 Nov. 1756 to John Strettell, attorney for John Beazly in Philadelphia. (PROB11/826). AWP.

Morris, Anna, wife of Cadwallader of Philadelphia. AWW 2 Jan. 1801 to John Brickwood. (PROB11/1352).

Morris, Hon. Charles of Halifax, NS. Will pr. 16 Dec. 1802. (PROB11/1384).

Morris, James of Dumfries, Gore District, [ON], gent. Will pr. 25 Jun. 1856. (PROB11/2234).

Morris, John of New Hanover, NC, merchant. Will pr. 2 Mar. 1778 by relict Elizabeth Morris. (PROB11/1040).

Morris, Thomas of E. FL, planter. AWW 15 Jun. 1797 to William Murdock and Horatio Clagett. (PROB11/1292).

Morse, Henry of Williamsburg, VA, intending a voyage to Britain for his health. Will 28 Aug. 1775 pr. 29 Dec. 1775 by Thomas Woodall of Hot Wells near Bristol. (PROB11/1014). AWP.

Mortier, Abraham of NYC, Deputy Paymaster of HM Troops. Will pr. 13 Jan. 1785 by brother David Mortier. (PROB11/1125).

Moreton, Anthony of Frederica, GA, Lieut. in Gen. Oglethorpe's Regiment of Foot. Will 7 Sep. 1747 pr. 11 Jul. 1749 by Niel Holland of Frederica. (PROB11/771). AWP.

Morton, John of London, merchant, who had a plantation in Carolina. Will 7 Aug. 1694 pr. 28 Apr. 1699 by Robert Cuthbert. (PROB11/450). AWP. Further grant 19 Mar. 1706.

Morton, Joseph Sr. of Carolina, landgrave. Will 14 Apr. 1685 AWW 20 Nov. 1688 to sons Joseph and John Morton. (PROB11/393). AWP.

Mott, William of Halifax, NS, gent. Will pr. 20 Jan. 1820. (PROB11/1624).

Motteux, Benjamin of London, jeweller, but late of SC, bachelor. Will 1 Jan. 1724 pr. 14 Dec. 1725 by brother John Anthony Motteux of London, merchant. (PROB11/606). AWP.

Mould, Henry of Dummer, Newcastle District, [ON]. Will pr. 6 Apr. 1833. PROB11/1814).

Moulson, Peter of St. Bartholomew the Less, London, whose brother Foulke Moulson was in VA. Will 29 May 1674 pr. 30 Jun 1674 by Margaret Blague. (PROB11/345). AWP.

Moult, William residing with James Jones of Nasswadax Creek, Accomack Co., VA, and who died in Accawacke, VA. Will 18 Sep 1653 AWW 20 Jun 1657 to brother Francis Moult of Ashby Folvill, Leics.. (PROB11/265). AWP.

Mountain, Rev. Jehosaphat, Rector of Christ Church, Montreal. Will pr. 26 Sep. 1818. (PROB11/1608).

Mountain, Rev. Salter Jehosaphat, Rector of Cornwall, [ON]. Will pr. 23 Apr. 1832. (PROB11/1798).

Mountain, Mary of QC City, spinster. Will pr. 6 May 1824. (PROB11/1686).

Mountain, Mary, formerly Mary Leach of QC, widow. Will pr. 27 May 1834. (PROB11/1831).

Mountain, Mary Anne of QC, spinster. Will pr. 20 Aug. 1856. (PROB11/2041).

Mowatt, James of Newhaven, CT. Will pr. 7 Dec. 1798. (PROB11/1316).

Moxon, Martha of Charlotte, Greece, Monroe Co., NY. AWW 18 Aug. 1831 to husband John Moxon. (PROB11/1789).

Moze, John of Lake Superior, [Canada]. Will pr. 12 Dec. 1804. (PROB11/1418).

Mullens, Richard of Western Bay, NL, bookkeeper. Will pr. 30 Sep. 1762. (PROB11/879).

Muller, Albert of Bristol who died in SC, bachelor. Will 21 Jun. 1724 AWW 21 Jan. 1729 to nephew Lyder Muller. (PROB11/627). AWP.

Mullett, Winifred of Charles Co., MD, widow. Will 20 Apr. 1685 AWW 3 Mar. 1697 to pc. James Amos. (PROB11/437). AWP.

Munday, Richard of Stepney, Mddx., master of merchant ship *Europa* who died in VA, bachelor. Will 3 Aug. 1737 pr. 2 Aug. 1738 by Samuel Bonham of Stepney. (PROB11/691). AWP.

Mundell, John of Newcastle Co., PA, merchant living in Boston, MA. Will 5 Dec. 1694 pr. 27 Apr. 1697 to brother William Mundell. (PROB11/437). AWP.

Munden, William of Brigus, Conception Bay, NL. Will pr. 7 Oct. 1851. (PROB11/2141).

Munro, Daniel of HMS *Carisfoot* who died in Long Island Hospital, NY. AWW to Daniel McCarthy, attorney for the creditor Cormick McHugh. (Jun. 1784).

Munro, Harry of Charleston, SC, but late of St. John the Evangelist Westminster, Capt. of 71st Regiment of Foot. Undated letter to "dear brother" [Simon Munro] accepted as will. Leg: son Gilbert Van Mater; eldest daughter Caty Disbrough, wife of Henry Disbrough; daughter Sarah Van Mater; third daughter Micah, wife of Daniel Polleamus; the children of Benjamin Van Mater. Exec: Charles Cooke. Will pr. 23 Jun. 1788 by named exec. (PROB11/1167).

Murdoch, Robert of Trenton, [NJ]. Will 29 Mar. 1758, witnessed by Robert Sterling and John Lees, appoints Rev. Hugh Dixon of Gray Abbey near Belfast, Ireland, and Mr. James Riddle of Cumberland near Belfast, merchant, as executors and to share his estate between their two families. The child said to be his by Rachel Stuart is to be treated kindly. Pr. 24 Jul. 1759 by Hugh Dixon and James Riddle. (PROB11/848). AWP.

Murray, Rev. Alexander of Philadelphia. Will pr. 24 Dec. 1795 by Rev. John Chalmers and Roderick McLeod. (PROB11/1269).

Murray, James of Newark, NJ. AWW 24 Jul. 1810 to William Taylor. (PROB11/1513).

Murray, John of St. John, NB. Will pr. 24 Oct. 1795. (PROB11/1266).

Murray, Margaret of Halifax, NS, widow. Will pr. 6 Sep. 1787. (PROB11/1157).

Murray, Thomas of St. John, NB. Will pr. 9 Feb. 1798. (PROB11/1302).

Musgrove *alias* **Musgrave, Bartholomew**, mariner of vicinity of Sydney, Cape Breton Island, NS. Will pr. 12 Dec. 1838. (PROB11/1904).

Musgrave, Michael of Pienketanck, Rappahannock River, Middlesex Co., VA. Will pr. 26 Jan. 1698 by Thomas Musgrave. (PROB11/443). VGE.

Myatt, Joseph, commander of Albany Fort, Hudson's Bay, widower. Will 6 Mar. 1728 pr. 7 Nov. 1730 by John Bird and Richard Staunton of London. (PROB11/641). AWP.

Mynterne, John. Will dated Manigo, VA, 15 Mar. 1618. Leg. wife Alice Mynterne to have share of ship *Consent*; cousin Elizabeth, dau of John Wills; brothers Samuel, William, Nathaniel and Byngey Mynterne; brother-in-law Thomas Gee. Wit: John Wynterne, Owen Pomerye and William Clement. AWW 6 Jan. 1819 to relict Alice Mynterne. (PROB11/133). AWP.

Myrick, Joseph who died at NY, master mariner. Leg: wife Anna Myrick of St. Ann, Mddx., who is to be exex. Will pr. 21 Feb. 1816 by relict. (PROB11/1577).

Nall, William of Boston, MA, but late of London, mariner of HMS *Greenwich*, bachelor. Will 22 Jan. 1696 pr. 22 Jun. 1696 by Henry Causton. (PROB11/433). AWP.

Nash, Paul of Petersburgh, VA, merchant. Will pr. 13 Jan. 1823. (PROB11/1665).

Needham, William of Montgomery Co., MD. Will pr. 27 Jul. 1826. (PROB11/1714).

Neeve, Mary, spinster, daughter of John Neeve, citizen and brewer of London, who died in VA. Will 17 Oct. 1661 pr. 13 Jan. 1674 by sister Sarah, wife of Stephen Lewis, citizen and stationer of London. (PROB11/344). AWP.

Neilson, Richard of Brigadier Guise's Regiment who died in Carolina, bachelor. Will [undated] pr. 22 Feb. 1743 by William Chancellor. (PROB11/724). AWP.

Nelson, Robert of Shadwell, Mddx., mariner who died in Carolina, bachelor. Will 23 Jun 1681 pr. 8 Jan 1683 by Dorcas Wellin. (PROB11/372). AWP.

Nelson, Paschall Esq., formerly of Boston, MA but late residing at St. Margaret Westminster, Mddx. Will 19 Jul. 1759 pr. 19 Sep. 1760 by nephew John Temple. (PROB11/859). AWP.

Nelson, Thomas of Rowley, MA. Will pr. 21 Feb. 1651 by Richard Dummer. (PROB11/215).

Nesbitt, William of Boston, MA, late Lieut. Col. of 4th Regiment of Foot. Letter to his brothers Arnold and Albert Nesbitt accepted as will. Deposition 14 Jul. 1783 by Alicia Wren and Maria Aylmer of Co. Kerry, [Ireland], confirming the handwriting of the testator. Leg: to wife Joyce Nesbitt of farm at Castle Corby, [Cumbria]. AWW 26 Jul. 1783 to relict Joyce Nesbitt. (PROB11/1106).

Netherclift, William, of Upper Canada, drummer in 9th Regiment of Infantry. Will pr. 31 Jul. 1817. (PROB11/1594).

Neufville. *See* **De Neufville**.

Nevett, Hugh of VA, bachelor. Will 27 Jul. 1673 AWW 5 Oct. 1680 to nephew John Nevett. (PROB11/364). AWP.

Nevill, John of St. Margaret Westminster, Mddx., Vice-Admiral of VA and who died there. Will 2 Nov. 1696 pr. 2 Nov. 1797 by relict Mary Nevill. (PROB11/441). AWP.

Nevile, Mary. *See* **Mercer**.

Nevin, James of NH. Will 31 May 1766 pr. 1 Jun. 1769 by Thomas Lane of London, merchant captain. (PROB11/949). AWP.

Nevin, John of East Port, ME. Will pr. 22 Oct. 1729 by nephew Samuel Gatliff. (PROB11/1762).

New, Thomas, Commander of brig *Faro* in port of Philadelphia. Will 30 May 1728 pr. 11 Jan. 1732 by relict Elizabeth Reynolds. (PROB11/649). AWP.

Newberry, Roger Esq. of Windsor, MA, Capt. in American Regiment who died in West Indies. Will 5 Sep. 1740 AWW 27 Aug 1744 to Christopher Kilby, attorney for relict Elizabeth Newberry and brother Roger Wolcott. (PROB11/734). AWP.

Newberry, Walter of Gracechurch Street, London who had family in Charles Town, SC, and Newport, RI. Will 22 Feb. 1734 pr. 4 Mar. 1737 by affirmation of Thomas Plumsted and Margaret Wyeth. (PROB11/682). AWP.

Newell, Andrew of Charlestown, MA, but late of Rotherhithe, Sy., mariner. Will pr. 4 Dec. 1741 by affirmation of Henron Brown of London, merchant. (PROB11/714). AWP.

Newman, Francis of Charles Co., MD. AWW 21 Aug. 1822. (PROB11/1660).

Newman, Robert of Halifax, corporal of HM sloop *Doterel*, now in sick quarters. Will pr. 13 Jun. 1835. (PROB11/1848).

Newman, Roger of Baltimore. Will 10 May 1704 AWW 30 Dec. 1704 to sister Susannah Coatsworth. (PROB11/479). AWP.

Newton, Francis of London now bound to VA, grocer. Will 24 Aug. 1660 pr. 11 Jan. 1662 by relict Mary Newton. (PROB11/307). NGSQ 69/307.

Newton, Hon. Henry of Halifax, NS, Collector of Customs. Will pr. 11 Dec. 1802. (PROB11/1384).

Newton, John of Annapolis Royal, NS, Lieut. in Royal Navy. Will pr. 27 Jul. 1821. (PROB11/1646).

Newton, Joseph, cook of the ship *Baltimore* bound for VA but who died on the *Dreadnaught*. Will 7 Feb. 1693 pr. 20 Oct. 1694 by Richard Martin. (PROB11/421). AWP.

Newton, Richard of St. John's, NL, gent and mariner. Will pr. 5 Mar. 1770. (PROB11/956).

Newton, Thomas, citizen and clothworker of London. Original will 24 Jul. 1640. Leg. and exex. wife Sarah Newton to have the lease of house in Gutter Lane, London; son Jonathan Newton and his children [unnamed] to have two shares of land in St. Martin's Hundred, VA, purchased from Mr. Hugh Evans, citizen and clothworker of London, turned over to the testator at a Quarter Court held on 13 Jan. 1622. Wit: Edward Osborne, John Horne and Roger Wilford. Pr. 13 Jan. 1643 by relict Sarah Newton. (Guildhall: MS 9052/11).

Newton, William of NYC, gent. Will pr. 22 Mar. 1790 to relict Mary Newton. (PROB11/1189).

Nicholas, William of HMS *Winchelsea* who died in VA, bachelor. Will 4 Jun. 1734 pr. 24 Oct. 1734 by Thomas Page. (PROB11/667). AWP.

Nicholls, John of Philadelphia who died at sea on the *Dorothy*. Will 8 Mar. 1745. pr. 1 Mar. 1751 by Charles Willing of Philadelphia. (PROB11/786). AWP.

Nicholls, Richard of NYC. Will 27 Sep. 1772. Leg. Joseph Wilson; Peter Middleton of NYC for his care of grandchildren Margaret and Ann Burges; daughters Mary Auchmuty; Elizabeth Colden; granddaughters Frances Montresor and Susanna Margaret Middleton; Mary Auchmuty's children by Rev. Samuel Auchmuty. Execs: Samuel Auchmuty, Alexander Colse- and Peter Middleton. Wit: Joseph Wilson, John Charlton, John Rice and Joseph Hildreth. AWW 3 Oct. 1783 to Francis Donaldson. (PROB11/1109).

Nicholls, Stephen of Salem, MA, mariner. Will 8 Feb. 1740 AWW 22 Aug. 1740 to Hannah Gobell. (PROB11/704). AWP. NGSQ 63/198.

Nichols, Stephen of Newport, RI, mariner of HMS *Vigilant* who died in Louisburg, NS, bachelor. Will 25 Mar. 1746 AWW 31 Jul. 1751 to Benjamin Wickham, attorney for Samuel Pool in Newport. (PROB11/789). AWP.

Nicholls, William of Newburyport, MA, seaman of HMS *Hecate* and *Leda*. Leg: James Smith, seaman of HMS *Leda* with his affidavit that the testator was an old man aged 70 who was born at Newburyport but had no relations living. AWW 11 Mar. 1817 to James Smith. (PROB11/1590).

Nicholson, Francis Esq., Governor of SC late residing in Hanover Square, Mddx. Will 4 Mar. 1728 pr. 5 Mar 1728 by Kingsmill Eyre Esq. PROB11/621). AWP.

Nicholson, Henry, Lieut. in Col. Amherst's Regiment of Foot, who died in Louisburg, NS, bachelor. AWW 3 Oct. 1758 to Sampson Barber, attorney for Capt. Richard Burton of Royal Dragoons in Germany. (PROB11/841). AWP.

Nicholson, John of Cecil Co., MD, who died on the ship *Anne*. Will 13 Nov. 1691 pr. 11 Aug. 1693 by the relict Catherine Nicholson. (PROB11/415). AWP.

Nicholson, Joseph of Charles Town, SC, merchant. AWW 19 Jun. 1783 to son Samuel Nicholson. (PROB11/1105).

Nicholson, William of Anne Arundel Co., MD, merchant. Will 25 Sep. 1719 pr. 5 Feb. 1720 by William Hunt. (PROB11/572). AWP.

Nickolls, James Bruce of Alexandria, DC. Will pr. by Rev. William Jackson and Phineas Janney. (PROB11/1800).

Nickols, Randolph of Charlestown, MA, mariner. Will 6 Aug. 1701 pr. 5 Dec. 1707 by wife Sarah Nickols. (PROB11/497). AWP. NGSQ 63/202.

Nicolls, Stephen of New England, mariner of HMS *Lyon*, bachelor. Will 8 Feb. 1740. AWW 22 Aug. 1740 to Hannah Gobell, wife and attorney of John Gobell. (PROB11/704). AWP.

Nickolls, William of Kent Co., PA. Will 13 Jan. 1697 pr. 21 Mar. 1700 by son William Nickolls. (PROB11/454). AWP.

Nicoll, Andrew of NYC, gent, Capt. Lieut. of Independent Company who died in NYC. Will 28 Jun. 1746 pr. 9 Feb. 1749 by Rev. James Orem. (PROB11/768). AWP.

Nighthamer, John of Charles Town, SC, mariner of HMS *Centurion*. Will of 2 Aug. 1757 witnessed by W. Mantle, John Craddick and William Rawden, appoints William Knight of Farley, Hants., mariner of the *Centurion* as sole legatee and executor. Pr. 28 Apr. 1760 by William Knight. (PROB11/855).

Nisbett, Sir John of Dean, Scotland, residing in Cheltenham, Glos. Will 6 May 1813 [very lengthy]. Leg: wife Dame Maria Nisbett residing in Charleston, SC, who has arranged for part of his estate to be set against claims; son John Nisbett; Rosina Byron, spinster, mother of John Nisbett aged 3; parish of St. John, Berkeley Co., SC. Trustees for disposal of US property: John Rutherfurd of Edgerton, Scotland and William Halberston of Edinburgh. Execs: John Rutherfurd and Charles Lord Sinclair. Pr. 28 Jun. 1828 by named execs. (PROB11/1742).

Noad, John of QC City, merchant grocer. Will pr. 10 Oct. 1843. (PROB11/1987).

Noel *alias* **Bushe, Mrs. Elizabeth** of NYC, widow. Will pr. 22 Jun. 1846 by mother Elizabeth Harriet Hellyer. (PROB11/2038).

Noore, John of Wapping, Mddx., mariner bound for VA. Will 2 Dec 1691 pr. 21 Jul. 1693 by relict Anne Noore. (PROB11/415). AWP.

Norquay, Omain *alias* **Oman**, settler on River Ossinibiran, Hudson's Bay. Will pr. 6 Mar. 1823. (PROB11/1668).

North, Stephen of Boston, MA, who died in St. Botolph Aldgate, London, son of the late Stephen North of Boston, vintner. Will 13 Jan. 1722 pr. 5 Jan. 1723 by uncle Francis North of St. Botolph Aldgate, apothecary

Nott, Edward, Gov. General of VA. Will pr.28 Nov. 1706 by Susan Leighton. (PROB11/491). VGE.

Nourse, William of Northumberland, [ON], Chief Trader in Hudson's Bay Co. Will pr. 9 Oct. 1856. (PROB11/2240).

Nowell, Thomas of St. Dunstan in West, London, gent., whose daughter Martha was wife of John Marshall in New England. Will 24 Jan. 1713 AWW 18 Mar 1713 to said daughter. (PROB11/532). AWP.

Nox, Thomas, master of HM sloop *Hornet*, who died in Brunswick, NC. Will 28 Sep. 1767 AWW 17 Mar. 1768 to Thomas Howard, attorney for cousins Michael Cashio Howard in Douai, Flanders, and Patrick Howard in Angiers, France. (PROB11/937). AWP.

Noyes, Peter of Sudbury, MA, now bound to sea. Will 10 Jan. 1698 AWW 10 Sep. 1699 to William and John Crouch. (PROB11/452). AWP.

Nugent, Thomas of NYC. Will pr. 31 Dec. 1833 by sister Eliza Skelly. (PROB11/1825).

Oakings, Hester of St. Botolph Aldgate, London, widow, whose son Joseph Oakings was in VA. Will 17 Oct. 1664 pr. 26 Jul. 1665 by Richard Norwood. (Guildhall: Ms 9052/15).

Oates, George of King Street, Charleston, SC, merchant. Will pr. 27 Feb. 1854. (PROB11/2186).

Oats, William of Boston, [MA], late of HMS *Boyne*. Letter to "Brother and Sisters" [accepted as will] of 22 Feb. 1774 having entered on *Somerset* going to America. Leg: siblings Richard, Margaret, Fanny and Elizabeth Oats; cousin Gracey Harvey. Affirmation 11 May 1777 by Nicholas Reseigh of St. Just, Corn., and Nicholas Weaver of Sennen, Corn., certifying the testator's handwriting. AWW 3 Jul. 1777 to Richard and Margaret Oats. (PROB11/1033).

Odell, William Franklin of Fredericton, Yorks Co., NB. Will pr. 10 Jun. 1845. (PROB11/2020).

Ogilvie, Rev. John, of NYC, doctor of physic. AWW 10 May 1786 to Margaret Ogilvie, widow. (PROB11/1142).

Ogden, David of Flushing, Long Island, NY. Will pr. 2 Oct. 1799 by son Nicholas Ogden. (PROB11/1331).

Ogden, Jonathan, Garrison surgeon of St. John's, NL. Will pr. 11 Sep. 1816. (PROB11/1584).

Ogden, Nicholas of NYC. AWW 21 Mar. 1823 to Gabriel Shaw. (PROB11/1668).

Ogden, Thomas of Precinct of St. Katherine, Mddx., master of *Thomas & Elizabeth* who died in VA. Will 11 Apr. 1700 pr. 7 Aug. 1704 by relict Alice Ogden. (PROB11/477). AWP.

Ogle, Samuel, Lieut. Governor of MD. Will 11 Feb. 1752 pr. 1 Sep. 1755 by Benjamin Tasker Esq. and Cp. Benjamin Tasker. (PROB11/818). AWP.

Oker, Abraham who died at sea on the *Bendish* bound for VA. Will 11 Mar. 1666 AWW 3 Aug. 1667 to pc Elianor Hitchcock. (PROB11/324). AWP.

Oliver, Peter of Middleborough, Plymouth Co., MA, but late of Birmingham, Warw. Leg: wife Mary Oliver; sons William, Peter and Andrew Oliver; the daughters of his deceased daughter Elizabeth Watson. Wit: Ba---- Pratt, Micah Bryant and Nathaniel Wilder. AWW 2 Nov. 1791 to son Peter Oliver. (PROB11/1211).

Opie, Thomas of Bristol, mariner, who died in VA. Will 16 Nov. 1702 asking for a tombstone to be sent to VA for his own and his grandfather's, David Lindsay's, grave. Will pr. 26 Jul. 1703 by sister Susannah Cole. (PROB11/370). AWP.

Orange, Thomas of NYC. Will pr. 15 Nov. 1824 by Henry Kermit. (PROB11/1692).

Ormandey, John of MD. Will 8 Feb. 1700 AWW 31 Aug. 1700 to Arthur Helme. (PROB11/456). AWP.

Ormsby, Eubule, Lieut. of 35th Regiment who died in W. FL. Will 23 Feb. 1756 pr. 2 Jun. 1768 by sister Mary Ormsby. (PROB11/940). AWP.

Orpwood, Mary of St. Margaret Westminster, Mddx., spinster, whose grandfather Edmond Orpwood was an inhabitant of Philadelphia. Will 4 Nov. 1746 AWW 15 Dec. 1747 to William Collins. (PROB11/758). AWP. NGSQ 64/288.

Osborn, Samuel of Freehold, NJ. Will 28 Feb. 1770. Leg: wife Kezia Osborn; brother Stophel Osborn to have his plantation purchased from John Longstreet and the plantation where he lives; the sons of Stophel Osborn named Samuel and William; sister Massy. Wit: Peter Forman, Edmund Harris and John Forman. AWW 25 Aug. 1801 to Samuel Osborn late of Hoxton, Shoreditch, Mddx., attorney for surviving exec. Stophel Osborn in NJ. (PROB11/1361).

Osborn, Thomas of NY Province, mariner of HMS *Lenox*. Will dated 8 May 1762 witnessed by Charles Lynd and George Rudd leaves a bequest to his brother William Osborn of NY. Pr. 6 Aug. 1764 by Henry Hall of NY. (PROB11/901).

Osgood, John of London, merchant, who had shares in NJ. Will 17 May 1694 pr. 15 Jun. 1694. (PROB11/421). NGSQ 53/135.

Osgood, Salem of London, merchant, who had lands in NJ. Will 10 Jun. 1703 pr. 9 Apr. 1706 by solemn declaration of relict Anna Osgood. (PROB11/488). AWP.

Oswin, Thomas, mariner of the *Essex,* who died in York River, VA. Will 5 Jan. 1721 pr. 16 Dec. 1721 by father Christopher Oswin. (PROB11/582). AWP.

Otway, Gresham of St. James Westminster, Mddx., but late of the environs of Boston, MA, spinster. Will 1 Nov. 1710 pr. 28 Nov. 1718 by uncle Edward Benskin. (PROB11/561). AWP.

Ottway, John of Horsham, Sussex, labourer, who died on passage to New England. Will 29 Mar. 1639 AWW 1 Mar. 1670 to Elizabeth, wife of Thomas Ernall. (PROB11/332). AWP.

Owen, David of Campo Bello, Charlotte Co., NB. Will pr. 16 Dec. 1833. (PROB11/1825).

Owen, Stephen of Wapping, Mddx., mariner bound for VA in merchant ship *Mary Ann*. Will 20 Apr. 1700. Leg. & exec: Thomas Watson of Wapping, mariner. Wit: Joseph Eardley, Ellinor Knowles and James Fancourt. Pr. 24 Dec. 1700 by Thomas Watson. (Guildhall: Ms 9171/50/174).

Owen, Thomas of Granville Co., SC, planter. Will 29 May 1735 pr. 14 Jul. 1738 by brother Jeremiah Owen. (PROB11/690). AWP.

Oyles, Philip, formerly of Flaunden, Herts., but late of MD, bachelor. Will 15 Mar. 1707 pr. 10 Nov. 1710 by solemn declaration of brother Thomas Oyles of Limehouse, Mddx., grocer. (PROB11/518). AWP.

Packe, Graves of London and VA, master of merchant ship *Gooch*. Will 16 Dec. 1728 pr. 14 Aug. 1731 by Edward Randolph of London, merchant. (PROB11/646). AWP.

Packharness *alias* **Peckharness,** John of NY, merchant. Will pr. 28 Nov. 1796 by Richard Packharness. (PROB11/1282).

Paddock, Adino of Boston, MA, Capt. of Foot Regiment in NJ. Will pr. 4 Aug. 1804 by James South, James Simpson and William Forman. (PROB11/1413).

Page, James of Great Placentia, NL, surgeon. Will pr. 13 Feb. 1777. (PROB11/1028).

Page, John of Gloucester Co., VA. Will 20 Apr. 1709 pr. 2 Jan. 1719 by son John Page. (PROB11/567). AWP.

Painter, John of QC, merchant. Will pr. 21 Mar. 1816. (PROB11/1578).

Painter, Nicholas of Anne Arundell Co., MD, gent., late residing in London. Will 8 Sep. 1684. Pr. 8 Oct. 1685 by Henry Bray. (PROB11/381). AWP.

Palmer, Anthony, Lieut. in Lieut. Gen. Dalziel's Regt. who died in Philadelphia. Will 24 Apr. 1746 pr. 8 May 1749 by Lieut. Robert Lowe. (PROB11/770). AWP. Further grant in 1750.

Palmer, Thomas of St. John's, King William Co., VA. Will 2 Sep. 1752 pr. 3 Nov. 1768 by son Nicholas Palmer. (PROB11/943). AWP.

Palmer, William Lamb of Boston, MA. Will 24 May 1823. Leg: wife Augusta Palmer; eldest son and exec. Charles Colley Palmer. Pr. 15 Sep. 1824 by named exec. Wit: Robert Sloper, John Hurd, late of Honiton, Devon, clerk to Mr. Sloper, and Lewis Penel. (PROB11/1690).

Panton, William of Pensacola, W. FL. Will pr. 29 Sep. 1804 by John Forbes and Adam Gordon. (PROB11/1418).

Pargiter, John of St. Martin in Fields, Mddx., whose cousin Sarah Lovell was at York River, VA. Will 10 Feb. 1688 pr. 24 Feb. 1688 by sons John and Samuel Pargiter. (PROB11/390). AWP.

Parish, George of Ogdensburg, St. Lawrence Co., NY. Will pr. 17 Aug. 1839 by Joseph Russell. (PROB11/1915).

Parke, Daniel Governor of Leeward Isles who had estate in VA. Will 29 Jan. 1710 pr. 15 May 1711. (PROB11/521). NGSQ 64/221.

Parker, Alexander of St. Edmund, Lombard Street, London, haberdasher who had real estate in PA. Will 6 Mar. 1689 pr. 25 Apr. 1689 by daughter-in-law Prudence Wager and daughter Mary Parker. (PROB11/396). AWP.

Parker, John of Morton, Thornbury, Glos., yeoman who died in PA, bachelor. Will 25 Mar. 1726 AWW 2 Apr. 1750 to cousin and next-of-kin Isaac Roach. (PROB11/778). AWP.

Parker, John of Bonavista Harbour, NL. Will pr. 13 Feb. 1786. (PROB11/1139).

Parker, Robert of St. John, NB. Will pr. 19 Nov. 1824. (PROB11/1692).

Parker, William of Stepney, Mddx., who died in MD. Will 3 Jan. 1672 pr. 24 Jul. 1673 by relict Grace Parker. (PROB11/342). AWP.

Parkes, Andrew of London, haberdasher, who died overseas. Will 2 Jul. 1628. Leg: brother John Parkes now in VA to have all goods on *Hopewell* in which the testator is embarked when it arrives in VA; aunt Sewzan Parkes of London, widow; aunt and exex. Elizabeth Warden of Christ's Hospital, London. Wit: Richard Merydale, Sir Anthony Mosley, John Clarke and Joseph Bryan. Pr. 13 Feb. 1630 by Elizabeth Warden. (PROB11/157). AWP.

Parkhurst, George of Ipswich, Suffolk, now bound to VA by the *Primrose* of London. Will 22 Jul. 1634. Leg: Anne Wonham who is to be exex. Wit: Thomas Draper, Richard Thoroton, Johan Browne, Humphrey Bruan and John Owsebie. Pr. 9 Feb. 1635 by Anne Wonham. (PROB11/167). AWP.

Parkin, Thomas of NYC. AWW 22 May 1795 to nephew Thomas Parkin. (PROB11/1261).

Parkins, Joseph Wilfred, of Newark, NJ, late Sheriff of London. AWW 18 Dec. 1843 to Thomas Colpitts Granger. (PROB11/1990).

Parnell, James of Lincolns Inn, Mddx., & PA. gent. Will 17 Dec. 1724 pr. 1 Oct 1725 by brother Ambrose Stevenson. (PROB11/216). AWP.

Parr, John, Governor of NS. Will pr. 31 May 1792. (PROB11/1219).
Parry, John of VA, bachelor. AWW 30 Jul. 1638 to brother William Parry. (PROB11/177). ACE.VGE.
Parsons, Ann of St. George's Bay, NL, widow. Will pr. 2 Nov. 1848. (PROB11/2083).
Parsons, James of Fortune Bay, NL, fisherman. Will pr. 12 Feb. 1813. (PROB11/1541).
Parsons, Margaret of Fortune Bay, NL. Will pr. 9 Dec. 1834. (PROB11/1840).
Parsons, William of St. George's Bay, NL, planter. Will 26 Feb. 1834. (PROB11/1828).
Partridge, John of Philadelphia but late of NYC, plasterer. Will pr. 31 Aug. 1827 by John Liptrott Graves. (PROB11/1730).
Passey, Samuel Aggs. *See* **Plummer.**
Passmore, William of Philadelphia, clothier. Will pr. 15 Feb. 1742. (PROB11/716).
Paston, John of Old Stratford, Warw., gent, who died in America. Will 10 Jan 1702 pr. 5 Jun. 1711 by mother Elizabeth Paston. (PROB11/521). AWP.
Paston, Robert, Capt. of HMS *Feversham* who had estate in NY. Will 12 Sep. 1711 AWW 13 Feb. 1713 to Benjamin Edmonds, attorney for Adolph Phillips and George Clarke of NY. (PROB11/531). AWP.
Patterson, John of Farmington, CT. Capt. of First CT Regiment of Foot who died in Havana. Will 11 May 1759 AWW 29 Jan. 1765 to Phineas Lyman, attorney for relict Ruth Patterson and son-in-law John Peirce in CT. (PROB11/905). AWP.
Pattison, George of Shadwell, Mddx., mariner of the *Betty*, who died in VA, bachelor. Will 28 Feb. 1719 pr. 26 Jan. 1722 by mother Jane Pattison. (PROB11/583). AWP.
Pattison, John of Rochester, Kent, mariner of HMS *Windsor* who died in SC. Will 15 Jul. 1732 pr. 8 Feb. 1742 by daughter Isabella, wife of George West. (PROB11/716). AWP.
Pattison, Mark of QC, First Lieutenant in Royal Artillery Regiment. Will pr. 5 Aug. 1797. (PROB11/1295).
Pattle, Eliza Henrietta of Brooklyn, NY, spinster. AWW 15 Feb. 1854 to Edward Beldam. (PROB11/2186).
Pawlett, William of Bicton, Hants., who had estate in MD. Will pr. 6 Mar. 1695 by relict Martha Pawlett. (PROB11/424). NGSQ 66/118.
Pawson, William of Montreal City, merchant. Will pr. 18 Aug. 1848. (PROB11/2079).
Payne, Edmund of Stepney, Mddx., who died in MD. Will 3 Jul. 1688 pr. 1 Jul. 1708 by relict Katherine Payne. (PROB11/502). AWP.
Payne, Jean of Goochland, VA, widow. Will pr. 3 Jun. 1808. (PROB11/1481).
Payne, John, formerly Lieut. of HMS *Chichester* but late of Winterbourne, Glos., who had lands in Carolina. Will 13 May 1750 pr. 4 Jul. 1750 by relict Martha Payne. (PROB11/781). AWP.
Payn, Robert of Christ Church, Berkeley Co., SC, bachelor, late of HMS *Aldborough.* Will dated 30 Jul. 1733 appointing John Murrell of the same parish as sole executor and universal legatee. Witnessed by Robert Jeffrys, John White and John Higgins. Commission of 24 Jul. 1734 to Isaac Cutforth to act as attorney for John Murrell in SC. (PROB11/666).
Peachy, Mary of St. Mary's parish, King & Queen Co., VA. Will pr. 18 Jan. 1717 by Thomas Walker. (PROB11/556). VGE.
Peacock, William of Carey's Fort, Cape Henry, [VA], commander of HMS *L'Aigle.* Letter with his signature written 3 Nov. 1782 in NYC accepted as will. AWW 13 Jun. 1783 to William Thomas Mousell, attorney for Pryce Peacock of Dublin, Ireland. (PROB11/1105).
Pearce, Andrew of Twillingate, NL. Will pr. 23 Jul. 1842. (PROB11/1965).
Peckham, John of Trinity, NL, planter. Will 9 May 1853. Leg: nephews Martin and John Peckham who are to be execs; sister Elizabeth Peckham. Wit: Benjamin Sweetland and George Sweetland. Pr. 28 Jan. 1854 by named execs. (PROB11/2193).
Peckharness. *See* **Packharness.**
Pecknell, Elizabeth of NYC but late of London, widow. Will 12 Jul. 1777. Leg: son George Pecknell; nephew Richard Pecknell; son-in-law William Orcher; daughter Rebecca, wife of William Orcher Hudleston, Capt. in Royal Artillery. Exec: William Orcher and Rebecca Hudleston. Wit: John Newton, David Naverro and Colin McKenzie. Pr. 13 Nov. 1786 by named execs. (PROB11/1147).

Pedley, James of Halifax, NS, gent. Will pr. 24 Sep. 1807. (PROB11/1467).

Peere, Robert of Clerkenwell, Mddx., butcher who died in VA and whose daughter Elizabeth was wife of Robert Rayment of VA, planter. Will 22 Jun. 1655 pr. 21 Oct. 1662. (Guildhall: Ms 9052/13).

Peirce, Tobias formerly of New England but late of London, mariner. Will 9 Dec. 1745 pr. 2 Jan. 1746 by Sarah Burrows. (PROB11/744). AWP. NGSQ 64/289.

Pelley *alias* Pelly, Richard of Hants Harbour, Trinity Bay, NL, planter. Will pr. 13 Jul. 1838. (PROB11/1898).

Penman, James of Charleston, SC. Will pr. 26 Nov. 1789 by William Drummond and Thomas Young. (PROB11/1185).

Penn, John of Philadelphia. Will pr. 23 Jan. 1796 by relict Anne Penn. (PROB11/1270).

Penn, Richard Esq. of Stanwell, Mddx., who had a quarter part of PA. Will 21 Mar. 1750 pr. 4 Mar. 1771 by relict Hannah Penn. (PROB11/965). AWP.

Penn, William of City of London but late in Patuxent River, MD, mariner. Will 20 Sep. 1696 pr. 18 Nov. 1697 by relict Elizabeth Penn. (PROB11/441). AWP.

Pennington, John of Amersham Woodside, Bucks., whose son Edward Pennington and grandson Isaac Pennington were resident in NJ. Will pr. 2 Jun. 1710. (PROB11/515). NGSQ 65/143.

Penny, William of English Harbour, NL, senior planter. Will pr. 4 Jul. 1854. (PROB11/2195).

Pepperell, Sir William of Kittery, MA. Will 1 Jan. 1759 pr. 10 Nov. 1768 by grandson William Pepperell, formerly William Pepperell Sparhawk. (PROB11/943). AWP.

Percival, Andrew of Westminster, Mddx. who had estate in Carolina. Will 20 Feb. 1696 pr. 27 Mar. 1696 by relict Essex Percival. (PROB11/430). AWP. New grant made in Jun.1730.

Percy, Rev. William of Charleston, SC, late of London & having estate at Leytonstone, Essex, and Chilvers Coton and Bedworth, Warw. Will 8 Dec. 1818. Debts of his late son William in Oxford to be paid. Leg: son Barnard Elliott Percy; son-in-law Thomas Jefson of West Bromwich, Staffs.; children of daughter Selina Percy Lewis. Execs: James Oldham and Thomas Bainbridge of London and son-in-law Thomas Jefson. AWW 15 Apr. 1820 to said execs. (PROB11/1628).

Perdriau, Lewis of Carolina who died in Barbados. Will 23 May 1694 pr. 12 Jul. 1697 by sister Judith, wife of Paul Faneuil, no executor having been named. (PROB11/439). AWP.

Perira, Emanuel of NY. Will pr. 15 Apr. 1780 by Emanuel Bandira. (PROB11/1064).

Perkins, Edward of Shadwell, Mddx, shipwright of the *Anne Fortune* bound for VA. Will 14 Jul. 1627. Leg: uncle Henry Holmes, citizen and clothworker of London, and Katherine his now wife, who are to be execs. Wit: Griffeth Edwards. Pr. 27 Apr. 1629 by Henry Holmes. (Guildhall: Ms 9171/25/287v).

Perroneau, Alexander of Charles Town, SC, gent. AWW 17 Sep. 1781 to Robert Wells and Aaron Loocock. (PROB11/1082).

Perroneau, Henry of Charles Town, SC, gent. Will 23 Jan. 1753 AWW 9 Aug. 1755 to James Crokatt of London, merchant, attorney for brother Alexander Perroneau, Benjamin Harriette and son Henry Perroneau in SC. (PROB11/817). AWP.

Perroneau, Mary Coffin of Charleston, SC, spinster. Will pr. 26 Nov. 1849 by William Henry Perroneau. (PROB11/2103).

Perry, James of Montreal, merchant. Will pr. 6 Nov. 1804. (PROB11/1417).

Persey, Abraham of Persey's Hundred, VA. Will pr. 10 May 1633. (PROB11/163). ACE.VGE.

Peter, William of Philadelphia. AWW 12 Jul. 1853 to John Thomas Henry Peter. (PROB11/2176).

Peters, Edward of Bristol, mariner bound overseas who had a tract in PA. Will 23 Oct. 1724 pr. 25 Feb. 1735 by mother Elizabeth Peters of Bristol. (PROB11/669). AWP.

Peterson, Gilbert of London, mariner, who died on the *Prince Royal* in VA, bachelor. Will 14 Aug. 1721 pr. 10 Jan. 1724 by James Carrack. (PROB11/595). AWP.

Petrie, John of Churchill, Hudson's Bay, labourer in Co. service. Will pr. 9 Jan. 1787. (PROB11/1149).

Pett, Arthur of Stepney, Mddx., master of the *Unity* of London but sick aboard the *Blessing* of Plymouth at James Town, VA. Will 30 Aug. 1609 pr. 19 Mar. 1611 by the relict Florence Pett, the named exec. Thomas Johnson renouncing. (Guildhall: Ms 9171/16/107).

Petty, Francis, mate of ship *Hope* bound for New England and West Indies. Will 12 Oct. 1692 pr. 30 Sep. 1693 by relict Sarah Petty. (PROB11/416). AWP.

Pewsey, George of Limehouse, Mddx., master of the *Marmaduke* and trader to VA. Will dated 19 Sep. 1634 aboard the *Assurance* at sea. Leg: wife & exex. Rebecca Pewsey; son (unnamed); mother Ursula Pewsey; sisters Martha and Annis Pewsey; dau. Joane Phillips. Pr. 16 Jan. 1637 by relict. (PROB11/173). AWP. NGSQ 68/116.

Philipps, Anne of Halifax, NS. Will pr. 13 Feb. 1837. (PROB11/1873).

Phillips, Caleb, sailmaker of New England, on HMS *Expedition.* Will 22 Jul. 1692 AWW to James Harris, mariner, during absence of relict Elizabeth Phillips overseas. (PROB11/413). AWP.

Philipps, Erasmus John. Account of credits and debits of Dec. 1776 drawn up by him to be sent to Mrs. Ann Philipps of Annapolis Royal, NS, Capt. of 35th Regiment of Foot. Deposition 7 Sep. 1780 by Elizabeth Adlam, wife of John Adlam of Marsham St., St. John the Evangelist, Mddx., and Esther Adlam, spinster, attesting to the testator's handwriting. AWW 9 Sep. 1780 to Ann Fenwick, widow, daughter and administratrix to Ann Philipps, widow. (PROB11/1069).

Phillipps, Giles Esq. of Ipswich, Suffolk but late of Pensacola, W. FL. Will 28 Sep. 1764 pr. 24 Jan. 1766 by relict Elizabeth Phillipps. (PROB11/915). AWP.

Phillips, Gillam of Boston, MA. AWW 19 Aug. 1782 to Samuel Prince. (PROB11/1094).

Phillips, Henry of Exeter, NH. Will pr. 17 Aug. 1813 by relict Elizabeth Phillips. (PROB11/1547).

Phillips, formerly Johnston, Mrs. Jane of QC City. Will pr. 4 Dec. 1772. (PROB11/983).

Phillips, Lewis of Huntingdon whose cousin John Throckmorton was in VA. Will 24 Aug 1668 pr. 3 Mar. 1669 by John Halley. (PROB11/332). AWP.

Phillips, Nathaniel of St. John's, NL, merchant. Will pr. 13 Sep. 1800. (PROB11/1347).

Philips *alias* **Phips, Neel** of St. Anne, [Limehouse], Mddx., mariner of merchant ship *Brunswick* who died in New England. Will 5 Dec. 1737 pr. 1 Feb. 1739 by William Thompson. (PROB11/694). AWP.

Phillips, Thomas of Montreal. Will pr. 4 Nov. 1853. (PROB11/2181).

Phillips, William of Boston, MA, merchant. Will 13 Oct. 1726 pr. 22 Dec. 1727 by John Lovelock of Chippenham, Wilts. (PROB11/618). AWP.

Phillips, William of NYC, Major General of Royal Regiment of Artillery. AWW 16 Apr. 1783 to William Collier. (PROB11/1102).

Phipps, Mary. *See* **Sergeant.**

Phips, Neel. *See* **Philips.**

Phipps, Sir William of Boston, MA, Governor of New England. Will pr. 29 Jan. 1697 by relict Lady Mary Phipps. (PROB11/436). ACE.GGE.

Pickance, Edward of St. John, NB, master mariner. Will pr. 17 Nov. 1854. (PROB11/2201).

Pickett, Richard Horton, master of ship *Sisters* who died at Charleston, SC. Will 18 Dec. 1801. Leg: wife Jane Pickett of Stepney, Mddx. and 3 children William, Janet and Richard Pickett. Wit: Samuel Watts and Jane Sterling. Pr. 7 Jul. 1806 by relict Jane Pickett. (PROB11/1446).

Pidgeon, Ann of Halifax, NS. Will pr. 2 May 1828. (PROB11/1741).

Pidgeon, Rev. George, Rector of St. John City, NB. Will pr. 21 Jun. 1819. (PROB11/1617).

Pike, John of NYC, late clerk on HMS *Iris,* whose legatees were John North and Jane his wife of NYC Will 6 Dec. 1781 pr. 2 Nov. 1782 by John North. (PROB11/1097).

Pike, Richard of Stoke Newington, Mddx., who had lands and kinsmen in PA. Will 2 Sep. 1752 pr. 5 Apr. 1755 by affirmation of Samuel Hoare and Nathaniel Newberry of London, merchants. (PROB11/815/111). AWP. NGSQ 61/34.

Pillgrem, Thomas Lambert of Trinity, NL. Will pr. 14 Jul. 1824. (PROB11/1688).

Pinckney, Charles Esq. of Charles Town, SC. Will 4 Jun. 1751 pr. 18 Mar. 1769 by son Charles Cotesworth Pinckney. (PROB11/947). AWP. NGSQ 63/292.

Pinckney, Charles Cotesworth of Charlestown, SC. AWW 11 Apr. 1827 to Benjamin Stead. (PROB11/1725).

Pine, Arthur, citizen and cordwainer of London whose daughter Hannah Johnson was of Accamack, VA. Will 1 Sep. 1665 pr. 6 Sep. 1665 by daughter Susanna Christmas. (Guildhall: Ms 9052/15).

Pipon, John Hodges of NS, Capt. of Royal Engineers. Will pr. 30 Jun. 1847. (PROB11/2058).

Pirsson, Joseph Poole of NYC, counsellor at law. AWW 4 Jan. 1848 to William Warren Hastings. (PROB11/2068).

Pitcher, James of NYC, Commissary of Masters of HM Forces. Will pr. 30 May 1783 by sister Grace Pitcher. (PROB11/1104).

Pitkin, James of Hartford, CT, late Lieut. of First Regiment of Foot who died in Havana. Will 2 Jun. 1761 AWW 29 Jan. 1765 to Phineas Lyman, attorney for brother Daniel Pitkin in CT. (PROB11/905). AWP.

Pittman, Margaret of Sop's Island, White Bay, NL, widow. Will pr. 14 Nov. 1846. (PROB11/2045).

Pittman, William of New Perlican, NL. Will pr. 7 Feb. 1837. (PROB11/1873).

Plesto, Edward of Kent Co., MD, carpenter & bachelor. Pr. 2 Aug. 1727 by the niece and next-of-kin Mary, wife of Charles Boardman, administratrix to the sister Catherine Eates *alias* Yeats deceased; the executors Thomas Smith and William Thomas renouncing. Revoked and granted 2 Aug. 1727 to William Yeates, son of Catherine Eates *alias* Yeates now deceased; Mary Boardman, Thomas Smith and William Thomas having died. (PROB11/616). AWP.

Plowden, Thomas of Lasham, Hants., who had lands in VA. Will 16 May 1698 pr. 10 Sep. 1698 by relict Thomazine Plowden. (PROB11/447). AWP.

Ployart, Jean Louis of Durham, Drummond, [ON], Lieut. Col. of Militia. Will pr. 22 Aug. 1853. (PROB11/2177).

Plummer, Benjamin Esq. of Portsmouth, NH. Will 7 May 1740 pr. 12 Mar. 1741 by brother Thomas Plummer of London. (PROB11/708). AWP.

Plummer *alias* **Passey, Samuel Aggs** of Philadelphia, teacher. Will pr. 8 Aug. 1829 by cousin Francis Gardner. (PROB11/1759).

Poinsett, Frances *alias* **Fanny, widow** of Charleston, SC. AWW 2 Aug. 1806 to Joel Richards Poinsett. (PROB11/1448).

Poizer, Thomas, soldier of 22nd Regiment who died in Mobile, W. FL, bachelor. Will 24 May 1764 pr. 13 Jun. 1767 by Elizabeth Chipman. (PROB11/929). AWP.

Pollard, Christopher of Capling Bay, NL, gent. Will pr. 10 Jan. 1693. (PROB11/413).

Pollard, John of Capling Bay, NL. Will pr. 28 Mar. 1717. (PROB11/557).

Poore, John of Gore District, [ON]. Will pr. 27 Aug. 1846. (PROB11/2041).

Pope, Francis of RI, now in England, mariner. Will 15 May 1772. Leg: John Harford and Thomas Powell of Mincing Lane, London, merchants, who are to be execs. Wit: M. Pitt, Peter Ravis and George Jemmett. Pr. 21 Jul. 1788 by John Harford. (PROB11/1167).

Pope, James of Madeira, merchant, whose cousin Francis Pope was in RI. Will 1743 pr. 6 Feb. 1746 by John Barrett of Madeira and Thomas Beckford of London, merchant. (PROB11/745). AWP.

Pope, Thomas of St. Philip & Jacob, Bristol, merchant, who had a plantation in Westmoreland Co., VA. Will pr. 20 Oct 1685 by Richard Gotley of Bristol. (PROB11/381). AWP.

Porter, Frederick Esq. of Roxbury, MA, Capt. in Royal American Regiment. Will 27 Dec. 1760 AWW 19 Feb. 1762 to William Hodshon, attorney for John Bowdoin, Matatiah Bourn and relict Mehettable in Boston, MA. (PROB11/873). AWP.

Porter, Samuel of Salem, MA. Will pr. 14 Mar. 1798. (PROB11/1304).

Porter, Thomas of NY. Will [of island of Curacao] 16 Jul. 1722 AWW 23 Jul. 1724 to George Streatfield and David Clarkson. (PROB11/598). AWP.

Potts, Joseph of Orphan House, Philadelphia, Lieut. of Royal Navy on half pay. Will 21 Oct. 1768 AWW 3 Sep. 1773 to Oliver Tomlin, attorney for the relict Meriam Potts in PA. (PROB11/991). AWP.

Pouillot. Marguerite of QC, widow. Will pr. 12 May 1741. (PROB11/1946).

Poulter, Hannah. *See* **Wallin.**
Powell, James of St. John's, NL. Will pr. 29 Mar. 1784. (PROB11/1115).
Power, William of Little Placentia, NL. Will pr. 18 Mar. 1752. (PROB11/793).
Pratt, John, formerly of VA, merchant, but late in Chelsea, Mddx., whose late nephew William Pratt was of Gloucester Co., VA. Will 12 Feb. 1731 pr. 22 Jul. 1731 by Joseph Windham, Roger Tublay and Philip Perry. (PROB11/646). AWP.
Predix, Gabriel of Stepney, Mddx., mariner who died in VA. Will 5 Jul. 1697 AWW 5 Jul. 1697 to pc. Peter Senth. (PROB11/439). AWP.
Prendergast, Thomas of Annapolis Royal, NS, late Capt. in Lieut. Gen. Phillips' Regiment. Will pr. 26 Mar. 1752. (PROB11/793).
Prentis, John of St. Martin in Fields, Mddx., but late of New London, CT, mariner. Will 24 Jul. 1746 pr. 5 Aug. 1746 by William Bowdoin of Boston, MA. (PROB11/1749). AWP.
Preston, James of Twillingate, NL. Will pr. 21 Apr. 1845. (PROB11/2016).
Preston, Richard of Patuxent, MD. Will 2 Dec. 1669 AWW 20 Aug. 1670 to son James Preston. (PROB11/333). AWP.
Prevost, William of Cincinnati, OH. Will pr. 19 Jan. 1830 by Thomas James. (PROB11/1765).
Priaux, William of NL. Will pr. 11 Oct. 1813. (PROB11/1548).
Price, Hopkin of Rappahannock River, Middlesex Co., VA. Will pr. 28 Nov. 1679 by Thurston Withnall. (PROB11/361). AWP.
Price, John, mariner of HMS *Mermaid* who died in SC, bachelor. Will 29 Mar. 1751 pr. 18 Jul. 1753 by Mary Rea of Greenwich, Kent, widow. (PROB11/803). AWP.
Prise, John of Shadwell, Mddx., mariner bound to VA by the *Recovery* of London. Will pr. 26 Sep. 1677 by relict Joanna Prise. (PROB11/354). AWP.
Price, Richard of St. Margaret Westminster, Mddx., citizen and vintner of London. Will 28 July 1630. Leg: son Richard Price to have lands in Hayes and Ruislip, Mddx; daughters Margaret, Ann and Olive Price; son of his sister Joan Dale, widow; brother John Price and his wife Mathewe; cousin Margaret Burgen, now wife of Henry Towers; cousin Thomas Burgen to lands due from testator's adventures in VA and the Society of St. Martin's Hundred there. Wit: Robert Wood, Richard Hilton and others. Pr. 5 November 1630 by relict Margaret Price. (PROB11/158). AWP.
Price, Roger, citizen and leatherseller of London, bound for VA on the *Salisbury*. Will pr. 2 May 1672 by brother Richard Price. (PROB11/339). AWP.
Prichard. James of Hyde Park, Dutchess Co., NY. AWW 28 May 1840 to James Prichard. (PROB11/1928).
Pritchard, John, formerly of All Hallows, Barking, London, and late of Bell Town, MD. Will 10 Feb. 1733 pr. 28 Jan. 1742 by Anthony Donne. (PROB11/715). AWP.
Primerose, Catharine of Charleston, SC, widow. Will pr. 28 Aug. 1841 by Christopher Gadsden and Hugh Perroneau. (PROB11/1950).
Primerose, Robert of Charleston, SC. Will pr. 20 Aug. 1825 by Christopher Gadsden and Hugh Perroneau. (PROB11/1702).
Primus, John of Shadwell, Mddx., mariner of HMS *St. Albans* who died in VA, bachelor. Will 10 Apr. 1693 pr. 8 Oct 1697 by Prudence Poulson. (PROB11/440). AWP.
Prise. *See* **Price.**
Probyn, Edward of NY. Will 10 Sep 1840. Leg: niece Ann Smith, daughter of testator's sister Margaret; testator's [unnamed] children when they are 21; residue to wife Ann Probyn who is to be exex. Wit: John Anthon and William W. Hodges. Pr. 13 Jan. 1846 by relict Ann Probyn. (PROB11/2030).
Proudfoot, William, Minister of the United Associate Secession Church of London, ON. Will pr. 27 Oct. 1851. (PROB11/2141).
Prout, Robert of Charles Town, SC, storekeeper. Will pr. 22 Aug. 1783 by brother William Prout. (PROB11/1107).
Provan, Joseph of Montreal, merchant. Will pr. 20 Jan. 1819. (PROB11/1612).
Provost, Elias of NY, carpenter, who died in VA. Will pr. 12 Jun. 1691 by John Castle of Deptford, Kent. (PROB11/405). AWP.

Prynn, Nicholas of Stepney, Mddx., mariner who died in VA. Will 11 Aug. 1682 pr. 5 May 1684 by relict Dorothy Prynn. (PROB11/376). AWP.

Pryor, Robert of Halifax, NS, sergeant of marines on HM sloop *Observateur*. Will pr. 12 Jun. 1812. (PROB11/1534).

Pudner, Edward of Bonavista, NL. Will pr. 7 Jan. 1819. (PROB11/1612).

Pudner, Mary of Bonavista, NL. Will pr. 5 Oct. 1822. (PROB11/1662).

Pye, Edward Henry of Charles Co., MD. AWW 12 Jan. 1826 to William Barksdale. (PROB11/1707).

Quarles, Aaron of St. John's, King William Co., VA. Will 19 Dec. 1767 pr. 23 Dec. 1771 by son John Quarles Jr. (PROB11/973). AWP.

Quin, Jeremiah of Trinity, NL, fisherman. Will pr. 29 Sep. 1835. (PROB11/1852).

Quiney, Richard of St. Stephen Walbrook, citizen and grocer of London, whose lands in VA he left to his son Richard Quiney. Pr. 3 Jan. 1657 by said son Richard Quiney. (PROB11/261). AWP.

Quinton, James of Newfoundland, planter, late of Ringwood, Hants. Will 10 Mar. 1780. Leg: wife Elizabeth Quinton; brother Henry Quinton; brother-in-law James Tuff; Thomas Wait of Ringwood, tallow chandler, to have care of testator's boats and other estate at Bonavista Harbour, NL, and schooner in Poole Harbour. Wit: Ann Green, widow, John Prabbits and Peter Slam(?). Pr. 26 Oct. 1780 by brother Henry Quinton. (PROB11/1070).

Radford, George of Dartmouth and Lympston, Devon, but who died in NY, mariner. Will 18 Apr. 1754 pr. 14 Mar. 1758 by relict Dorothea Radford. (Mar. 1758).

Rae, James of Stirling, Scotland, merchant, late in London but who died in MD. Will 28 Nov. 1699 pr. 12 Mar. 1703 by John Glissel of London, merchant. (PROB11/469). AWP.

Rae, William Glen, of Vancouver Island, BC, in Hudson's Bay Co. service. Will pr. 26 Jun. 1849. (PROB11/2095).

Ramsay, Charles, mariner of HMS *Harwich* who died in America, bachelor. Will 3 Nov. 1757 AWW 5 Feb. 1761 to Henry Mills, attorney for brother John Ramsay in NY. (PROB11/863). AWP.

Randolph, Benjamin of VA. AWW 3 Sep. 1818 to James Randolph. (PROB11/1608).

Randolph, Edward of Acquamat, VA, Surveyor General of Customs of America, about to make his seventeenth voyage to America. Will 15 Jun. 1702 AWW 7 Dec. 1703 to Sarah Howard. (PROB11/473). AWP.

Randolph, Hon. Peter of Chatsworth, Henrico Co., VA, Surveyor General of Customs. Will 4 May 1767 AWW 21 Oct. 1768 to William Robertson Lidderdale, attorney for Col. Archibald Cary, Richard Randolph, John Wayles and Seth Ward Sr. in VA. (PROB11/943). AWP.

Rankin, James of Little Lake, Hallowell Township, Midland District, [ON], schoolmaster. Will pr. 3 Jun. 1834. (PROB11/1833).

Ranney, William Parker of St. John, NB, merchant. Will pr. 18 Oct. 1844. (PROB11/2006).

Ranolds, Samuel of Stepney, Mddx., mariner of HMS *Fox* who died in SC, bachelor. Will 10 Aug. 1730 pr. 7 Aug. 1732 by Richard Miller of Stepney. (PROB11/653). AWP.

Rapalje, John, formerly of Long Island and now of NYC. Leg: niece Catherine, wife of George Woltdon of London. Wit: Silvanus Miller. Will pr. 24 Nov. 1819 by Catherine Woltdon with powers reserved to John Carpenter. (PROB11/1522).

Raper, Robert of Charles Town, SC. AWW 31 Oct. 1789 to William Raper. (PROB11/1184).

Ratliffe, Thomas of Notre Dame St., Montreal. Will pr. 8 Nov. 1855. (PROB11/2222).

Rattry *formerly* **Beardsley, Martha** of St. John's, NL, widow. Will pr. 22 Apr. 1818. (PROB11/1603).

Rawlins, Joseph of Baltimore but formerly of St. Christopher's. Will pr. 5 Apr. 1797 by William Manning. (PROB11/1289). AWP.

Rayment, John Sedden of Montreal. Will pr. 22 Nov. 1830. (PROB11/1778).

Reade, Alexander of Middlesex Co., VA, gent. Will 11 Dec. 1759 pr. 15 Jul. 1767 by George Thornburgh of London. (PROB11/930). AWP.

Read, George of Whitechapel, Mddx., mariner of the *Swallow* but who died on the *Culpepper* in VA. Will 27 Nov. 1682 pr. 14 Oct. 1685 by relict Margaret Read. (PROB11/384). AWP.

Read, John of Bristol, VA, mariner. AWW 6 Jul. 1688 to relict Mary Read. (PROB11/392). GGE.

Read, Robert of St. Olave, Southwark, Sy., mariner of *Baltimore* bound for VA, Will 15 Jan. 1703 pr. 17 Dec. 1705 by relict Elizabeth Read. (PROB11/485). AWP.

Read, Thomas of Colchester, Essex, carpenter, whose son Thomas Read and son-in-law Samuel Bacon married to Mary, daughter of the testator, were in New England. Will 13 Jul. 1665 pr. 3 Mar. 1666 by son Isaac Read and John Clarke. (PROB11/320). AWP.

Read, William of New England, mariner of *Granada*. Will pr. 12 Sep. 1692 by Elizabeth Harlock. (PROB11/411). GGE.

Reading, Richard of Aurora, Erie Co., NY. Will pr. 10 Jul. 1851 by nephew Thomas Reading. (PROB11/2136).

Redwood, Langford of Flushing, Queens, NY. AWW 4 Sep. 1844 to John Coles Symes, James Trecothick and John Henry Roper Jr. (PROB11/2005).

Redwood, William Jr. of Newport, RI, merchant. Will 5 Apr. 1766. Exex: wife and sole legatee Sarah Redwood. Wit: Josias Lyndon, Philip Wanton and Mary Lyndon. Pr. 26 Jul. 1790 by relict Sarah Redwood. (PROB11/1194).

Reed, Isaac of Boston, MA, mariner of HMS *Tiger*. Will 11 Oct 1695 pr. 21 Nov. 1695 by Mark Pooyd. (PROB11/428). AWP.

Reed, William of HMS *Southampton* at James River, VA. Will 22 Nov. 1702 pr. 21 Jul. 1703 by David Cluny. (PROB 11/470). AWP.

Reeks, Nicholas, mariner of the *William & Sarah* who died in MD. Will 21 Jan. 1734 pr. 17 Oct. 1734 by Samuel Spurrier. (PROB11/667). AWP.

Rees, John of Halifax, NS, butcher. Will pr. 2 Jan. 1829. (PROB11/1750).

Reeves, Richard of Toronto, carpenter. 22 May 1857. (PROB11/2252).

Reid, Andrew of Charles Town, SC. AWW 28 Jun. 1784 to John Tunno. (PROB11/1118)/

Reid, George, Assistant Surgeon at the Hospital of St. John's, NL. Will pr. 6 Apr. 1784. (PROB11/1116).

Reid, Henry Solomon of Darlington, Newcastle District, [ON]. Will pr. 1 Sep. 1855. (PROB11/2219).

Remnant, John of Kingston on Thames, Sy., lighterman and waterman, late mariner of HMS *Pearl* who died in VA, bachelor. Will 19 Jun. 1741 pr. 16 Feb. 1743 by John Mackey. (PROB11/724). AWP.

Remsen, Peter of NYC, merchant. Will pr. 12 Jul. 1792 by son Simeon Remsen. (PROB11/1221).

Rennell, John of St. John's, NL, surgeon. Will pr. 30 Aug. 1820. (PROB11/1633).

Renton, Joseph of Northumberland, surgeon of merchant ship *Rose* who died in VA, bachelor. Will 16 Feb. 1739 pr. 20 Jul. 1742 by Cuthbert Birkley. (PROB11/). AWP.

Reynolds, John of Halifax, NS, carpenter of HM sloop *Vulture*. Will pr. 31 May 1758. (PROB11/838).

Reynolds, William of Halifax, NS, Clerk of the Cheque of Ordnance Department. Will pr. 23 Aug. 1813. (PROB11/1547).

Rice, David, Lieut. Gov. of Garrison of Annapolis, NS. Will 6 Jan. 1722 pr. 14 Sep 1724 by relict Anne Rice. (PROB11/599). AWP.

Rice, John of Philadelphia but now residing in Bath, Som.Will 13 Sep. 1789 pr. 15 Dec. 1790 by relict Joanna Rice. (PROB11/1199). NGSQ 63/48.

Richards, William of St. Martin in Fields, Mddx., carpenter of transport ship *George* in HM service who died on merchant ship *Easter* in Carolina. Will 13 May 1709 pr. 30 Jun. 1722 by relict Elizabeth Richards. (PROB11/585).

Richardson, William Jr. of MD, mariner who died in Rotherhithe, Sy. Will 17 Sep. 1731 pr. 13 Mar. 1732 by affirmation of Thomas Plumsted. (PROB11/650). AWP.

Richardson, William Esq., formerly of Kensington, Mddx., and Cross Oak, Wilts., who died in Pensacola, W. FL. Will 29 Aug. 1760 AWW 16 Feb. 1769 to sister Mary, wife of Rev. William Robinson. (PROB11/946). AWP. Further grants in 1794 and 1828.

Richardson, Zachariah, formerly of Bermondsey, Sy, but late of Philadelphia. Will 21 Dec. 1735 pr. 23 Feb. 1736 by affirmation of relict Rebecca Richardson and Thomas Binks. (PROB11/675). AWP.

Richman, Francis Henry of Cooperville, Philadelphia. Will pr. 3 Jun. 1856 by Emanuel Loury and relict Hannah Richman. (PROB11/2234).

Ricketts, Henry *alias* Marshall, Ricketts of Halifax, NS, ship master. Will pr. 18 Mar. 1853. (PROB11/2169).

Rider, Richard of Bonavista, NL. Will pr. 5 Jan. 1831. (PROB11/1780).

Ridley, Anna Barbara of QC, widow. 29 Aug. 1836. (PROB11/1866)

Ridout, Joseph of Rogues' Harbour, NL, planter and widower. Leg: sons Joseph and Gillbart Ridout; daughters (unnamed). Wit: James White and John Nobel. AWW 26 Apr. 1844 to William Tarbet, attorney for natural children Giles, Joseph and Gilbert Ridout at Rogues' Harbour. (PROB11/1997).

Rieusset, John of NC, widower. Will pr. 26 May 1744. (PROB11/733).

Ripley, Francis of Shadwell, Mddx., who died in VA on the *Francis & Edward*. Will 10 Dec. 1694. Wit: Mary Clover, John Cosin and Samuel Willis. AWW 17 Sep. 1697 to relict Elizabeth Ripley, the named exex. Mary Cole of Shadwell, widow, renouncing. (Guildhall: Ms 9171/48/455).

Ripley, John who died at Fort Augustus, E. FL. Will dated Tower of London 10 Nov. 1769. pr. 7 Sep. 1773 by mother Judith Ripley. (PROB11/991). AWP.

Rivet, Daniel of Stepney, Mddx., weaver, but late of GA. Will 8 Sep. 1733 pr. 19 May 1739 by relict Barbe Rivet. (PROB11/696). AWP.

Robe, Alexander Watt of St. John's, NL, Lieut.Col. in Royal Engineers. Will pr. 19 Sep. 1849. (PROB11/2100).

Roberts, Elias, of St. Benet Fink, citizen and merchant tailor of London. Leg: wife Sarah Roberts to have lands in Martin's Hundred, VA; son Elias Roberts in VA; his three daughters [unnamed] to have a share of lands in Somer Islands and St. David's Island; lector in Welsh language to be funded for Queen's Hope parish, Flintshire; his lands in Ireland to go to the Merchant Tailors' Co. Wit: Elias Roberts and Ephraim Cathrell. Will pr. 20 Feb. 1627 by relict Sarah Roberts. (Guildhall: Ms 9171/143).

Roberts, Humphrey of Portsmouth, Norfolk Co., VA. AWW 13 Apr. 1793 to William Roberts. (PROB11/1231).

Roberts, Josiah of Mile End, Mddx., gent, whose daughter Mary married Matthew Randall of Philadelphia. Will 3 May 1795 pr. 19 Dec. 1796 by son Nathaniel Roberts and William Hainworth. (PROB11/1283). NGSQ 70/113.

Roberts, Elizabeth of London, widow whose daughter Elizabeth Shrimpton, widow, was in New England. Will 26 Feb. 1701 pr. 13 Jan. 1702 by daughter Mary Breedon. (PROB11/463). AWP. NGSQ 63/200.

Roberts, Robert of St. Mary, Beverley, East Riding of Yorks. but late of NY, physician of HM Hospital about to embark for Great Britain. Leg: brother William Roberts; wife Catherine Roberts. Will pr. 24 Apr. 1801 by relict Catherine Roberts. (PROB11/1356).

Roberts, Thomas of Brigus Island, NL. Will pr. 11 Oct. 1836. (PROB11/1868).

Roberts, William of Ferryland, NL, fisherman. Will pr. 9 Nov. 1677. (PROB11/355).

Robertson, Gilbert, HM Consul for Philadelphia. Will pr. 31 Oct. 1837. (PROB11/1885).

Robertson, James of Churchill Factory, Hudson's Bay. Will 23 Dec. 1810. Leg: brother David Robertson; Janet Robertson, daughter of testator's deceased brother Edward Robinson, to have ground in Sandwick, Orkney; children of deceased brother John Robertson. Wit: Thomas Topping, John L. Couper, Thomas Halorow and Thomas Corston. Pr. 25 Feb. 1715 by nephew James Robertson. (PROB11/1565).

Robertson, John of Charles Co., MD. Will pr. 30 Dec. 1824. (PROB11/1693).

Robertson, Neil of Montreal, gent. Will pr. 19 May 1817. (PROB11/1603).

Robertson, Peter of Halifax, NS, Assistant Surgeon to the Forces. Will pr. 26 Jul. 1847. (PROB11/2060).

Roby, Anthony who died in Carolina, illegitimate. AWW 12 Jul. 1688 to the brother Thomas Roby; the named exec.early alias Avelyn Roby having died. (PROB11/392). GGE. (PROB11/392).

Robey, Thomas Jr. of Derby who died in Philadelphia. Will 7 Mar. 1754 pr. 10 Apr. 1754 by Francis Green. (PROB11/898). AWP.

Robey, Thomas Jr. of Denby, Derbys., but late of Philadelphia. Will 7 Mar. 1754 with codicils of 6 Mar. 1755 and 8 Nov. 1755. Exec: Francis Green, father Thomas Robey and James Dolling. Sentence 14 May 1767 for validity of will and declaring James Dolling to have "contumaciously absented himself" from the legal proceedings. (PROB11/934).

Robins, Francis of Exeter, Devon, serge maker, whose nephew Francis Robins resided in Boston, MA. Will 7 May 1764 pr. 7 Dec. 1767. (PROB11/934). AWP.

Robinson, George of NYC, mariner. Will pr.10 Mar. 1802. (PROB11/1372).

Robinson, Joseph of Charlotte Town, Queen's Co., PE. Will pr. 27 Jan. 1808. (PROB11/1473).

Robinson, Thomas of NS. Will pr. 9 Aug. 1788. (PROB11/1169).

Robinson, Thomas Francis of St. John's, NL. Will pr. 14 Aug. 1818. (PROB11/1607).

Robinson, William of MD. Will 29 Nov. 1696 pr. 14 Aug. 1697 by William Colvert. (PROB11/439). AWP.

Robotham, George of Talbot Co., MD. Will 28 Feb. 1698 AWW 8 Nov. 1698 to nieces Mary Erp, Ann Cooke and Ann Cotton. (PROB11/448). AWP.

Robson, Isaac of Stepney, Mddx., mariner of merchant ship *Britannia* who died in VA. Will 17 Feb. 1704 pr. 27 Sep. 1710 by relict Mary Robson. (PROB11/518). AWP.

Roby. *See* **Robey.**

Roche, James of Warwicksquick, Isle of Wight, VA, planter, late of Queen Camel, Som. Will 22 Aug. 1652. Leg: eldest brother [Robert] Roche, vicar of Queen Camel, who is to be exec; servant Thomas North who is to manage testator's cattle; Capt. George Fadding of Warwicksquick who is to be attorney in trust. Wit: Ed. Gillhew, John Marton and William Stephens. Pr. 18 Sep. 1652 by brother Robert Roche. (PROB11/224).

Rock(e), John of NL, mariner. Will pr. 9 Jul. 1771. (PROB11/969).

Roe, John Sr. of Hazelwood, Madison, Licking Co., OH. Will pr. 31 Dec. 1849 by son Dr. Thomas Henry Roe. (PROB11/2105).

Rodgers, James of Charlestown, SC, mariner. Will Jan. 1762 pr. 9 Jun. 1763 by John Beswicke. (PROB11/889). AWP.

Rogers, Richard of St. Michael, Crooked Lane, London, Controller of H.M. Mint, born in Little Ness, Salop. Leg: wife Joane; son Edward Rogers to have lands in VA which are then to pass to grandson Richard Rogers; dau. Anne, wife of Jasper Draper; kinsmen Abraham and John Rogers; grandchildren Edward and Lidia Rogers; son-in-law William Hewson. Wit: Robert Hanson, scrivener, Bartholomew Hill, William Salisburie, John Smith and William Stevens. Pr. 8 Sep. 1636 by Edward Rogers and Jasper Draper. (PROB11/172). AWP.

Rogers, Theophilus of Northampton whose nephew John Rogers became a ship's captain in the Guinea trade, emigrated to VA in 1754 but thereafter was never heard of again. Will 30 Jan. 1730 pr. 11 Sep. 1730 by brother Robert Rogers and William Beevor. (PROB11/640). AWP. NGSQ 62/205.

Rogers, William of NYC. Will pr. 31 Oct. 1829 by John Wesley Hall. (PROB11/1762).

Rolfe, John of James City, VA. Will pr. 21 May 1630. (PROB11/157). ACE.GGE.

Rolle, Francis of MD. Will 17 Nov. 1724 pr. 7 Dec. 1724 by Arnault Hawkins of MD. (PROB11/600). AWP.

Rome, George of Newport, RI, who died in Lisbon, merchant. Leg: brothers Christian, John, Richard and William Rome; sisters Ann and Elizabeth Rome; natural children Charles, Charlotte and Chester born of Hannah White; natural daughter Betsy born of Lucy Buckler; Elizabeth Sands of Newport. AWW 20 Apr. 1793 to brother William Rome. (PROB11/1231).

Romerille, Francis of Broad Cove, Conception Bay, NL. Will pr. 26 Mar. 1807. (PROB11/1458).

Romman, William of Woodborough, Wilts., who died in Philadelphia, bachelor. Will [undated] pr. 1 Mar. 1722 by brother Richard Romman. (PROB11/584). AWP.

Rooke, Samuel of St. John's, NL, merchant. Will pr. 13 Jan. 1727. (PROB11/613).

Rootes, Thomas Reade of VA, merchant lately residing in St. Faith's, London. Will 10 Feb. 1766 pr. 21 Mar. 1766 by John Hyndman. (PROB11/917). AWP. Further grant in Mar. 1767.

Rose, Walter of York Township, [ON]. Will pr. 14 Sep. 1844. (PROB11/2005).

Ross, David of Richmond, VA. AWW 27 Apr. 1722 to John Fallowfield Scott. (PROB11/1656).

Ross, Elizabeth of Elizabeth City, NC. Will 20 Sep. 1756 pr 28 Nov. 1768 by son-in-law Anthony Hawkins. (PROB11/944). AWP.

Ross, George of Shelburne, NS, merchant. Will pr. 2 Jun. 1818. (PROB11/1605).

Ross, John, formerly of Wapping, Mddx., but late of New England, mariner. Will 11 Apr. 1766 pr. 27 Oct. 1770 by John Thompson of Shadwell, Mddx., ropemaker. (PROB11/961). AWP.

Ross, Malcolm of Churchill Factory, Hudson's Bay, but late of South Ronaldsay, [Orkneys]. Will 6 Sep. 1799. Leg: natural son George Ross born by an Indian woman inn Hudson's Bay; brother Charles Ross; Helen Ross alias Forbaster, widow of Samuel Forbaster. John Ballenden of York Factory and David Geddes of Stromness, [Orkneys] to be guardians of testator's children. Wit: Thomas Topping and George Charles. Pr. 12 Feb. 1802 by David Geddes. (PROB11/1370).

Rowe, Charles Joseph of South Orillia, Simcoe District, [ON], gent. Will pr. 26 Apr. 1856. (PROB11/2231).

Rowland, John of Shadwell, Mddx., mariner of New England who died on passage from France to London. Will 15 Sep. 1709 AWW 19 Jul. 1714 to Francis Cane, attorney and husband of the mother Abigail Cane of New England. (PROB11/541). AWP.

Rowsell, Sarah of Halls Bay, NL, widow. Will pr. 18 Feb. 1822. (PROB11/1653).

Roydon, William, citizen and grocer of London who had estate in PA and died in Philadelphia. Will 20 May 1692 pr. 3 Jan. 1696 by John Tizack of London. (PROB11/433). AWP.

Royse, John of London, merchant who traded with NY but died in Gravesend , Kent. Will 18 Jun. 1683 pr. 9 Dec. 1686 by father Daniel Royse. (PROB11/385). AWP.

Ruggles, George, sailor of *Due Return* bound for VA who died overseas. Nuncupative will Mar. 1625 AWW 3 May 1625 to Henry Furton. (Guildhall: Ms 9171/24/422).

Ruggles, Timothy of Wilmot, Annapolis, NS. Will pr. 22 Jul. 1796. (PROB11/1277).

Rundle, Daniel of Philadelphia, merchant. AWW 17 Sep. 1795 to Robert Barclay. (PROB11/1266).

Rush, John of NY, hatter. Will 13 May 1743 pr. 1 Jun. 1743 by Edward Daniel. (PROB11/727). AWP.

Russell, Elizabeth of Marblehead, MA, widow. Will 15 Aug. 1770 pr. 2 Jan. 1772 by Russell Trevet of Marblehead. (PROB11/974). AWP.

Russell, Elizabeth of York, York Co., [ON], spinster. Will pr. 6 Oct. 1825. (PROB11/1704).

Russell, Henry, mariner of HMS *Aldborough* who died in SC, bachelor. Will 20 Jun. 1730 AWW 30 Aug. 1734 to John Pick, attorney for William Randal of Charles Town, SC. (PROB11/666). AWP.

Russell, John Esq. of Brunswick, Cape Fear, NC, Captain of HM sloop *Scorpion*. Will 13 Dec. 1752 pr. 6 Jul. 1753 by relict Alice Russell. (PROB11/803). AWP.

Russell, William Esq. of Savannah, GA, late residing in Whitechapel, Mddx. Will 21 Feb. 1768 pr. 6 Mar. 1769 by relict Jane Russell. (PROB11/947). AWP.

Russell, William of Cape Breton [NS]. Will pr. 16 Apr. 1789. (PROB11/1178).

Rutherford, John of Edgerston, Bergen Co., NJ. Will pr. 4 Oct. 1741 by daughter Mary Rutherford. (PROB11/1953).

Ryley, John, mariner of HMS *Winchelsea* and HMS *Chester* who died in Boston, MA. Will 31 Mar. 1712 pr. 16 Jun. 1713 by Bryan Northen. (PROB11/534).

Rymer, Duncan *alias* **McNab, Rymer** of Bytown District, Bathurst, [NB]. Will pr. 1 Feb. 1839. (PROB11/1907).

Rymes, Edward of St. Botolph Bishopsgate, marine of HMS *Royal Sovereign* who died in NY. Will 3 May 1691 pr. 14 Feb. 1704 by relict Elizabeth Rymes. (PROB11/475). AWP.

Sabbeston, Hugh of York Factory, Hudson's Bay. Will dated 20 Nov. 1810 at Carlton House, Red River. Leg: reputed wife Peggy Sabbeston; reputed children (unnamed). Wit: Alexander Kennedy, James Halero and James Morwick. Pr. 2 Dec. 1814 by William Auld and William Sinclair. (PROB11/1563).

Sadler, John, late of St. Stephen Walbrook, London, and late of Hunsdon, Herts., who had a plantation near James River, VA. Will 2 Jan. 1799 pr. 16 Nov. 1716 by Sir Charles Ingleby. (PROB11/555). AWP.

Sadler, Mary of Mayfield, Sussex, widow, whose daughter Mary Sadler and her children she supposed to live in New England. Leg: daughter and exex. Elizabeth James; son John Sadler; dau. Ann Allin; grandchildren Mary and Thomas Russell, Mary and Elizabeth James. Wit: John Ricken and Mathew Hudley. Pr. 13 Nov. 1647 by Elizabeth James. (PROB11/202). AWP.

Sale, Nathaniel of London who died in Charles Town, SC, merchant. Will 18 Mar 1709 pr. 5 Jun. 1711 by Mary Johnson. (PROB11/521). AWP.

Salisbury, Nicholas of Boston, MA, shopkeeper. Will 4 Apr. 1748 AWW 7 Nov. 1749 to Thomas Lane, attorney for the relict Martha Salisbury in Boston. (PROB11/775). AWP.

Salle, Antonia, seaman of HMS *Aeolus* in Naval Hospital at Halifax, NS. Will pr. 23 Sep. 1814. (PROB11/1516).

Salmon, William Warren of Marnhull, Dorset, but late of Bell Island, NL, planter. Will 10 Sep. 1807. Leg: wife Racheal Salmon; daughter Susannah Salmon; Joseph Bird of Sturminster Newton, Dorset, and Henry Creasy to take care of property left to the testator by his father William Salmon lately deceased. Wit: W. Mahon, Henry Duggan and John Vincent. Pr. 22 May 1813 by Joseph Bird. (PROB11/1544).

Salvador, Joseph of Charles Town, SC. Will pr. 24 Nov. 1788 by daughters Abigail, Elizabeth and Susanna Salvador. (PROB11/1172).

Salwey, Anthony of Ann Arundel Co., MD, gent. Will 23 Oct. 1668 pr. 23 Aug. 1672 to brother Richard Salwey. (PROB11/339). AWP.

Sansom, Joseph of Philadelphia. AWW 10 May 1828 to Richard Van Heythuysen. (PROB11/1741).

Sampson, George of Sandwich, Barnstable Co., MA, mariner of HMS *York*. Will dated 25 Jul. 1740 appoints Jarvis Pinkney of York Town, [VA?], mariner, universal legatee and sole executor. Witnessed by George Ryall, Lieut. Thomas Prifits and Francis Donovan. Pr. 31 Oct. 1740 by Jarvis Pinkney. (PROB11/705).

Sampson, Henry of Bruton, Som., Lieut. in 31st Regiment who died in FL. Will 14 Dec. 1757 pr. 30 Dec. 1772 by brother Thomas Sampson of Bruton, apothecary and surgeon. (PROB11/983). AWP.

Sanders, James of Bonavista, NL. Will pr. 22 Nov. 1770. (PROB11/958).

Saubere, Samuel of Philadelphia. AWW 30 Apr. 1849 to Henry Lloyd Magan. (PROB11/2092).

Saunders, Joseph of King's Cove, Bonavista Bay, NL, planter. Will pr. 12 Dec. 1850. (PROB11/2124).

Saunders, Thomas of Newport, RI, book-keeper of HMS *Guernsey*. Will 7 Feb. 1761 AWW 6 Apr. 1765 to Clark Gayton, attorney for Sgt. Edward Wright in Gibraltar. (PROB11/908). AWP.

Sargeant, John of Philadelphia. Will pr. 20 Dec. 1822 by mother Margaret Sargeant, widow. (PROB11/1664).

Sarvener *alias* **Savenier, James** of St. John, NB, Lieut. in NJ Volunteers. Will pr. 7 Oct. 1805. (PROB11/1432).

Savage, Perez of Salem, MA, mariner. Will dated Mackeness, Barbary, 23 May 1694 AWW 21 May 1702 to nephew Thomas Thatcher. (PROB11/464). AWP.

Saxton, John of Montreal, gent. Will pr. 21 Nov. 1809. (PROB11/1506).

Schmitz, Franz Jacob of San Francisco, CA. AWW 27 Dec. 1853 to daughter Mathilda Schmitz. (PROB11/2183).

Scholes, James of Brooklyn, NY. AWW 1 Jul. 1850 to William Pike. (PROB11/2117).

Schouborg, Ann of Yonkers, NY. AWW 20 Jan. 1857 to Joseph Delevaute. (PROB11/2245).

Schuyler, John Cortlandt of Watervliet Co., Albany, NY, merchant. AWW 2 Aug. 1797 to brother William Schuyler. (PROB11/1295).

Scott, Alexander of Lancaster City, PA. AWW 16 Mar. 1824 to Charles Robert Turner. (PROB11/1683).

Scott, Edward of HMS *Nightingale*. Will dated Annapolis, MD, 4 Sep. 1714 AWW 27 Mar. 1716 to brother William Scott. PROB11/551). AWP.

Scott, Elizabeth of Niagara Falls, ON. Will pr. 17 Jul. 1851. (PROB11/2136).

Scott, John of South Hampton, Long Island, NY, mariner. AWW 4 Jun. 1692 to William Clapcott. (PROB11/410).

Scott, John of Mattox, Westmoreland Co., VA, merchant. Will 28 May 1700 AWW 19 Dec. 1702 to Elizabeth Scott, wife and attorney of nephew Gustavus Scott. (PROB11/467). AWP.

Scott, John of Charleston, SC, gent. AWW 30 Aug. 1791 to John Shoolbred. (PROB11/1208).

Scott, Mary of VA, spinster. AWW 30 Jul. 1781 to Ann Anderson. (PROB11/1080).

Scott, Walter of MD but late residing in St. Benet Gracechurch, London, merchant. Will 6 Feb. 1752 pr. 14 Mar. 1752 by James Armour and John Stewart of London, merchants. (PROB11/793). AWP.

Scott, William of St. Mary Abchurch, London, but late of Charles Town, MA, surgeon. Will 18 Aug. 1752 pr. 30 May 1754 by Philip Hall of London, grocer. (PROB11/808). AWP.

Scott, William of St. Andrew's, Charlotte Co., NB, gent. Will pr. 17 Jun. 1839. (PROB11/1912).

Scottow, Thomas of Boston, MA, surgeon, bound to sea in *Gerrard* of London. Will pr. 4 Sep. 1699 by Margaret Softly, widow. (PROB11/452).

Skottowe, Thomas of Charles Town, SC. Will pr. 29 Dec. 1788 by brother Nicholas Skottowe. (PROB11/1173).

Scovell, Phillip of Hudson's Bay, carpenter. Will pr. 1 Feb. 1688. (PROB11/390).

Seager, Stephen of Canonsburgh, Washington Co., PA. Will pr. 5 Jan. 1808 by Andrew Munro. (PROB11/1473).

Seaman, Benjamin of St. John, NB. Will pr. 2 Oct. 1786. (PROB11/1147).

Seaman, George of Charles Town, SC, gent. Will 14 Jan. 1769 pr. 24 Jul. 1769 by John Deas. (PROB11/950). AWP.

Seaman, John of St. Dunstan in East, citizen and cooper of London who died in MD. Will 31 Aug. 1696 pr. 7 Oct. 1692 by relict Elizabeth Seaman. (PROB11/411). AWP.

Selby, Edward of Shadwell, Mddx. Will 16 May 1694. Leg: son Edward Selby to have plantation of 150 acres called Selby's Purchase near Bush River, MD, which the testator's wife is to manage until the son is 21; children Precilla, Elizabeth and Mary Selby. Wit: Butler Oliver, Mary Brooking, Theo. Pomeroy and Thomas Porter. Pr. 22 May 1694 by relict Mary Selby. (Guildhall: Ms 9171/46/167v).

Sergeant, Dame Mary, late Phipps of Boston, MA. Will 19 Feb. 1704 AWW 29 Jan. 1707 to John Metcalfe, attorney for adopted son Spencer Phipps *alias* Bennett in NY. (PROB11/492). AWP.

Service, John of NY, midshipman on HMS *Belliqueux*. Will pr. 8 Oct. 1782. Wit: Andrew Service and James Fraser. Execs. and legatees Robert and George Service of NYC. Pr. 27 Jan. 1784 by George Service. (PROB11/1112).

Sewell, Adam of Shadwell, Mddx., mariner of HMS *Phoenix* who died in Carolina, bachelor. Will 1 Dec. 1737 pr. 1 Jul. 1741 by George Powers. (PROB11/710). AWP.

Sewell, Henrietta. *See* **Smith.**

Shairp, Alexander Mordaunt of Dowes, Newcastle, [ON], of Royal Navy. Will pr. 19 Jan. 1849. (PROB11/2087).

Shambler, James of Bonaventure, NL. Will pr. 11 Feb. 1769. (PROB11/946).

Sharp, Simon of Scothorne, Lincs., mariner of frigate *Grantham* in America in State service. Will 20 Sep. 1657 pr. 31 Mar 1659 by Charles Brandon, steward of said ship. (PROB11/289). AWP.

Sharp, Thomas of Bristol, mariner, but late of Philadelphia, bachelor. Will 25 Feb. 1723 pr. 2 Dec. 1743 by John Thomas of Bristol, baker. (PROB11/730). AWP.

Sharples, James of NYC. Will pr. 23 Jul. 1811 by relict Ellen Sharples. (PROB11/1524).

Shaw, Lachlan of Prince William parish, SC, Lieut. of an Independent Company of Foot. Will 20 Feb. 1761 AWW 6 Feb. 1765 to George Urquhart, attorney for son Lachlan Shaw in Scotland. (PROB11/906). AWP.

Shaw, Richard of Wapping, Mddx., mariner bound to Guinea and VA and who died in VA. Will 21 Nov. 1698 pr. 4 Jun. 1700 by Moses Lacy. (PROB11/456).

Shearer, William of London, master of the *Friendship* who died in Boston, MA. Will 31 Mar. 1762 pr. 2 Dec. 1763 by brother-in-law John Freeman of London. (PROB11/894). AWP.

Shedden, William *alias* **Ralston** of NY, merchant. AWW 28 Jul. 1852 to son Patrick Ralston Shedden. (PROB11/2156).

Shemans, Benjamin of Stepney, Mddx, mariner who died in Carolina on HMS *Dolphin*. Will 31 Oct. 1722 pr. 2 Aug 1723 by Mary Jordan, widow. (PROB11/592). AWP.

Shepherd, James, Sheriff of QC. Will pr. 4 Dec. 1822. (PROB11/1664).

Sheppard, John of Towcester, Northants., mercer. Will 16 Jul. 1643. Leg: eldest son William Sheppard in New England to have all goods shipped to him by *Concord* and his house in Banbury; sons John, Samuel and Daniel Sheppard to have houses and lands in Towcester; brother John Waples. Wit: William Pitchford, Andrew Paine and Peter Deakin. Pr. 6 Jun. 1646 by relict Frances Sheppard. (PROB11/196). AWP.

Shepherd, Joseph, deputy chaplain to 21st Regiment who died in W. FL. in 1766. Will 12 Jun. 1765 pr. 1 Aug. 1769 by Capt. Archibald Grant. (PROB11/950). AWP.

Sherley, William, citizen and apothecary of London, who died in VA, bachelor. Will 16 Jun. 1746 pr. 16 Jul. 1750 by Edward Bathirst. (PROB11/781). AWP.

Sherwin, George of Boston, MA, Capt. in 6th Regiment of Foot. AWW 6 Mar. 1777 to brother John Sherwin. (PROB11/1029).

Shexam, William, mariner of HMS *Pendennis* of St. Mary's Bay, NL. Will pr. 13 Dec. 1703. (PROB11/473).

Shillitoe, Charles formerly of NY and late of Commercial Road, Bedford Place, Mddx. Will 28 Nov. 1837 & codicil 8 Dec. 1837. Leg: Wife Emma Shillitoe to have premises in Chicago used to soap and candle making and other lands in Michigan City, Lower Canada and NY State; entitlement under the will of Varley Beilby to go to Spearman Johnstone and Joseph Maulby of York who are to be execs. with testator's wife; children Mary, Ann and Charles Shillitoe. Wit: A.H. Heighley, James Haigh, Joseph Maulby and Jane Salmon. Pr. 20 Nov. 1838 by relict Emma Shillitoe. (PROB11/1889).

Shipley, George of NYC, cabinet maker. AWW 16 May 1804 to William Remington. (PROB11/1409).

Shoolbred, Elizabeth of QC City, widow. Will pr. 14 Apr. 1821. (PROB11/1642).

Short, James Esq. of Surrey Street, London, and late of VA and Lisbon. Will10 Aug. 1773 pr. 21 Feb. 1774 by Mungo Baikie of Leicester Fields and Joseph Clarke of of Tavistock Street, London. (PROB11/995). AWP.

Shortt, William Charles of Upper Canada. Lieut. Col. of Army and Col. of 41st Regiment of Foot. Will pr. 12 Nov. 1824. (PROB11/1692).

Shoveler, Sarah of Southwark District, Philadelphia, widow. AWW 3 Mar. 1800 to Joseph Hancock by solemn affirmation. (PROB11/1339).

Shoveler, Sturges of Philadelphia, mariner. Will 6 Apr. 1773, wits. Bowl. Brook, John Parrock and Peter Thomson. Pr. 9 Jan. 1779 by relict Sarah Shoveler. (PROB11/1049).

Shower, Nathaniel of Boston, MA, purser of HMS *Blandford*, widower. Will 26 Jul. 1755 AWW 13 Nov. 1761 to daughter Elizabeth Shower. (PROB11/870). AWP.

Shrimpton, Samuel of Boston, MA. Will 5 Jun. 1697 AWW 3 Jun. 1700 to Elizabeth Roberts. (PROB11/456). AWP.

Shrubsole, William of St. George, Hanover Square, Mddx., gent., late of SC. Will 19 Jul. 1748 pr. 16 Mar. 1759 by Elizabeth Shrubsole. (PROB11/845). AWP.

Shute, Samuel of St. Peter, Cornhill, London, who had trading partners in NY. Will 8 Apr. 1684 pr. 15 Dec. 1685 by relict Anne Shute. (PROB11/381). AWP.

Sibbet, Robert of St. Luke, Mddx., mariner who died in MD, bachelor. Leg: Catherine Stringfellow who is to be exex. Wit: Arthur Parker and John Palmer. Pr. 24 Mar 1737 by Catherine Stringfellow. (PROB11/582). AWP.

Silsby, Daniel formerly of MA, then of GA and SC, but late of Christ Church, Surrey, gent., whose family were inhabitants of Boston. Will 11 Jan. 1791 pr 14 Feb. 1791. (PROB11/1202). NGSQ 63/201.

Simpson, Alexander, of Norfolk, VA, master of HMS *Swallow.* Will 14 Sep. 1767 AWW 12 Jun. 1771 to John Gathorne, attorney for relict Ann, now wife of William George. (PROB11/968). AWP.

Simpson, Emilius of Fort Vancouver, Columbia River, [WA], in the service of Hudson's Bay Co. Will pr. 27 Jun. 1832. (PROB11/1802).

Simpson, Patrick of St. John's Island, SC. Will pr. 3 Mar. 1792 by John Simpson. (PROB11/1216).

Simson, Thomas Esq., who was born in Jamaica, late of St. Martin in Fields, Mddx., NY & Philadelphia but who died in Jamaica. Will 7 Jul. 1725 pr. 19 Feb 1730 by Nathaniel St. André. (PROB11/636). AWP.

Simpson, Thomas of Fort Confidence, Rupertsland, Hudson's Bay. Will pr. 23 Feb. 1841. (PROB11/1941).

Sinckler, John of Shadwell, Mddx., mariner of the *Owners Adventure* who died in VA, widower. Will 30 Jan. 1692 pr. 1 Jul. 1697 by Anne Hill. (PROB11/439). AWP.

Singer, Francis of NS. Will pr. 30 Jun. 1823. (PROB11/1672).

Skeffington, Joseph of Bonavista, NL. Will pr. 31 Jan. 1789. (PROB11/1175).

Skene, William of Annapolis Royal Garrison, NS, surgeon. Will pr. 11 Mar. 1773. (PROB11/986).

Skinner, Alexander of St. Augustine, E. FL, Superintendent for Indian Affairs. AWW 22 Feb. 1800 to James Simpson. (PROB11/1337).

Skinner, Cortland of Bristol, Glos., but formerly of NJ. Will 7 Sep. 1794 pr. 17 Apr. 1799 by relict Elizabeth Skinner. (PROB11/1323). NGSQ 63/41.

Skynner, Henry of St. Augustine, E. FL, barrackmaster, gent. Will pr. 3 Nov. 1784 by Ann Samuel. (PROB11/1123).

Skinner, Richard of Mansack on banks of MS River, W. FL. Will dated Charles Town, SC, 22 Apr. 1774 AWW 30 Sep. 1775 to brother Robert Skinner. (PROB11/1011). AWP.

Skinner, Stephen of Perth Amboy, NJ, Lieut. in Royal Navy. Will dated Punta Delgado, St. Michael's Island, [MD], 20 Apr. 1806. Leg: father Stephen Skinner of Shelburne, NS, to have all English funds; sister Catherine Skinner; Catherine, widow of late brother John Skinner. Execs: friends Peter Mackie Sr. and William Tyrrell of NY. Wit: William Harding, British Consul, and Thomas Kenyon, British merchant. AWW 19 Jan. 1808 to James Halford. (PROB11/1473).

Skinner, Stephen of Shelburne, NS. Will 11 Apr. 1807. Leg: daughter Catherine Skinner; the daughter of William Terril of NY, merchant; Catherine Skinner, widow of testator's son John Skinner. Execs: Peter Mackie of NYC and said Catherine Skinner, widow. Wit: Anne Maria Gracie, Thomas B. Rowland and Thomas Crowell. AWW 29 Jan. 1810 to George Leckie, attorney for Catherine Skinner in NS. (PROB11/1507).

Skinner, Thomas of London, shoemaker, who died in MD. Will 14 Nov. 1695 pr. 12 Dec. 1706 by brother John Skinner. (PROB11/491). AWP.

Skottowe. *See* **Scottow.**

Slater, James of Red River Settlement, Rupertsland, Hudson's Bay. Will pr. 28 Oct. 1857. (PROB11/2259).

Slater, John of Annapolis Royal Garrison, NS, gent. 8 Nov. 1742. (PROB11/722).

Slater *alias* Mayo, Mary, widow of Col. Henry Slater of NY. Will 14 Sep. 1704 AWW 13 Mar. 1705 to Charles Lodwick, attorney for Mary Leaver in NY. (PROB11/481). NGSQ 64/48.

Slaughter, William of St. John's, NL, boat keeper. Will pr. 1 Dec. 1736. (PROB11/680).

Sloggett, Henry of Plymouth Dock, gent., whose daughter Frances was wife of John Bernard Houseal of Prince William parish, SC. Will pr. 20 Sep. 1804. (PROB11/1414). NGSQ 72/293.

Slone, James of London, merchant, who died in Boston, MA. Will 4 Mar. 1735 pr. 3 Aug. 1737. (PROB11/690). AWP.

Smart, John of Rotherhithe, Sy., surgeon, who died in MD. Will 24 May 1712 pr 21 Jun. 1720 by relict Ann Smart. (PROB11/474). AWP.

Smile, John of HMS *Greyhound* who died in NY. Will 16 Aug. 1722 pr. 11 Dec. 1724 by Alexander Bibb. (PROB11/601). AWP.

Smith, Alexander of Wapping, Mddx., mariner of HMS *Suffolk* who died in VA on the *Richard & Mary*. Will 27 Nov. 1689. Leg: wife Anne Smith who is to be exex. Wit: Thomas Markes and Fra. Soaker. AWW 30 Jun. 1697 to cr. Stephen Lade. (Guildhall: Ms 9171/48/398).

Smith, Barlow. *See* **Smith, William.**

Smith, Benjamin of Charleston, SC. AWW 3 Jun. 1791 to John Simpson. (PROB11/1206).

Small, Edith of London District, [ON]. Will pr. 28 May 1853. PROB11/2173).

Smith, Edward of St. John the Baptist, London, but late of HM Artillery in NY, bachelor. Will 22 Oct. 1754 pr. 18 Jul. 1758 by uncle James Hannam of St. John the Baptist, smith. (PROB11/839). AWP.

Smith, Elizabeth of Wethersfield, CT, widow. Will pr. 14 Mar. 1786 by brother John Scott. (PROB11/1140).

Smith, George of VA who died in St. George Martyr, Mddx.. Will 7 Oct. 1728 pr. 28 Jan. 1729 by Sarah & Richard Tayler. (PROB11/627). AWP.

Smith, George of Wapping, Mddx., mariner of transport ship *Hercules* who died in NY, bachelor. Will 26 Apr. 1761 pr. 13 Apr. 1763 by Bearend Ehlers. (PROB11/887). AWP.

Small, George of Andering, NL, boat keeper. Will pr. 23 Feb. 1811. (PROB11/1519).

Smith, George Clement Fearn of Philadelphia, engraver. AWW 24 Dec. 1844 to relict Harriot Elizabeth Lake. (PROB11/2009).

Smith, George Hamilton, of St. John, NB, Officer in H.M. Customs. Will pr. 8 Apr. 1846. (PROB11/2035).

Smyth, George Stracey, Lieut. Governor of NB and Maj. General of Fredericton, York Co. Will pr. 24 Jul. 1823. (PROB11/1673).

Smith *alias* **Sewell, Henrietta** of QC City, widow. Will pr. 29 Oct. 1849. (PROB11/2102).

Smith, James of Burlington, NJ, late Secretary of NJ. Will 17 Mar. 1721 pr. 22 Apr. 1736 by Sir Thomas Mackworth. (PROB11/657). AWP.

Smith, James of PE, merchant. Will pr. 23 Sep. 1822. (PROB11/1661).

Smith, Janet of QC, widow. Will pr. 11 Jan. 1821. (PROB11/1638).

Smith, Jehosaphat, citizen and ironmonger of London who died in Boston, MA. Will 23 Jul. 1677 pr. 29 Jul. 1678 by brother Jacob Smith. (PROB11/357). AWP.

Smith, John of Hartford, CT, merchant, late in Cork, Ireland. Will 18 Nov. 1731 pr. 17 Jan. 1732 by David Williams. (PROB11/649). AWP.

Smith, John of VA, mariner of HM schooner *Sultana*. Will pr. 31 Dec. 1772. (PROB11/983).

Smith, John of Niagara Garrison, ON. Will pr. Will pr. 3 Nov. 1783. (PROB11/1110).

Smith, John Edward *alias* **Patrick** of South Hampton, Suffolk Co., NY. Will pr. 1 Oct. 1855 by James Harlow Payne and brother James Patrick. (PROB11/2221).

Smith, Joseph of NYC, merchant. Will 7 May 1792. Leg: wife Dorothy Smith and daughter Elizabeth Smith; Martha, daughter of Joseph and Mary Roberts of Harlow, Essex. Execs: William Kemson and Frederick Rhinelander, merchants, and Robert Carter, all of NY, cabinet maker. Wit: Daniel Parcutt, Francis Child Jr. and Francis Child. AWW 17 Sep. 1795 to Keene Stables. (PROB11/1266).

Smith, Oliver of Stepney, Mddx., mariner, who died in VA on the *Susanna*. Will 26 Nov. 1680 pr. 4 Oct 1686 by relict Mary Smith. (PROB11/385).

Smyth, Rev. Peter of Brentford Butts, Mddx., chaplain of HMS *Tibury* who died in America, widower. Will 19 May 1749 pr. 8 Dec. 1757 by Rev. William Chilcott of New Brentford. (PROB11/834). AWP.

Smith, Peter of Halifax, NS, merchant. Will pr. 19 Jul. 1816. (PROB11/1582).

Smith, Richard of Stepney, Mddx., mariner of the *Duke of York* who died in VA. Will 17 Feb. 1670 pr. 9 Jun 1680 by Elizabeth Davis. (PROB11/363). AWP.

Smith, Robert of Savannah, GA. Will pr. 9 Apr. 1778 by brother Thomas Smith. (PROB11/1041).

Smith, Rt. Rev. Robert, Bishop of SC. AWW 28 Feb. 1842 to Edward Western. (PROB11/1958).

Smith, Samuel of London, haberdasher, whose brother Daniel Smith was resident in Charlestown, MA. Will 24 Mar. 1690 pr. 17 Nov. 1705 by relict Dorothy Smith. (PROB11/485). NGSQ 63/199.

Smith, Susanna of QC, widow. Will pr. 12 Oct. 1855. (PROB11/2112).

Smith, Thomas of PA, midshipman of HMS *Cumberland.* Will 29 May 1757 pr. 6 Jun. 1763 by Samuel Cherry. (PROB11/889). AWP.

Smith, Thomas of QC, soldier in 68th or Durham Regiment of Light Infantry. Will pr. 3 Mar. 1825. (PROB11/1607).

Smith, Hon. William of NYC. Will 7 Dec. 1796. Leg: lands in Moone Town left by John Plenderleath, married to testator's daughter Janet, when he sailed away in 1776; wife Janet Smith; other children. Wit: Thomas Smith, Robert Whyte and James Smith. Pr. 15 Feb. 1796 by Janet Plenderleath with similar powers to the relict Janet Smith; children William, Mary, and Harriet Smith.(PROB11/1271).

Smith, William of QC City. Will pr. 8 Jul. 1848. (PROB11/2078).

Smith, William of H.M. Ordnance of St. John, NB, civil engineer. Will pr. 29 Apr. 1854. (PROB11/2190).

Smith, William *alias* **Barlow** of British Hollow near Potosi, WI, brewer. AWW 12 Dec. 1856 to Edwin Chadwick. (PROB11/2243).

Smithett, Robert of Bermondsey, Sy., mariner of HMS *Lumley Castle* who died in Boston, MA. Will 19 Jan. 1693 pr. 4 Oct 1695 by relict Proteza Smithett. (PROB11/427). AWP.

Snell, Catherine of St. James Goose Creek, SC, spinster. Will 19 Sep 1741 AWW 5 Dec. 1743 to James Crokatt, attorney for Rev. Timothy Millechamp and Hugh Grange in SC. (PROB11/730). AWP.

Snelling, William Handfield of Halifax, NS, Deputy Commissary-General of H.M. Forces. Will pr. 13 Aug. 1838. (PROB11/1900).

Snook, Morgan of Fortune Bay, NL. Letter dated 30 Mar. 1808 from him to Jonathan Hickman asking him to provide for Ann Snook after his death. Affidavit by George Read of Sturminster Newton, Dorset, testifying to handwriting of deceased. AWW 17 Mar. 1820 to Joseph Bird, attorney for sole exec. Jonathan Hickman at Grand Bank, Fortune Bay, NL. (PROB11/1627).

Solomon, Elias, of New England but late of Rotherhithe, Sy., mariner. Will 14 Sep. 1725 pr.28 Aug. 1732 by Sarah Pike, widow. (PROB11/653). AWP.

Soumaien, Simeon of Philadelphia, PA, Lieutenant of Capt. Horatio Gates' Independent Company who died in America. Will 28 May 1753 pr. 22 Dec. 1755 by relict Aleathea Soumaien. (PROB11/819). AWP.

Southcott, Leonard, Quartermaster of the *Loyal Rebecca* in York River, VA. Will 18 Dec. 1676 pr 21 Jun. 1677 by Thomas Short. (PROB11/354). AWP.

Southell, Seth of Albemarle Co., NC. Will 25 Jan. 1690 AWW 8 Feb. 1697 to pc William Bowtell. (PROB11/436). AWP.

Southwell, George. *See* **Steel.**

Southwick, Thomas of London, mariner who died in VA. Will 4 Feb. 1742 pr. 1 Dec. 1743 by Mary Hare of Clerkenwell, Mddx. (PROB11/730). AWP.

Spangle, Francis of Newcastle, VA, mariner of HM sloop *Snake.* Will pr. 9 Sep. 1779. (PROB11/1057).

Sparrow, Samuel of Charleston, SC. AWW 7 Jan.1804 to relict Sarah Acres. (PROB11/1404).

Spears, Ferguson of QC, Capt. in 24th Regiment of Foot. Will pr. 10 Dec. 1799. (PROB11/1334).

Speermaine, Launce of Stepney, Mddx., mariner of HMS *Royal William* who died in VA. Will 6 May 1697 pr. 24 Jun. 1700 by Elizabeth Speermaine. (PROB11/456). AWP.

Spelman, Thomas of VA, gent. AWW 24 Apr. 1627. (PROB11//151). ACE.GGE.

Spence, James of York Fort, Hudson's Bay. Will pr. 26 Nov. 1796. (PROB11/1282).

Spence, Patrick, formerly of Copely parish, Westmoreland Co., VA, late of Allington, Dorset. gent. Will 25 Mar. 1710 pr. 4 May 1710 by Daniel Gundry. (PROB11/515). NGSQ 62/209. AWP.

Spencer, Mottrom of Nomini, Westmoreland Co., VA. Will 24 Oct. 1691 AWW 15 May 1703 to brother Capt. William Spencer. (PROB11/471). AWP.

Spencer, Nicholas of Nominy, Westmoreland Co., VA. Will 25 Apr. 1688 AWW 15 Jan. 1700 to John Rust. (PROB11/454). AWP.

Spencer, Thomas, mariner of the *Isabella*, having lands in George Town, MD. Will 8 Oct. 1771 pr. 4 Feb. 1778 by sisters Elizabeth and Beata Spencer of Bideford, Devon. (PROB11/1039). NGSQ 63/136.

Spicer, Arthur of Sittenburne, Richmond Co., VA. Will 18 Sep. 1699 AWW to the mother Alice Spicer during the minority of the only son John Spicer. (1700). Will in TNA:C5/312/47. NGSQ 67/212

Spooner, John of Boston, MA, merchant. Will 11 Feb. 1761 AWW 22 Jun. 1764 to Sir William Baker, attorney for Thomas Green and son John Spooner in Boston. (PROB11/899). AWP.

Spooner, John of Boston, MA, merchant. Will 23 Jul. 1768 AWW 19 May 1769 to Abraham Dupuis, attorney for Andrew Oliver and Arnold Welles of Boston. (PROB11/948). AWP.

Spotswood, Alexander Esq. of Orange Co., VA, late Col. of American Regiment. Will 19 Apr. 1740 AWW 23 Feb. 1742 to Robert Cary, attorney for relict Butler Spotswood, Elliott Benger and Robert Rose in VA. (PROB11/716). AWP.

Springer, Benjamin of St. Augustine, E. FL., planter, but late of London. Will 28 Dec Nov. 1786. Leg: wife Mary Springer; daughter Mary wife of Rev. Mr. Jean to have a shilling; son Charles Springer to have a shilling "as they all appear independent of me." Exec: Richard Dabbs. Wit: John Hasler, Thomas Wilkin and Thomas Debbridge. Pr. 2 Dec. 1786 by Richard Dabbs. (PROB11/1148).

Sproule, George of Fredericton, NB. Will pr. 10 Jun. 1818. (PROB11/1605).

Sprowle, Andrew of Gosport, Norfolk, Co., VA. Will pr. 14 Mar. 1782 by George Logan, George Surdy and John Hyndman. (PROB11/1089). ALC.

Spurzheim, Gaspar of Boston, doctor of physic. AWW 25 Feb. 1835 to Mathias Hermesdorf. (PROB11/1835).

Squire, Daniel of NYC. AWW 14 Dec. 1786 to George Moor. (PROB11/1148).

Stacey, Mary of Waltham Holy Cross, Essex, widow of Henry Stacey, merchant of London. Will 26 May 1686. Leg: her four children [unnamed] to have lands in NJ inherited under her husband's will. Execs: son Samuel Stacey and brother James Nevell, citizen and merchant tailor of London. Wit: Samuel Coddington, Margaret Nevell and Francis Warner. Pr. 28 Sep. 1686 by James Nevell. (Guildhall: Ms 9171/40/187).

Stacy, Samuel of HMS *Nightingale* who died in Annapolis, MD. Will 18 Aug. 1715, pr. 9 Mar. 1716 by father John Stacy. (PROB11/551). AWP.

Stanford, Joseph of Detroit, MI. AWW 14 Feb. 1851 to brother John Stanford. (PROB11/2128).

Staines, Rev. Robert John, clerk of Victoria, Vancouver Island, BC. Will pr. 25 Jul. 1855. (PROB11/2216).

Stanley, Hugh of MD. Will 30 Jul. 1667 AWW 8 Dec. 1671 to Elizabeth Stanley. (PROB11/337). AWP.

Stanser, Rt. Rev. Robert, rector of St. Paul's, Halifax, NS. Will pr. 17 Jun. 1829. (PROB11/1757).

Stanton, Jeremiah of Richmond Co., NY. Will 3 Oct. 1767 AWW 3 Jul. 1772 to Isaac Lascelles Winn, attorney for relict Louisa Teresia Stanton. (PROB11/979). AWP.

Stanton, John Jr. of Groton, CT, Capt. of First Regiment of Foot who died in Havana. Will 21 May 1762 AWW 29 Jan. 1765 to Phineas Lyman, attorney for execs. in CT. (PROB11/905). AWP.

Stanway, Henry of St. John, NB, Capt. in Royal Artillery. Will pr. 14 Nov. 1846. (PROB11/2045).

Staples, William of Greenbush, Rensselaer Co., NY, chairmaker. AWW 24 Jan. 1826 to son Thomas Staples. (PROB11/1707).

Stapylton, Francis Samuel of Habberdown, NY, Capt. in 9th Regiment of Foot. AWW 24 Nov. 1779 to sister Ann Bree. (PROB11/1058).

Starbuck, Samuel of Sherborne, Nantucket, MA, merchant. Will pr. 2 May 1805. (PROB11/1426).

Starke, Thomas of London, merchant, who left his estate in VA to his son John Starke. Will pr. 4 Mar. 1706 by relict Sarah and son John Starke. (PROB11/497). AWP. NGSQ 70/39.

St. Clair, Sir John of Elizabeth Town, NJ, Deputy Quartermaster-General to HM Forces in America. Will 26 Oct. 1767 AWW 15 Sep. 1769 to Richard Mowland, attorney for the relict Elizabeth, now wife of Dudley Templer, and Andrew Elliott, both resident in America. (PROB11/951). AWP.

Strachey, William of St. Augustine, London, merchant, whose daughter Arabella, wife of John Waters, planter, was in VA. Will 27 Oct. 1686 pr. 21 Mar 1687. (PROB11/386). AWP.

Stedman, Robert of SC, peruke maker and planter. AWW 16 Mar. 1769 to relict Sarah Stedman. (PROB11/953).

Stedman, Solomon of Boston, MA, mariner. AWW 1 Dec. 1697 to Henry Cole. (PROB11/442).

Steel, Allen if Boston, MA, mariner of HMS *Comet Bomb*. Will 7 May 1747 AWW 7 Dec. 1754 to Henry Sanders, attorney for relict Deborah Steel in Boston. (PROB11/812). AWP.

Steel *alias* Southwell, George of QC, gunner of 4th Battalion of Royal Artillery. Will pr. 13 Nov. 1824. (PROB11/1692).

Steel, John of St. Philip's, Charles Town, SC, vintner, who died in Plymouth, Devon. Will 3 Dec. 1742 pr. 5 Jun 1745 by relict Mary Steel. (PROB11/740). AWP.

Stegge, Thomas of Henrico Co., VA. Will pr. 15 May 1671. (PROB11/336). GGE.

Sterry, William of Bristol but late in Boston, MA, mariner. Will 30 Aug. 1684 AWW 26 Oct. 1685 to pc. Giles Merricke in Boston. (PROB11/384). AWP.

Stephens, Alexander of Frederick Co., VA, Lieut. in Royal Americans. Will 12 Jan. 1768 AWW 8 Jan. 1770 to John Russell, attorney for brother John Stephens in VA. (PROB11/958). AWP.

Stevens, Charles of 100 Cumberland Street, Brooklyn, NY, gent. Will pr. 23 Nov. 1857 by sister Eliza Ann and Angelina Margaret Stevens. (PROB11/2261).

Stephens, Francis of Barking, Essex, who had estate in Truro, Gloucester Co., NY. Will pr. 24 Jan. 1792 by Richard Forman of the Tower, London, Joseph Dillon on the ship *Sandwich Packet* and Rev. Robert Dillon of Penryn, Corn.. (PROB11/1213).

Stevens, George of NL. Will pr. 2 Jan. 1767. (PROB11/925).

Stevens, James of Chipppenham, Wilts., who died in NY, Capt. in Royal Regiment of Artillery. Will 30 Oct. 1767 AWW 3 May 1769 to mother Ann Stevens, widow. (PROB11/948). AWP.

Stevens, Robert of St. James Goose Creek, SC. Will 8 Sep. 1720 pr 7 Nov. 1722 by John Vicaridge. (PROB11/588). AWP. NGSQ 63/195.

Stevens, William of Stepney, Mddx., joiner, bound to Thomas Odell, a VA planter embarked for a voyage overseas. Leg: if both the testator and Odell should die, the testator's wife Izett Stevens should receive £200 and the residue of the estate; cousins John, William and Ruth Stevens. Wit: John Rose, Mary Marsden and John Marsden. Pr. 4 Sep. 1691 by Thomas Odell. (Guildhall: Ms 9171/43/266).

Stevens, William of Hampton, VA. Will pr. 12 Mar. 1803. (PROB11/1389).

Stevenson, Allen of City of Chester, merchant about to make a voyage to America with friend Andrew Symme. Will 8 Mar. 1699 pr. 3 Jan. 1700 by Robert Sparke. (PROB11/454). AWP.

Stevenson, Cornelius of NYC, merchant. AWW 3 Mar. 1806 to Effingham Lawrence. (PROB11/1440).

Stephenson, Enoch of NYC. Will 3 Feb. 1736 AWW 1 Dec. 1753 to Robert Lindsay, attorney for relict Catherine Stephenson and brother Pennington Stephenson, and Peter Valert and Joseph Robinson of NY. (PROB11/1805). AWP.

Stevenson, James of Salem, MA, gent. Will pr. 19 Nov. 1728 by cr. Jocelyn Dansey. (PROB11/626).

Stewart, Alexander of Maj. Gen. James Oglethorpe's Regt. who died in Frederica, GA. Will 7 Nov. 1747 pr. 5 May 1748 by brother James Stewart. (PROB11/761). AWP.

Stuart, Charles, President of Mobile, W. FL. Will pr. by Elizabeth Hatfield, widow, 5 Sep. 1781. (PROB11/1082).

Stewart, Charles of Charlotte Town, PE. Will pr. 26 Jan. 1819. (PROB11/1612).

Stewart, Charles James, Bishop of QC. Will pr. 25 Jul. 1837. (PROB11/1882).

Stewart, George Esq. of Boston, MA, Capt. of a Company who died in West Indies. Will 20 Sep. 1740 AWW 27 Aug. 1744 to Christopher Kilby, attorney for Benjamin Faneuil. (PROB11/745). AWP.

Steuart, James of Woolwich, Kent, shipwright who died in Charles Town, SC. Will 6 Jul. 1749 pr. 17 Oct. 1755 by Mungo Murray Jr. of Limehouse, Mddx., gent. (PROB11/818). AWP.

Stewart, James of Oxford, Warren Co., NJ, Capt. of N.J. Volunteers. AWW 27 Apr. 1820 to James Tidbury. (PROB11/1628).

Stewart, James, Judge of Supreme Court of NS. Will pr. 30 Jun. 1830. (PROB11/1773).

Stewart, James of Halifax, NS, gent. 30 Aug. 1833. (PROB11/1820).

Stuart, John of Pensacola, W. FL. Will pr. 10 Jul. 1783 by relict Sarah Stuart. (PROB11/1106).

Stewart, John of Mount Stewart, PE. Will pr. 25 Sep. 1840. (PROB11/1934).

Stuart, John, factor of Hudson's Bay Co. for Indian Territories. Will pr. 21 Aug. 1851. (PROB11/2138).

Stewart, Peter of Stewart Lodge, Canton, Greene Co., NY. AWW 25 Aug. 1836 to Robert Samuel Palmer. (PROB11/1866).

Stuart, Ruth of Boston, MA, widow. Will 5 Mar. 1752 pr. 14 Jul. 1752 by son Sir John Stuart. (PROB11/796). AWP.

Stuart, William, resident of Boston, MA, mariner. Will 14 Oct 1724 AWW 3 Feb. 1729 to John Dod, attorney for Thomas Steel Esq. of Boston. (PROB11/628). AWP.

Stewart, William of QC, Surgeon to H.M. Forces. Will pr. 23 Feb. 1830. (PROB11/1767).

Stockdale *alias* **Hawkes, Priscilla**, formerly of Pembroke, Bermuda, and late of Buffalo, NY. Will 31 Aug. 1827. Leg: sisters Frances Tucker and Sarah Beach; nieces Elizabeth Hawkes Tucker and George Germain Beach. Affidavit by Sarah Beach of Pembroke that when she was in Buffalo she saw her sister write her will in pencil. Affidavit by John Roxburgh of St. George, Bermuda, that when the testatrix was in Bermuda she was also called Priscilla Hawkes. AWW 3 Sep. 1855 to Robert Tucker, attorney for the sister Sarah Beach. (PROB11/2219).

Stocker, Joseph of Wiveliscombe, Som., mercer, whose son Ephraim Stocker embarked for VA in about 1688 but was never again heard of. Will 5 Mar 1679 pr. 28 May 1679 by relict Mary Stocker. (PROB11/359). AWP. NGSQ 67/212.

Stocking, Francis of Hilborough, Norf., who inherited a plantation in Philadelphia by the will of his son Thomas Stocking. Will 27 Jan. 1730 pr. 7 Feb. 1730 by nephew John Stocking. (PROB11/636). AWP.

Stolpys, John of Wapping, Mddx., mariner who died in VA. Will 20 Nov. 1690 pr 18 Apr 1692 by Albert Albertson. (PROB11/409). AWP.

Stone, James of Philadelphia, surgeon's mate in 63rd Regiment of Foot. Will dated 5 Nov. 1758 witnessed by Philip Cookworthy, Benjamin Cookworthy and Rachell Cookworthy leaving bequests to his guardian Mr. Evan Morgan of Philadelphia, his sister Sarah Sallows of Philadelphia, and his cousin Mrs. Mary Emerson, peruke maker near Wapping, London. William and Mary Penny, children of William Penny of Newton Abbot, Devon, are to be executors. Pr. by William Penny 7 Jan. 1764. (PROB11/895).

Stone, Margaret of St. Peter le Poor, London, widow, whose husband William Stone went to VA in about 1670. Nuncupative will 2 Nov. 1676 pr. 21 Nov. 1676 by brother-in-law Joseph Godwin. (PROB11/352). AWP.

Stone, William of Philadelphia. AWW 17 Jul. 1788 to William Vaughan. (PROB11/1168).

Story, Ralph of Wapping, Mddx., mariner, who died in VA. Will 14 Aug. 1663, pr. 1 Jun 1664 by relict Avis Story. (PROB11/314). AWP.

Stout, Richard of Sydney Island, Cape Breton, NS. Will pr. 31 Jul. 1821. (PROB11/1646).

Stratfold, Thomas formerly of Bierton, Bucks., yeoman, but late of VA. Will 26 Mar. 1701 pr. 7 May 1706 by Henry Ilmore. (PROB11/488).

Stott, Thomas of QC, formerly Paymaster of 4th Royal Veteran Battalion, now merchant of QC. Will pr. 7 May 1830. (PROB11/1771).

Strawbridge, William of Lower Providence Township, Montgomery Co., PA, gent. AWW 6 Dec. 1830 to Horatio G. Jones of Roxborough, PA. (PROB11/1779).

Street, John, Controller of Customs of NL. Will pr. 8 Jun. 1811. (PROB11/1523).

Street, William of Clifton, Niagara Falls, Lincoln Co., [ON], gent. Will pr. 16 Jul. 1835. (PROB11/1850).

Stringer, Samuel of Epsom, Sy., doctor of physick, whose son [unnamed] was in MD. Will undated pr. 26 Jul. 1738 by relict Louisa Stringer. (PROB11/690). AWP.

Stripling, John of St. John's, NL. Will pr. 13 Jan. 1781. (PROB11/1073).

Strong, Thomas J. of Baldwin Co., AL. AWW 21 Jan. 1826 to pc James Jones. (PROB11/1707).

Strudwick, Martha of Orange Co., NC, widow. AWW 20 Sep. 1820 to Peter Browne. (PROB11/1634).

Strudwick, Samuel of New Hanover Co., NC. Will pr. 29 Mar. 1797 by relict Martha Strudwick. (PROB11/1288). NGSQ 63/136.

Struthers, William Esq., of Chatham Co., GA, planter, but late of Waltham Abbey, Essex. Leg: former partner John Miller of East Hackney Road, Mddx; Mrs. Agnes Douglas of Belfast, Ireland, relict of William Douglas; partner James McGillivray of GA, planter. Wit: Thomas Sanders of Cheshunt, Herts; Thomas Coleman of Waltham Abbey and Peter Maltby of Fishmongers' Hall, London. Pr. 22 Jun. 1803 by John Miller. (PROB11/1395).

Stuart. *See* **Stewart.**

Sturdy, William of Stafford Co., VA, bachelor. AWW 12 May 1715 to Robert Sturdy. (PROB11/546). VGE.

Suggitt, John, formerly of Newcastle-upon-Tyne, master and mariner, late of Northampton Co., VA. Will 16 Mar. 1763 AWW 9 Oct. 1771 to Jane Selby, widow, mother of relict Jane Suggitt. (PROB11/972). AWP.

Sullivan, Bartholomew of Halifax, NS, merchant. Will pr. 28 Aug. 1813. (PROB11/1547).

Sutherland, Charles, Lieut. Col. in Army, Major in NL Regiment of Fencible Infantry of QC. Will pr. 23 Oct. 1812. (PROB11/1538).

Sutherland, George of Red River Settlement, Hudson's Bay. Will pr. 8 Nov. 1852. (PROB11/2159).

Sutherland, James of York Factory, Hudson's Bay. Will pr. 10 May 1808. (PROB11/1480).

Swan, John of Wapping, Mddx., mariner who died at sea near New England. Will 13 Dec. 1695 pr. 8 Aug. 1701 by Richard and Margaret Heading. (PROB11/461). AWP.

Sway, Henry, of NY, mariner serving in the *Star Bomb*. Will dated Port Royal, Jamaica, 5 Dec. 1711 appointing Morgan Williams of the same ship as sole executor and legatee. Wit: Charles Trewbody, John Kirkdell and Henry Antrobus Jr. Pr. 20 Nov. 1712 by Morgan Williams. (PROB11/529). AWP.

Sweet, John, of Trinity, NL. Will pr. 18 Jul. 1792. (PROB11/1221).

Sweet, Mary, of Trinity, NL. Will pr. 18 Jul. 1792. (PROB11/1221).

Sweetapple, Timothy of Battle Harbour, Labrador. Will pr. 13 Jan. 1847. (PROB11/2049).

Sweetland, Henry of Ferryland, NL, merchant. Will pr. 29 Feb. 1792. (PROB11/1215).

Swett, Joseph of Boston, MA, cooper of HMS *Defiant*. Will 20 Aug. 1689 pr. 25 Jan. 1696 by John Gill. (PROB11/433). AWP.

Swift, James of St. Mary Abchurch, London, who died in Hackney, Mddx., trader to New England. (PROB11/376).

Tale, Moncrief of Fort York, Hudson's Bay, servant of Co. Will pr. 21 Mar. 1782. (PROB11/1089).

Tarry, Samuel of Raleigh, Amelia Co., VA. Will 10 Jun. 1757 AWW 22 Dec. 1768 to John Tarry of Petersburgh, VA, attorney for cr. Peter Johnston and Thomas Yuille in VA. (PROB11/944). AWP.

Tarte, Thomas of Lake Huron, [ON], Assistant Surgeon to Royal Navy. Will pr. 2 Jul. 1819. (PROB11/1618).

Tasker, Hon. Benjamin of Annapolis, MD. Will 22 Oct. 1764 pr. 2 Jun. 1769. (PROB11/944). AWP.

Tattnall, Edward Fenwick of Chatham Co., GA. AWW 13 Aug. 1846 to brother Joseph Tattnall. (PROB11/2041).

Tavernor, Robert of London, merchant, who died in VA having goods in MD. Will 18 Oct. 1675 pr. 31 Jan. 1677 by Bridget Fowlkes of Barbican, London. (PROB11/353). AWP.

Tawse, Thomas of Savannah, GA, late Lieut. of 71st Regiment of Foot. AWW 27 Jul. 1781 to Gavin Young. (PROB11/1080).

Taylor, Abraham Esq. of Philadelphia but late of Bath, Somerset. Will 8 May 1764 pr. 10 Mar. 1772 by son John Taylor. (PROB11/976). AWP.

Taylor, Bryan of St. Stephen, Coleman Street, London, merchant who died in MD, bachelor. Will 16 Jan. 1731 AWW 13 May 1737 to brother Freeman Taylor. (PROB11/583). AWP.

Taylor, Charlotte Ann of Detroit Wayne, MI. Will pr. 7 Jul. 1840. (PROB11/1931).

Taylor, Eleazer of Parrsborough, King's Co. near River Macau, NS. Will pr. 24 Apr. 1803. (PROB11/1391).

Taylor, Freeman of Mincing Lane, London, whose late nephew Everard Taylor resided at Leonard's Creek, Patuxent River, MD. Will 1 Jan. 1765. Wit: Martin Smith and B. Daniel. Pr. 17 Jun 1766 by Wakelin Welch. (PROB11/920).

Taylor, George of QC, Lieut. Col. on half pay, aide de camp to Capt. Gen. the Earl of Dalhousie. Will pr. 3 Feb. 1827. (PROB11/1722).

Taylor, Humphrey of PA but late of Stepney, Mddx., who died in NY, widower. Will 29 Nov. 1710 pr. 16 Oct. 1716 by mother Elizabeth Taylor, widow. (PROB11/554). AWP.

Taylor, John, formerly of Whitehaven, Cumberland, but late of Savannah, GA., shipwright. Will 19 Feb. 1765 pr. 2 Oct. 1772 by brother William Taylor. (PROB11/982). AWP.

Taylor, John of QC City, Deputy Secretary of Lower Canada. Will pr. 22 Jun. 1820. (PROB11/1631).

Taylor, Thomas, seaman and planter of NL but late of Litchett Minster, Dorset. Will 23 Mar. 1695. Leg: wife Elizabeth Taylor; daughter Elizabeth Taylor; sons John and Thomas Taylor who are to have plantation in NL. Overseers for NL: Henry Corban and William Green, planters at Perlican, NL. Wit: Mary Rogers, Elizabeth Grant and John Moores. Pr. 21 Feb. 1698 by relict Elizabeth Taylor. (PROB11/444).

Taylor, Thomas of Gore, [ON]. Will pr. 22 Jan. 1840. (PROB11/1922).

Taylor, William of Hackney, Mddx., citizen & haberdasher of London, whose brother Robert Taylor in the Somer Islands had a son Samuel Taylor in New England. Will pr. 19 Jul. 1651 by son Samuel Taylor. (PROB11/217). AWP. Further grant in 1674.

Taylor, William of Perth Amboy, NJ. AWW 12 Jul. 1808 to Daniel Coxe. (PROB11/1483).

Taylor, William of Shelburne, NS. Will pr. 25 Jun. 1811. (PROB11/1523).

Teere,Thomas of St. Botolph Aldgate, London, citizen and blacksmith whose son Thomas Teere was resident in New England. Will 28 Nov. 1681 pr. 31 May 1682 by relict Elizabeth Teere. (Guildhall: Ms 9052/23).

Temple, Sir John of NY. AWW 4 Feb. 1799 to Charles Rivington Broughton. (PROB11/1319).

Temple, Joseph of King William Co., VA. Will 20 Dec. 1744 AWW 28 Jan. 1762 to son William Temple. (PROB11/872). AWP.

Temple, William, late of King William Co., VA, but late resident in Bristol. Will 15 Mar. 1763 pr. 2 May 1767 by John Snow of Bristol, merchant. (PROB11/929). AWP.

Tenant, James of Princess Ann Co., VA, clerk. Will 23 Dec. 1726 AWW 1 Mar. 1727 to Thomas Sandford, attorney for relict Elizabeth, now wife of Lewis Conner in VA.. (PROB11/634). AWP.

Tennant, Robert of York Fort, Hudson's Bay. Will pr. 8 Nov. 1794. (PROB11/1252).

Terrell, Robert of Reading, Berks, clothier, (whose sons Richmond and William emigrated to New Kent Co., VA). Original will 8 Jun. 1643. Leg: his six children Robert, Richmond, William, Marie, Margaret and John Terrell; wife Janet Terrell. Overseers: brother-in-law Richard Stampe and friend Thomas Baldwin. Execs: wife Janet and son John Terrell. Wit: Richard Stampe, Richard Hunt, Thomas Warner and Edward Wilmer, Jr. Pr. 27 Sep. 1643 by named execs. (PROB10/639/350).

Terrell, Robert of London, merchant.Will 26 Oct 1677. Leg: cousin William Terrell, son of brother William Terrell; cousins Mary and John Alpen; brother Richmond Terrell; sister Mary Mew. Exec. Robert Allen who is to settle accounts in VA with Mr. Johnson and others. Wit: Anthony Horsmonden, Richard Wicking, John Wicking and Elizabeth Wicking. Will pr. 23 Nov. 1677 by cousin Robert Alpen, citizen and cook of London. (PROB11/355). AWP.

Terrington, John, Civil Officer of HM Ordnance of St. John's, NL. Will pr. 28 Nov. 1832. (PROB11/1808).

Teulon, Peter Hensman of Montreal. Will pr. 30 May 1839. (PROB11/1911).

Tew, Mark McLeod of Halifax, NS, Major in 34th Regiment of Foot. Will pr. 20 Dec. 1837. (PROB11/1888).

Tew, Richard of Newport, RI, yeoman. Will pr. 27 Mar. 1674 by brother John Tew. (PROB11/344).

Thatcher, Barthomew of Kingwood, Hunterdon Co., NJ. AWW 23 May 1818 to James Tidbury. (PROB11/1604).

Thomas, James of Philadelphia who died in London. Will 22 Jul. 1706 AWW 11 Feb. 1712 to John Askew. (PROB11/525).

Thomas, John of Stepney, Mddx., sailor. Will written at Perlican, NL. Leg: William Startout; Richard Burd; sons Thomas and Mathew Thomas. Exec: William Thomas. Wit: Thomas Smith, Robert Chester and William Starbuck. Pr. 29 Jan. 1610 by relict Jane Thomas. (Guildhall: Ms 9171/21/221v).

Thomas, John of Montreal. Will pr. 3 Feb. 1823. (PROB11/1667).

Thomas, Nathaniel of Windsor, NS. Will pr. 6 Dec. 1823. (PROB11/1679).

Thomas, Nathaniel Ray of Windsor, Hampshire Co., NS. Will pr. 5 Oct. 1789. (PROB11/1184).

Thomas, William of Llantwit Major, Glamorgan. Will 15 Jan. 1647. Leg: lands and goods in West Indies and America worth £500 to wife (unnamed) or the child she may be carrying; brothers Samuel and Alexander Thomas; testator's wife's children by her first husband. Wit: John Lloyd, William Tobee and Jane Sander. Pr. 6 Jun. 1649 by brother Alexander Thomas. (PROB11/209). AWP.

Thomas, William of Albany Factory, Hudson's Bay. Will 10 Jan. 1817. Leg: reputed wife Catherine Thomas; reputed sons Richard and Charles Thomas; reputed daughters Elenor, Charlotte, Matilda and Catherine Thomas; nephew William Thomas, son of brother Frederick Thomas of London. Execs: Alexander Lean of Fenchurch Street, London, and John Bowley of Moose Factory, Hudson's Bay. Pr. 27 Nov. 1819 by Joseph Bowley. (PROB11/1622).

Thomlinson. *See* **Tomlinson**

Thompson, Andrew, son of Thomas Thompson of Auchterhouse near Dundee, Scotland, late of St. Botolph Aldgate, London, bound for VA on the ship *Jacob*, mariner. Will 2 Feb. 1624. Leg: brother Walter Thompson; sisters Christian, Mary, Margaret and Elizabeth Thompson; friend John Cannady of East Smithfield, London, gun maker. Wit: Robert Chapman, John Varley and Henry Rouse. Pr. 1 Apr. 1725 by John Kannadie. (Guildhall: Ms 9051/6/143).

Thompson, Anna of Charleston, SC, widow. Will pr. 24 Aug. 1849 by children Susan Eliza Gaillard, widow, Sarah Maria Kiddell, widow, and Robert Thompson. (PROB11/2098).

Thompson, Cornelius of NYC, seaman of HMS *Dolphin*. Will dated 13 May 1772 witnessed by David Dalzell, John Colpoys and Joseph Milburn. Pr. 8 Jul. 1775 by surviving executor John Healy of Bury in Cork, Ireland, the other executor Philip Nicholson of Whitehaven, Cumberland, having died. (PROB11/1010).

Thomson, David of Carolina, merchant, late in London but who died in York Town, VA. Will 26 Jun. 1746 pr. 29 Dec. 1749 by cousin Joseph Davidson of London, bookseller. (PROB11/775). AWP.

Thompson, Isaac of New London, CT, late Lieut. of First CT Regiment of Foot who died in Havana. Will 6 Jun. 1761 AWW 29 Jan. 1765 to Phineas Lyman, attorney for brother Samuel Thompson in New London. (PROB11/905). AWP.

Tompson, Jacob of Bristol, mariner of ship *Sarah*. Nuncupative will dated VA Sep. or Oct. 1698 AWW 18 Aug. 1699 to relict Susanna Tompson. (PROB11/452). AWP.

Thomson, James of St. Botolph Aldgate, London, mariner of HMS *Rose* who died in Carolina, bachelor. Will 19 Nov. 1733 pr. 18 Dec. 1738 by William Livingston. (PROB11/693). AWP.

Thompson, John of Surry Co., James River, VA, at present in London, merchant. Will pr. 16 Mar. 1699 by Thomas Haistwell. (PROB11/450). VGE.

Thompson, John of Bermondsey, Sy., distiller, whose cousin Alexander Thompson was a distiller in RI. Will 6 Apr. 1740 pr. 2 May 1740 by relict Jane Thompson. (PROB11/702). AWP.

Thomson, John of Seigniory of Rigaud St. Magdeleine, [QC]. Will pr. 18 Apr. 1833. (PROB11/1815).

Thompson, Joseph of Natchez, W. FL. Will pr. 17 Dec. 1781. (PROB11/1085).

Thomson, Samuel of Shadwell, Mddx., mariner who died in VA. Will 3 Dec. 1691 pr. 6 Jun. 1694 by Thomas Anderson. (PROB11/421). AWP.

Thomson, Mrs. Selina Harriett Cotton of Sorel, [QC]. Will pr. 17 Sep. 1844. (PROB11/2005).

Thomson, Thomas of Scotland bound for MD. Will 10 Apr. 1711 pr. 23 Jun. 1736 by brother James Thomson in Scotland. (PROB11/677). AWP.

Thompson, William of St. Katherine Creechurch, citizen and haberdasher of London. Will 22 Apr. 1639. Leg: wife Johane Thompson who is to be exex; his children Samuel, Peter, John and Mary Thompson who are to have his lands and adventures in VA and St. Christopher's and lands in Thorpe Market, Roughton and Gunton, Norfolk; his son Richard Thompson who has already received his inheritance; his daughter Mary, wife of Casper Clayton; the poor of Thorpe Market, Norfolk, and St. Katherine Creechurch; his brothers John Thompson at Colby, Norfolk, and Rowland Thompson; sister Elizabeth Thompson; cousin Martha Thompson. Overseers Thomas Free of Mark Lane, London, George Dann and Richard Glover, apothecary. Wit: William and John Frithe, John Brand, John Bassano and John Hare. Codicil of 23 Aug. 1639. Pr. 28 Oct. 1643 by relict Johane Thompson. (Guildhall: Ms 9171/29/149).

Thompson, William of Upminster, Essex, innholder but late sailmaker, whose exec. Basil Cowper was resident in GA. Will pr. 7 Jan. 1774. (PROB11/994).

Thompson, Zacharias of QC City. Will pr. 9 Dec. 1780. (PROB11/1072).

T'Hooft, Thomas Cunningham of Middleburgh, [NY]. Will pr. 6 Jun. 1749. (PROB11/770).

Thorn, James Kerslake of London District, [ON], gent. Will pr. 5 Feb. 1848. (PROB11/2070).

Thorn, Richard of London Town, [ON], gent. Will pr. 3 Nov. 1849. (PROB11/2103).

Thorpe, Henry, late of Liverpool, Lancs., but late of Knowsley, Lancs., who had lands and houses in PA. Will 19 Jun. 1710 pr. 18 Jan. 1711 by solemn declaration of brother Thomas Thorpe. (PROB11/519). AWP. Further grant in 1733.

Thorpe, Thomas of Stepney, Mddx., mariner who died in VA. Will 9 Mar. 1722 pr. 13 Feb. 1724 by relict Jane Thorpe. (PROB11/596). AWP.

Throckmorton, Raphael of St. Gregory, London, whose wife's brother William Walthall was living in VA. Will 10 Sep. 1669 pr. 3 May 1670 by cousin Edward Throckmorton. (PROB11/332). AWP.

Throckmorton, Robert of Little Paxton, Hunts., who had plantations in VA. Will 1 Mar. 1699 pr. 3 May 1699 by father-in-law Thomas Bromsall and uncle Edward Mason. (PROB11/450). AWP.

Thrum, Henry of NS, marine in Gen. Cornwallis Regiment. Will pr. 1 Dec 1753. (PROB11/805).

Thurman, Susanna of NYC, widow of Francis Thurman of NYC, merchant. Will 23 Aug. 1758 pr. 26 Jan. 1760 by brother-in-law John Thurman. (PROB11/852). AWP.

Thurmur, John, living in Calvert Co., MD. Will 4 Apr. 1668 AWW 10 Feb. 1669 to son Thomas Elwes. (PROB11/329). AWP.

Tidy, Francis Skelly of Montreal, Col. of 24ᵗʰ Regiment of Foot. Will pr. 29 Jun. 1836. (PROB11/1863

Tiffin, Simon of Orleans Island, QC. Will pr. Will pr. 20 Nov. 1760. (PROB11/861).

Tilden, Joseph of St. Stephen Walbrook, London, citizen and girdler. Will 1 Feb. 1643. Leg: brother Freegift Tilden; two daus. of testator's brother [Nathaniel] Tilden now married and in New England; niece Sarah Smith. Exec: nephew Joseph Tilden. Wit: Henry Randall, Francis Nelmes and Val. Crome. AWW 18 Mar. 1643 to brother Hopestill Tilden during the absence overseas of the nephew Joseph Tilden. (PROB11/191). AWP.

Tilly, George of VA. Will pr. 22 Jan. 1743. (PROB11/723).

Tilsed, William of Lamaline, NL, seaman. Will pr. 28 Apr. 1820. (PROB11/1628).

Tilson, John of Boston, MA, chief mate of the *Blackey* who died while bound from St. Kitts to London. Will 28 Jul. 1757 pr. 2 Aug. 1757 by Richard Comport of Milton next Gravesend, Kent, innholder. (PROB11/832). AWP.

Tilsted, John of Shoe Cove, Cape John, NL, planter, but late of Wimborne Minster, Dorset, gent. Will 28 Feb. 1831. Leg: grandson John Harris of Christchurch, Hants; granddaughter Eliza Harris; Caroline, daughter of George Lambert of Lougham, Hants. Execs: John Harris, John Smith Miller and John Vey of Wimborne. Wit: Henry Brodribb, Samuel C. Scott and John Thorn. Pr. 30 Apr. 1835 by grandson John Harris and John S. Miller. (PROB11/1846).

Timbrill, William of Barbados who had lands in Chester Town, MD. Will 25 Jul. 1743 AWW 10 Dec. 1762 to Joseph Price, husband of the testator's daughter Sarah. (PROB11/882). NGSQ 63/135.

Timson, William of Bruton parish, York Co., VA. Will 25 Apr. 1726 AWW 2 Jun. 1736 to Neil Buchanan, exec. of brother John Timson deceased. (PROB11/677). AWP.

Tobin, Hon. James of Halifax, NS, merchant. Will pr. 16 Jul. 1839. (PROB11/1914).

Tobin, Hon. Michael of Halifax, NS. Will pr. 6 Aug. 1844. (PROB11/2004).

Tobin, Nicholas, gunner of HMS *Pluto* now in St. John's Harbour, NL. Will pr. 19 Apr. 1804. (PROB11/1408).

Todd, Humphrey of Wapping, Mddx, mariner of HMS *Deptford* who died on HMS *Adventure* in Boston, MA. Will 11 Feb. 1709 pr. 4 Feb. 1714 by John Slater. (PROB11/538). AWP.

Todd, Thomas Sr. of Baltimore. Will 22 Feb. 1675 pr. 30 Mar. 1678 by son Thomas Todd. (PROB11/356). AWP.

Todd, William of Red River Settlement, Rupertsland, Hudson's Bay. Will pr. 8 Nov. 1852. (PROB11/2162).

Tolmie, Normand of NYC, mariner. Will 29 Oct. 1765 Leg: wife and exex. Phoebe Tolmie. Wit: Rudolphus Rittzamer, Robert R. Livingston Jr. and Michael Jeffrey. Pr. 1 Apr. 1788 by relict Phoebe Tolmie. (PROB11/1165).

Tolmie, Phebe of NYC, widow. AWW 16 Aug. 1796 to Samuel Douglas. (PROB11/1278).

Tomlins, Sarah of Philadelphia, spinster. Will pr. 26 Jul. 1856 by Jesse Brush. (PROB11/2236).

Tomlinson, Edward of Rotherhithe, Sy., mariner of merchant ship *Rappahannock Merchant* who died in VA, widower. Will 28 Oct. 1740 pr. 28 Jul. 1743 by daughter Ann Tomlinson. (PROB11/728). AWP.

Thomlinson, Robert of Boston, MA, merchant. Will 11 Apr. 1739 AWW 29 Jan. 1741 to brother Richard Thomlinson. (PROB11/707). AWP.

Tompkins, Russell, formerly HM Storekeeper of Jamaica, late on the *Ruby* of Philadelphia who died in PA. Will 17 Jul. 1749 pr.12 Jan. 1750 by brother John Tompkins. (PROB11/776). AWP.

Toms, William of Topsham, Devon, mariner who died in VA. Will 19 Aug. 1675 AWW 14 Jul 1680 to Elizabeth Evans. (PROB11/367). AWP.

Tookerman, Richard of SC, gent. Will 11 Dec. 1723 pr. 22 Apr. 1726 by Thomas Mathew and Nathaniel Barnardiston. (PROB11/608). AWP.

Tookey, Job of HMS *Newport*, mariner and bachelor. Will 26 Nov. 1695 pr. 11 Dec. 1696 by Henry Fitzhugh, brother and attorney of Robert Fitzhugh of Boston, MA. (PROB11/435). AWP.

Tooley, formerly Fry, Mrs. Susannah of NYC. AWW 31 Aug. 1854 to James Eldridge. (PROB11/2196).

Topping, Joseph of Islington, Mddx., merchant who had houses and land in VA. Will 4 Sep. 1692 pr. 14 Oct. 1692 by siblings Samuel and Hannah Topping. (PROB11/411). AWP.

Topping, Samuel of Stepney, Mddx., weaver, who had houses and lands in VA inherited by the will of his late brother Joseph Topping. Will 10 Dec. 1692 pr. 4 May 1693 by sister Hannah Topping. (PROB11/414). AWP.

Topping, William, surgeon of merchant ship *Boughton* who died on merchant ship *New York Postilion* in NY. Will 14 Aug. 1707 pr. 21 Jan. 1718 by relict Ann Topping. (PROB11/562). AWP.

Torkington, Joseph of VA. Will pr. 26 Apr. 1652 by brother Samuel Torkington. (PROB11/231). ACE.VGE.

Toulmin, Amy of AL, widow of John Butler Toulmin. Will 21 Sep. 1824. Leg: friends William Collier and Joseph Treffry of Plymouth, Devon, and William Crouch of Falmouth, Corn., to receive my estate for the benefit of daughter Amy Jane Treffry Toulmin; sister Mary Honeychurch; cousin Anna Newton and her son Benjamin Wills Newton; brother-in-law Harry Toulmin and his present wife Martha Toulmin. Wit: Abraham Bell and William Hitt of NY. AWW 12 Nov. 1824 by William Collier, Joseph Treffry and William Crouch. (PROB11/1692).

Toulmin, Harry of Washington, AL. Will pr. 10 Feb. 1825 by relict Martha Toulmin and brother John Butler Toulmin. (PROB11/1695).

Tovey, Nicholas formerly of St. George's, [Bristol] Som.. but who died in Cecil Co., MD, mariner. Will 9 Jan. 1675 AWW 23 Feb. 1675 to relict Anne Tovey. (PROB11/348). AWP.

Towle, George of Bethnal Green, Mddx., who died on ship *Mary* in NY, bachelor. Will 3 May 1756 pr. 1 Dec. 1757 by Matthew Stamford of Bethnal Green, coal merchant. (PROB11/834). AWP.

Townsend, Gregory of Halifax, NS, Assistant Commissary. Will pr. 22 Jan. 1799. (PROB11/1318).

Townsend, Joseph Cuthbert of Cobourg, Newcastle District, [ON]. Will pr. 27 Jun. 1852. (PROB11/2155).

Townsend *alias* Dudgeon, Patrick of Whitechapel, Mddx., but late of Boston, MA., who died in the West Indies. Will pr. 14 Jul. 1702 by brother William Townsend. (PROB11/465). AWP.

Townshend, Hon. William of Charlotte Town, PE. Will pr. 6 Mar. 1826. (PROB11/1710).

Towsey, John of Boston, MA, bachelor. Will 10 Mar. 1699 AWW 19 Sep 1709 to Benjamin Smith, attorney for brother Thomas Towsey in Boston. (PROB11/511). AWP.

Traiell, James of Shadwell, Mddx., mariner who died in VA on HMS *Shoreham*. Will pr. 26 Jun. 1718 by relict Margery Traiell. (PROB11/564). AWP.

Traweek, Robert of Butomocke (Potomack), VA, mariner of HMS *Plymouth*, widower. Will 10 May 1729 AWW 17 Aug. 1730 to Thomas Bignall, guardian of the son George Traweek. (PROB11/639). AWP.

Treen, George of St. John's, NL. Will pr. 12 Apr. 1768. (PROB11/938).

Trench, Alexander of Granville Co., NC, merchant. Will 1 Jan. 1730 pr. 4 Dec. 1733 by Benjamin Whitacre. (PROB11/662). AWP.

Trent, James of Inverness, Scotland, mariner, citizen of Sweden but late of City of London, Capt. of ship *Charles* in Crown service who died in PA. Will 26 Nov. 1695. Leg: brother William Trent of Philadelphia, merchant to have one-eighth of the *Charles* pr. 6 Apr. 1698 by mother Isabella Stuart of Inverness, Scotland: revoked in 1699 and admon. granted to brother William Trent. (PROB11/445). AWP.

Trevett, Russell of Marblehead, MA. Will pr. 12 Sep. 1803 by son Russell Trevett and Samuel Hooper. (PROB11/1399).

Try, Ralph, cooper of merchant ship *Fairfax* bound to Guinea and died in York Town, VA. Will 20 Sep. 1697 pr. 7 May 1701 by relict Frances Try. (PROB11/460). AWP.

Tucker, Mrs. Elizabeth of Trenton, NJ. AWW 17 Mar. 1790 to James Allan and Thomas Dickason. (PROB11/1190).

Tucker *alias* **Williams, John** of Port Hope, [ON]. 25 Jul. 1855. (PROB11/2217).

Tucker, William of Bonne Bay, NL, planter, and late of Sturminster Newton, Dorset. Will 14 Dec. 1823. Leg: niece Deborah Tucker, daughter of late brother Luke Tucker; sister-in-law Elizabeth, widow of late brother John Tucker, and Dorothy, daughter of late brother James Tucker. Execs: Joseph Bird of Sturminster Newton, merchant, and Richard King of Wincanton, Somerset. Wit: Edward Russ, William Jeanes and Robert Dyke. Pr. 27 Mar. 1823 by Joseph Bird. (PROB11/1668).

Tuff, Sarah of Western Bay, NL, widow. Will pr. 8 Mar. 1842. (PROB11/1960).

Tuff, William of Western Bay, NL, blacksmith. Will pr. 5 Sep. 1832. (PROB11/1806).

Tull, Richard of London but late of MD, bachelor. Will 27 Jan. 1682 AWW 13 Oct. 1699 to pc. Daniel Biddle. (PROB11/452). AWP.

Tulloch, George of Halifax, NS, furrier. Will pr. 30 Dec. 1854. (PROB11/2203).

Tunney, Rev. Robert William of Kingston, [ON], chaplain to Forces. Will pr. 15 Sep. 1832. (PROB11/1806).

Turnbull, George of NY, formerly Lieut. Col. of NY Volunteers. AWW 22 Jan. 1812 to David Davies. (PROB11/1529).

Turnbull, George of New Haven, CT, Commander in Royal Navy. Will pr. 5 Jul. 1826 by relict Margaret Turnbull, John Day and Henry Wilkes. (PROB11/1715).

Turner, David of Kincardine, [ON]?, bachelor, mariner of HMS *Porcupine.* Will pr. 9 Aug. 1762.

Turner, John of Bagendon, Glos., yeoman, late of Whitechapel, Mddx., who died in MD, bachelor. Will of 12 Oct. 1717. Sentence for validity of will 9 Sep. 1724 AWW 4 Dec. 1724 to Thomas Eycott, father of Rachel Eycott. (PROB11/598). AWP.

Turner, Thomas who died in NY, late Lieutenant in the Royal Navy and commander of HM Packet *Wellington.* Will 3 February 1826. Leg: brother Charles and sister Philippa Turner. Exec: John Hingman of Bloomsbury, London, Navy Agent. Wit: William Ellis and James Richardson. AWW 24 Oct. 1826 to cr. William Broad, John Hingman renouncing. (PROB11/1718).

Turner, William of Keels, NL. Will pr. 25 May 1820. (PROB11/1630).

Turner, Dr. William of Canada, doctor of medicine. Will pr. 25 Jan. 1838. (PROB11/1890).

Turpin, James of Liberty of the Tower, London, tobacconist and widower who died in VA. Will 27 Nov. 1675 pr. 30 May 1678 by brother-in-law John Smith. (PROB11/357). AWP.

Tute, John of London, commander of the *Hope,* who died on James River, VA. Will 9 Apr. 1736 pr. 7 Jul. 1738 by Thomas Parr of London. (PROB11/690). AWP.

Tuttie, John of St. Bartholomew by the Exchange, citizen and fruiterer of London, son of the late William Tuttie of London and brother of Hannah Knight of New England who had children there. Pr. 3 October 1657 by relict Rachel Tuttie. (PROB11/268). AWP.

Tyng, William of Gagetown, Queens Co., NB but residing at Gorham, MA. Will 18 Jan. 1805. Leg: wife Elizabeth Tyng. AWW 15 Jan. 1810 to Edward Goldstone. (PROB11/1507).

Tynte, Edward, Governor of Carolina. Will 19 Jul. 1709 pr. 6 Oct. 1710 by Frances Kilner of St. Giles in Fields, Mddx. (PROB11/517). AWP.

Uniacke, Norman Fitzgerald of Halifax, NS. Will pr. 15 Feb. 1847. (PROB11/2051).

Uniacke, Richard John of Halifax, NS, H.M. Judge. Will pr. 7 Jan. 1836. (PROB11/1857).

Upington, Walter of Bristol, mariner who died in MD. Will 4 Dec. 1691 pr. 6 Sep. 1692 by George Tice and Roger Bagg. (PROB11/411). AWP.

Uriell, George of London, master of *William* who died in MD. Will 5 Mar. 1731 pr. 8 Dec. 1738 by Rebecca Iredell, widow. (PROB11/693). AWP.

Utting, Ashby Esq. of SC, Capt. of HMS *Aldborough.* Will dated Charles Town, SC, 27 Sep. 1745 pr. 13 Jan. 1747 by relict Amy Utting. (PROB11/752). AWP.

Vallens, William of Burnt Island, NL, trader. Will pr. 22 Aug. 1816. (PROB11/1583).

Van Cortlandt, Philip of QC. Will pr. Will pr. 12 Dec. 1833. (PROB11/1825).

Vandeput, George of Halifax, NS, Admiral and Commander-in-Chief. Will pr. 19 Aug. 1800. (PROB11/1346).

Vanderdussen, Alexander of SC who died in Hoxton, Shoreditch, Mddx.. Will of 4 Jul. 1749 witnessed by John Golcock, William Butler and Job Milner. Leg: his servant Charles Murine; Anne Kirkpatrick when she is 21; the children of Mary Nisbit. Execs: John Cleland, James Michie and Daniel Welshmysen. AWW 8 Jun. 1762 to William Higginson, attorney for Thomas Wallace, husband and administrator of Elizabeth Wallace, formerly Nisbit, deceased, for the benefit of Thomas Wallace now on a voyage overseas, the named executors having died. (PROB11/877).

Van Horne, Cornelius Garret of NYC, merchant. Will 3 Sep. 1747 AWW 3 Mar. 1770 to John Exley, attorney for son Augustus Van Horne in NYC. (PROB11/956). AWP.

Van Mater, Daniel of Freehold, Monmouth Co., NJ. Will pr. 9 Aug. 1778. (PROB11/1169).

Vanneck, Thomson of Three Rivers, [QC]. Will pr. 15 Sep. 1855. (PROB11/2220).

Vansittart, Henry, Rear Admiral of London District, [ON]. Will pr. 26 Feb. 1844. (PROB11/1994).

Van Swieten, Ouzeel of NY but now in London, bachelor. Will 23 Jan. 1694 AWW 2 Jan. 1703 to Jacob Myna Cruger. (PROB11/468). AWP. Further grant in Jly. 1705.

Van Veghten, John of Albany, NY, Major in NY forces who died in the Havannah. Will 19 May 1762 AWW 9 Apr. 1764 to Thomas Harris, attorney for relict Annatje Van Veghten in NY. (PROB11/898). AWP.

Van Wyck, Elizabeth of Baltimore, widow. Will 14 May 1814. Leg: husband William Van Wyck to have houses and lots in Baltimore; daughter Frances Akers Van Wyck. Execs: son-in-law Richard Cooke Tilghman, son John Charles Van Wyck and Louis Barney. Wit: Samuel Storett, Charles Wirgman and Peter Wirgman. AWW 27 Aug. 1821 to Rebecca Hutchinson Thomas, widow, attorney for named execs in North America. (PROB11/1647). NGSQ 72/290.

Vavasour, Henry of Montreal, Col. in Royal Engineers. Will pr. 20 Dec. 1851. (PROB11/2144).

Venables, Thomas of Northern Liberties of Philadelphia. Will 21 May 1750 AWW 20 Aug. 1752 to Daniel Moore, attorney for relict Rebecca Venables in Philadelphia. (PROB11/796). AWP.

Verge, John of Trinity NL, planter. Will 21 Dec. 1825. Leg: granddaughters Susanna Lanigan and Susanna Lanigan Cook; son-in-law George Cook of Trinity; sister Mary Bugdon; grandsons Philip and Richard Cook; nephew John Verge, son of testator's late brother Thomas Verge. Wit: George Buchanan Jr. and Will Goodfellow. Pr. 11 Oct. 1828 by George Skelton. (PROB11/1747).

Vernod, Mary of SC, widow, now in Blackmore Street, Mddx. George Cock Esq. is to take care of the education and maintenance of her son George Vernod who is to be her universal legatee. Will witnessed by Blanch Bromley and Thomas Harrison pr. 22 Jul. 1739. (PROB11/696).

Vernon, Christopher of MD, planter, who died at St. Dunstan in the West, London. Will 8 Dec. 1724 pr. 14 Dec. 1724 by aunt Anne Vernon. (PROB11/600). AWP.

Vidal, Richard Emeric of Port Sarnia, Sainston, [ON], Commander in Royal Navy. Will pr. 7 Mar. 1855. (PROB11/2209)

Waddington, John of Philadelphia, merchant. AWW 12 Dec. 1815 to cr. John Hain. (PROB11/1575).

Wade, Joseph. *See* Ward.

Waggoner, Joseph of York, Hudson's Bay. Will pr. 31 Oct. 1766. (PROB11/923).

Waggoner, Rowland of Albany Fort, Hudson's Bay, chief factor. Will pr. 4 Dec. 1740. (PROB11/706).

Wagstaff, Charles Eden of Boston, MA, engraver. Will pr. 22 Feb. 1853 by relict Ann Randall Wagstaff. (PROB11/2168).

Wain, Richard of NYC, fringe and fancy trimmer. Will 19 Jun. 1804. Leg: wife Ann Wain who is to be sole exex. Wit: William Rose, Thomas W. Smith and Samuel Rose. Pr. 23 Nov. 1808 by relict Ann Wain. (PROB11/1489).

Wakeham, Joseph of Bexhill, Sussex, yeoman who hade estate in New England. Will6 Sep. 1714. Leg: sister Sarah, wife of Richard Carswell of Hastings, Sx., tailor; mother Ann Longly, widow. Wit: William Saxby, Dorothy Britten and Edward Lidlow. Pr. 23 Nov. 1715 by relict Elizabeth Wakeham. (PROB11/549).

Wakeman, Joseph of Montreal, keeper of steak & chop house. Will pr. 22 Feb. 1856. (PROB11/2228).

Walbank, Edward of Philadelphia. Will 16 Apr. 1733 pr. 18 Jun. 1735 by relict Agnes Walbank. (PROB11/671).

Walden, John. *See* **Walton.**

Walker, Flower of MD. Will 10 Jun. 1700 pr. 12 Feb. 1709 by Richard Walker with similar powers reserved to Thomas Walker and George Dunn. (PROB11/506). AWP.

Walker, George of St. Giles, Cripplegate, London, cook of HM hospital ship *Pembroke* but who died in VA on HMS *Pearl.* Will 29 Mar. 1709 pr. 13 Aug. 1719 by George Chapman. (PROB11/570). AWP.

Walker, Nathan, Ensign late of Col. Gooch's American Regt. Will dated Augusta, GA, 25 Nov. 1744 pr. 15 Oct. 1746 by Andrew Carre. (PROB11/750). AWP.

Walker, Thomas of St. Michael Bassishaw, London, citizen and salter whose son Thomas Walker was in Boston, MA. Will 20 Apr. 1661 pr. 2 Dec. 1663 by relict Hannah Walker. (Guildhall: Ms 9052/14).

Walker, Thomas of Bay Bulls, NL. Will pr. 10 Feb. 1731. (PROB11/636).

Walker, Thomas of Belle Isle, Detroit, Capt. of Engineers and Government Secretary. Will dated 28 Apr. 1762 witnessed by John Haigh naming his brother William Walker. Deposition of 20 Oct. 1762 by Lydia Walker of St. James Westminster, Mddx., relict of the testator, that she received a copy of his will from Mr. George Walker of Belle Isle. AWW granted 19 Oct. 1762 to the said Lydia Walker, attorney for George Walker at Belle Isle. (PROB11/880).

Wallace, William Alexander of NYC, merchant. Will pr. 29 Jul. 1840 by relict Susan Wallace. (PROB11/1931).

Waller, Henry of Mount Pleasant, Westchester Co., NY. Will pr. 24 Mar. 1835 by son Joseph Fernando Waller. (PROB11/1845).

Walley, Mary of Williamsburg, VA, but late of St. Margaret Westminster, Mddx., widow. Will 16 Feb. 1742 pr. 1 Feb. 1743 by James Franceys. (PROB11/724). AWP.

Wallin *alias* **Poulter, Hannah** of St. Andrew Undershaft, London, spinster, who left £10 to Thomas Poulter in VA, brother of Mary Poulter, daughter of her cousin John Poulter of Hitchin, Herts. Will 15 Mar 1662 pr. 7 Aug. 1663 by Joseph Alston. (PROB11/312). AWP.

Wallis, Richard of Toronto. Will pr. 8 Aug. 1843. (PROB11/1985).

Walsh, John. *See* **Welsh.**

Walter, John Esq. of Tooting, Sy., who had lands in Granville Co., SC. Will 30 Dec. 1734 pr. 5 Jun. 1736 by son Abel Walter. (PROB11/677). AWP.

Walter, Richard of New England. AWW 25 Feb. 1654 to relict Sarah Walter. (PROB11/239). ACE.

Walter, Rev. William, Rector of Boston, MA. AWW 26 Jun. 1801 to John Lane. (PROB11/1359).

Walters, David of Charlestown, MA, seaman of HMS *Britannia* but on board the hospital ship *Smirna Factor.* Will 15 Jun. 1703 pr. 30 Oct. 1703 by Thomas Pyke of Boston, MA.. (PROB11/472). AWP.

Walthoe, Nathaniel Esq. of Williamsburg, VA. Will pr. 13 Jun. 1772 by Thomas Waller of London, stationer. (PROB11/979). AWP.

Walton, Jacob of NYC, Capt. in Royal Navy. Will 29 Mar. 1832. Leg: wife Sarah Walton and son to be execs. and he to inherit estate in Delaware and Herkimer(?) Cos., NY; two sons, James de Launy Jacob and Charles Johnston Walton; two daughters, Sarah Georgette Mary

Anne Gerardine and Catherine Jane Eliza Walton. Wit: W.H. Porter, Robert Scott and R. Adams. Pr. 4 Dec. 1844 by relict Sarah Walton. (PROB11/2009).

Walton *alias* **Walden, John** of St. Francis Harbour, Labrador Island, NL. Will pr. 16 Apr. 1804. (PROB11/1408).

Wampers, John. *See* **White.**

Wanson *alias* **Wansen, Joseph** of Cape Ann, Gloucester Co, MA, belonging to HM sloop *Otter*. Will dated 5 Jun. 1748 appoints as sole executrix his friend Mary Prin of Foy, Corn. Witnessed by Capt. William Crust and Henry Middleton, master. Pr. 14 Sep. 1748 by Mary Townsend, wife of George Townsend, formerly Prin. (PROB11/764). GGE.

Wanton, William of St. John City, NB. Will pr. 19 Oct. 1816. (PROB 11/1585).

Waple, Thomas, formerly of London, distiller, but late of MD, bachelor. Will 4 Apr. 1713 pr. 8 Apr. 1715 by brother Henry Waple and brother-in-law Jonathan Forward. (PROB11/545). AWP.

Ward *alias* **Wade, Joseph,** lately mariner of HMS *Mary* of Boston, MA. Will dated 21 Oct. 1691 leaving estate in New England to Frances Gibbs of Boston, spinster. Witnesses John Marshall, Edward Mobrye and Richard Hazard. Execs: Thomas Linch, Valentine Baker, George Golden and William Barton. Pr. 17 Oct. 1692 by George Golden with similar powers reserved to the other named execs. (PROB11/411).

Ward, Thomas of New England who died in Lisbon, mariner of merchant ship *Industry*. Will 13 May 1710 AWW 16 Jan. 1710 to Joanna Keast. (PROB11/513). AWP.

Warden, Thomas, formerly of Cranborne, Dorset, and NL, planter, but late of Ringwood, Hants. Leg: William Rittier and Moses Rittier Jr. of Ringwood, Hants; brother Roger Warden of Cranborne, cordwainer and his two daughters; Susanna Warden, natural daughter of testator's late sister Susanna Warden of New Sarum, [Wilts]; George, Thomas and Sarah Osbaldiston, children of sister Mary Osbaldiston of [Wimborne] St. Giles, Dorset. Execs: Henry Warn, James Middleton and John Middleton. Pr. 30 Dec. 1764 by William and Moses Rittier. (PROB11/904).

Warden, William of Charles Town, SC, but late of Whitechapel, Mddx., mariner. Will 15 Apr. 1746 pr. 18 Nov. 1746 by William Legoe. (PROB11/751). AWP. NGSQ 64/289.

Wardrobe, Harriet Louisa of Savannah, GA, widow. Will pr. 5 Dec. 1856. (PROB11/2243)

Wardrobe, William of GA, Lieut. Col. Will 23 Feb. 1813. Leg: children of late brother John; natural daughter Edwarda; sister Christian ____?____ Pr. 23 Feb. 1713 by John Macfarlan. (PROB11/1542). [Registry copy badly stained].

Wardrop, John of Calvert Co., MD, merchant late of All Hallows Staining, London. Will 22 Sep. 1758, pr. 1 Jul. 1767 by James Russell of London. (PROB11/931). AWP.

Waring, formerly Lloyd, Sarah of St. James Goose Creek, SC, widow. Will 24 Jan. 1755 AWW 4 Jul. 1760 to Sarah Nickelson, widow, attorney for Peter Taylor, George Austin, Benjamin Waring and Robert Hume in SC. (PROB11/857). AWP.

Warkman, Mark. *See* **Glocester.**

Warner, Edward of St. Botolph Aldgate, citizen and distiller of London, who had lands in MD. Will pr. 20 Mar. 1724 by son Edward Warner. (PROB11/596). AWP. NGSQ 63/39.

Warnett, Thomas of James City, VA, merchant. Will pr. by relict Thomazine Warnett 8 Nov. 1630. (PROB11/158). ACE.GGE.

Warren, Samuel of Detroit, MI. Will 26 Sep. 1850 pr. by Charles Christopher Trowbridge. (PROB11/2120).

Warren, Thomas of Boston, MA, merchant. Will pr. 10 Oct. 1850 by son Thomas Benjamin Warren. (PROB11/2121).

Washington, Lawrence of Washington parish, Westmoreland Co., VA, gent. Will 11 Mar. 1698 pr. 10 Dec. 1700 by daughter Mildred, wife of John Gale. (PROB11/458). AWP.

Waterhouse, Peter of Halifax, NS, Major in 81st Regiment of Foot & Brevet Lieut. Col. Will pr. 14 Jul. 1823. (PROB11/1673).

Waters, Edward of Elizabeth City, VA, gent. AWW 18 Sep. 1630 to son William Waters. (PROB11/158). ACE.

Waters, Richard of Somerset Co., MD. Will 21 Apr. 1720 AWW 13 Nov. 1722 to Jonathan Scarth, attorney for relict Elizabeth and son William Waters in MD. (PROB11/588). AWP.

Waters, William of Northampton Co., VA. Will 3 Jul. 1720 pr. 22 Oct. 1722 by son William Waters. (PROB11/587). AWP.

Waterton, Anne of NYC and late of Demarara, (widow of Christopher Waterton) who died on 29 Aug. 1821 about to depart for Europe. Will 6 May 1812. Leg: son Robert Waterton to have estate called Woodlands in Yorks.; children Agnes, Matilda, George and Henry Waterton; son Francis Birmingham; guardians to children, brother Sir John Waddell Bedingfield and John Wingat of London. AWW 30 Jun. 1823 to son Edward Birmingham. (PROB11/1672). Further grants of 21 Mar. 1834 and 19 Aug. 1845.

Watkins, Charles of SC, planter, who died at sea on merchant ship *Dolphin*. Will 25 Aug. 1742 AWW 19 Oct. 1742 to brother William Watkins. (PROB11/721). AWP.

Watkins, Michael of Annapolis Royal, NS, gunner. Will pr. 15 Aug. 1722. (PROB11/586).

Watkinson, Samuel of Middleton, CT. Will pr. 13 Nov. 1819 by son David Watkinson. (PROB11/1819).

Watson, Elizabeth De Conty. *See* **Gravina.**

Watson, Henry of Prince George Co., MD, gent., late residing in London. Will 17 Mar. 1736 AWW 7 Nov. 1767 to son John Watson. (PROB11/934). AWP.

Watson, John pf London, master mariner who died in MD, bachelor. Will 10 May 1743 pr. 23 Jun. 1746 by Christopher Marshall of London. (PROB11/748). AWP.

Watson, Richard of St. Margaret Westminster, Mddx., whose late wife's son, Robert Boodle, was at Rappahannock River, VA. Will 18 Apr. 1685 pr. 6 Jan. 1686 by Bruno Clench. (PROB11/382). AWP.

Watson, William of Baton Rouge, LA. Will pr. 23 Jul. 1782 by David Rose and William Watson. (PROB11/1094).

Watt, John of Northern Liberties, Pittsburgh Co., Allegheny, PA, hawker and pedlar. AWW 1 Jun. 1837 to George Cox. (PROB11/1881).

Watts, John of Workington, Cumberland, mariner bound to sea and who died in MD. Will 4 Apr. 1728 pr. 1 Oct. 1736 by brother Richard Watts. (PROB11/679). AWP.

Watts, John of NY, having real estate at No. 3 Broadway, NYC, and at Rose Hill and Sherburn, NY. Will 13 May 1836. Leg: daughter Elizabeth Watts; grandson Philip Kearney; grandson John Watts de Peyster, son of late daughter Justina, and her husband Frederick de Peyster; kin of late brother Stephen Watts; Robert Watts, son of late brother Robert Watts; Wits. of NYC: Dan Lord Jr., of Beach St., Andrew Hamersley of 53 Greenwood St. and Frederick Prime of 12th Ward. Pr. 16 Aug. 1850 by Frederick de Peyster. (PROB11/2118).

Watts, Richard of Bear Cove, NL. Will pr. 24 Jan. 1833. (PROB11/1811).

Watts, Robert of Westchester, NY, gent. AWW 25 Feb. 1852 to Sarah Maria Cruger. (PROB11/2148).

Waugh, David of Stafford Co., VA, planter. AWW 20 Feb. 1694 to Henry Bowen. (PROB11/422). VGE.

Way, Catharine of Trinity, NL. Will pr. 25 Jun. 1823. (PROB11/1672).

Way, Richard, mariner of New England who died on HMS *Namur*. Will 1 Jun. 1735 pr. 29 May 1736 by John Nightingirl for benefit of relict Hannah Way in New England. (PROB11/676). AWP.

Wayte, John of Worcester, glover, who had lands in PA. Will 13 Aug. 1691 pr. 14 Nov. 1691 by relict Elizabeth Wayte. (PROB11/407). AWP.

Weare, Thomas of Charfield, Glos., yeoman, whose brother Peter Weare was in York, [MA]. Will 20 Dec. 1684 pr. 3 Oct. 1685 by Peter Weare. (PROB11/384). AWP.

Weatherall, Joseph of Trinity, NL, boat keeper. Will pr. 2 May 1818. (PROB11/1604).

Weaver, John of Bristol who died in Charles Co., MD. Will 17 Jun. 1705 AWW 1 Nov. 1705 to the sister Mary Weaver; the named executor John Pikswort renouncing. (PROB11/485). AWP.

Webb, Daniel of Monkton Farley, Wilts., whose late brother Isaac Webb was in New England. Will 13 Feb. 1732 pr. 8 Jun. 1733 by son-in-law Edward Seymour. (PROB11/660). AWP.

Webb, Gilbert of Cornwall, Orange Co., NY. Will pr. 23 Nov. 1834 by Peter Roe. (PROB11/1692).

Webb, Matthew, marine of HMS *Guerriere,* now a patient in Naval Hospital, Halifax, NS. Will pr. 7 Jun. 1614. (PROB11/1558).

Webb, William of Bristol but residing in MD, mariner. Will 20 Oct. 1710 pr. by relict Sarah Webb 30 Oct. 1711. (PROB11/523). AWP.

Webber, Daniel of Stepney, Mddx., mariner intending a voyage to New England. Will 19 Feb. 1724 pr. 26 Apr. 1731. (PROB11/644). AWP.

Webber, John of NL, bachelor and planter. Will pr. 14 Jun. 1764. (PROB11/899).

Webber, Jonathan of Harbour Grace, Conception Bay, NL. Will pr. 3 Mar. 1787. (PROB11/1151).

Webber, Samuel of Marblehead, MA, mariner of HMS *Assistance.* Will pr. 16 Sep. 1745. IPROB11/742).

Wedgwood, Joseph of Halifax, NS, hospital sergeant of 38th Regiment of Foot. Will pr. 29 Apr. 1852. (PROB11/2152).

Weedon, John of Boston, MA. mariner of the *Mary.* AWW 18 Jun. 1702 to Thomas Dummer. (PROB11/463).

Weedon, William of St. Botolph Bishopsgate, London, whose nephew William Weedon was of Pocomoke River, MD. Will 20 Sep. 1696 pr. 2 Nov. 1692 by nephew William Weedon. (PROB11/412). AWP.

Wells, Richard of Anne Arundel Co., MD. Will pr. 14 Nov. 1668. (PROB11/328). GGE.

Welch, Francis of NYC but late of Knightsbridge, Westminster, Mddx., merchant. Will 2 Jan. 1775 pr. 2 Mar. 1775 by Richard Neave of London, merchant. (PROB11/1006). AWP.

Welsh *alias* **Walsh, John** of Little Placentia Island, NL, publican. Will pr. 27 Feb. 1775. (PROB11/1005).

Welsh, Richard of Great Placentia, NL, merchant. Will pr. 6 Mar. 1771. (PROB11/965).

West, John of Boston, MA, but formerly of NY. Will pr. 25 Nov. 1691 by relict Anne West. (PROB11/407). GGE.

West, John of St. Sepulchre, citizen and girdler of London who had tenements in PA. Will 20 May 1698 pr. 1 Jul. 1699 by son Richard West. (PROB11/451). AWP.

Westley, Ambrose of Charles Town, SC, soldier in 65th Regiment of Foot. Will 19 Aug. 1759 AWW 27 Oct. 1763 to mother Mary Westley of Aston Clinton, Bucks. (PROB11/893). AWP.

Weston, Francis Marion of All Saints, George Town, SC. AWW 28 Nov. 1855 to William John Slade Foster. (PROB11/2223).

Wharton, Richard of Boston, MA, merchant. Will 10 Jul. 1687 pr. 15 Apr. 1690 by Samuel Read and Nathaniel Whitfield. (PROB11/401). AWP.

Wharton, Richard of Williamsburg, VA. Will 26 Jul. 1712 AWW to brothers Thomas and John Wharton. (PROB11/532). AWP.

Whearley, Henry of Barbados but bound for England and whose brother Abraham Whearley was in PA. Will 3 May 1685 pr. 26 Apr. 1689 by brother Daniel Whearley of London. (PROB11/395). AWP.

Wheeler, Francis of London, merchant, now bound for VA. Will 6 Oct. 1656 pr. 14 Mar. 1660 by son Francis Wheeler. (PROB11/297). AWP.

Whetstone, Robert, of NY, late of HMS *Mentor,* now of HM Navy Yard. Will 5 Nov. 1782. Wife Mary to be universal exec. and legatee. Wit: John Burgess and William Frazer. AWW 29 Mar. 1784 to John Turner, husband and attorney for relict Mary Turner residing in NS. (PROB11/1115).

Whitaker, Alexander of Blackfriars, London, setting out for VA. Will 16 Feb. 1611 pr. 4 Aug. 1617 by brother William Whitaker. (Guildhall: Ms 9171/23/750) and, on his death, admon. in PCC to sister Susan Lothrop. (PROB11/130/95).

Whitbourne, Elizabeth of St. Botolph Aldgate, London, widow, whose niece Elizabeth was wife of William Erby of VA, planter. Will 17 Nov. 1690 pr. 18 Aug. 1692 by John Strong, citizen and woodmonger of London. (Guildhall: Ms 9052/29).

Whitborn, John, formerly of West Teignmouth, Devon, mate of the *Brislington,* but late of SC, bachelor. Will 1 Sep. 1756 AWW 1 Apr. 1760 to brother Peter Whitborn. (PROB11/855). AWP.

White, Benjamin of Princes Square, London, but late of Boston, MA, master in Royal Navy on half pay. Will 3 Oct. 1765 pr. 23 Mar 1774 by Henry Cort of Crutched Friars, London. (PROB11/996). AWP.

White, Betty of Cleveland, OH, widow. AWW 29 Jan. 1836 to William Rossiter. (PROB11/1857).

White, Mrs. Elizabeth of New Brunswick, NJ. Will pr. 22 Dec. 1785 to John Watts. (PROB11/1136).

White, formerly Wright, Mrs. Helen of Yarmouth, NS. Will pr. 29 Dec. 1845. (PROB11/2028).

White, James of Barbados but who died in Boston, MA, merchant. Will 10 Sep. 1666 pr. 11 Feb 1668 by brother William White. (PROB11/326). AWP.

White alias Wampers, John of Boston, MA. Will pr. 1 Oct. 1679 by John Blake. (PROB11/361). GGE.

White, John of Ratcliffe, Mddx., shipwright who died in VA on ship *Preservation*. Will 8 Aug. 1689. Leg: wife Mary White who is to be exex. Pr. 8 Oct. 1697 by relict Mary White. (Guildhall: Ms 9171/48/488v).

White, John of Boston, MA. gent. AWW 21 Jan. 1796 to Thomas Latham. (PROB11/1271).

Whyte, Dr. Joseph of Godmanchester, Beauharnais Co., Montreal. Will pr. 17 Mar. 1855. (PROB11/2209).

White, Limpany, Lieut. of Col. Gooch's Regiment of Foot who made a bequest to Katherine Duron of Second River, NJ. Will 3 Apr. 1741 AWW 5 Mar. 1747 to sister Martha White. (PROB11/753). AWP. NGSQ 64/286.

White, Robert of NY, Commissary of Stores at Pensacola, W. FL, bachelor. Will 30 Mar. 1767 pr. 8 Nov. 1774 by brother Rev. Nathaniel White of Bow Churchyard, London. (PROB11/1992). AWP.

White, Thomas of Philadelphia. AWW 6 Mar. 1786 to Richard Peters. (PROB11/1140).

White, Thomas of NYC. AWW 13 Aug. 1822 to Matthew White. (PROB11/1661).

White, William of Stepney, Mddx., mariner of the *St. Albans* who was drowned in VA. Will 9 Aug. 1692 pr. 7 Sep. 1697 by Edward Daniel. (PROB11/440). AWP.

White, William of Wimborne Minster, Dorset, late planter of NL. Will 4 Dec. 1765. Charles and William Anstey, sons of Charles Anstey of Poole to have a plantation in Willingate, NL; nephew William White, son of brother Richard White to have house in Wimborne; brother Robert White; daughters-in-law Mary wife of James Ormerod and Anne Brenton; sister Katharine White; Mary Dewy of Wimborne, widow; George Rogers of Wimborne, cordwainer; residue to sister Dinah wife of Samuel Bowden. Wit: William King, Thomas Green and Richard Corpe. Pr. 18 Feb. 1766 by Dinah Bowden. (PROB11/916).

White, William of Charleston, SC, shopkeeper. Will pr. 21 Jan. 1795 by William Smith. (PROB11/1255).

Whitefield, Rev. George of St. Luke, Mddx., who died at the Orphan House, GA, widower. Will 22 Mar. 1770 AWW 5 Feb. 1771 to Charles Hardy, Daniel West and Robert Keen. (PROB11/964). AWP.

Whitehead, Mary of Binfield, Berks., widow, whose son Richard Whitehead was in VA. Will 28 Feb. 1679 pr. 2 May 1679 by daughter Philadelphia Whitehead. (PROB11/359).

Whitehead, Richard of Windsor, CT. Will pr. 26 Jun. 1645 by John Andrewes. (PROB11/193). ACE.GGE.

Whitehorne, George of Whitechapel, Mddx., mariner who died in Boston, MA. Will 23 Feb. 1714 pr. 16 Aug. 1722 by Benjamin Thorp, citizen and weaver of London. (PROB11/586). AWP.

Whitehurst, Thomas of Brunswick, NC, bachelor, Lieut. in Royal Navy. Will 22 Mar. 1765 pr. 7 Oct. 1766 by sister Ann Whitehurst. (PROB11/923). AWP.

Whitley, Roger of Fort King George, SC, Ensign of Gen. Nicholson's Independent Company. Will 7 Oct. 1726 AWW 10 Dec. 1729 to William Livingston, attorney for Alexander Nisbett in Edinburgh, Scotland. (PROB11/634). AWP.

Whitmore, Benjamin of Middletown, CT. Will 25 Jun. 1696 AWW 30 Sep. 1696 to Isabel Edwards. (PROB11/434). AWP.

Whitpaine, Richard of St. Clement Eastcheap, citizen and butcher of London. Will 27 Apr. 1689. Leg: wife Mary Whitpaine to sell testator's 7000 acres in PA, mansion house in Philadelphia on River Delaware, and land called Whitpaine's Crook in Philadelphia Co; sons John and Zachariah Whitpaine; grandson Thomas, son of Thomas Lee. Overseers: Richard Mow of Ratcliffe, Mddx., biscuit baker, John Edridge of St. Mary at Hill, London, distiller, Thomas Cox of Whitechapel, Mddx., vintner, and Thomas Lee of Little Tower Hill, London, haberdasher. Wit: Thomas Hattersly, Robert Richardson and Jonah Cranwell. Pr. 29 May 1689 by relict Mary Whitpaine. (Guildhall: Ms 9171/41/363v).

Whittingham, William of Boston, MA, gent. Will pr. 15 Apr. 1672 by Nathaniel Hubbard. (PROB11/340).

Whyte. *See* **White.**

Wickeat, Jacob, mariner of HMS *Hampton Court,* bachelor, who was born of Indian parents in New England. Will 22 Mar. 1741 AWW 30 Sep. 1741 to Alexander Godwin, attorney for Richard Jeffery. (PROB11/712). AWP.

Wickham, Moses of Southampton, master of HMS *Soulings* now in NY. Will 13 Apr. 1713 pr. 22 Jan. 1715 by Thomas Orr. (PROB11/544). AWP.

Wier, Daniel of Commissary General of Army, NYC. Will pr. 9 Feb. 1782 by Jacob Wilkinson. (PROB11/1088).

Wigington, Henry of Villiers Street, Mddx., but late of SC. Will 27 May 1722 pr. 17 Dec. 1722 by Robert Hume. (PROB11/588). AWP. NGSQ 62/210.

Wilcocks, Capt. John of Accomack, VA. Will pr. by Temperance Wilcocks 30 Jun. 1628. (PROB11/153). ACE.GGE.

Wilkes, John De Ponthieu of NYC, notary public. AWW 24 Mar. 1846 to Edmund John Scott. PROB11/2033).

Wilkinson, Joseph of Calvert Co., MD, merchant. Will 25 Apr. 1734 AWW 22 Jul. 1736 to William Torver, attorney for relict in MD. (PROB11/678). AWP.

Willdon, Rev. Thomas, clerk of Trinity, NL. Will pr. 28 Jan. 1803. (PROB11/1386).

Willdy, Benjamin of London, factor, but late of Carolina. Will 17 Dec. 1694 AWW 15 Feb. 1697 to sister Martha Wood, the mother Martha Dogget having died.

Willett, John Esq., formerly of St. Christopher's but late of NYC, merchant. Will pr. 9 Jan. 1767 by relict Frances Willett. (PROB11/925). AWP.

Willett, Margaret of Westchester, NY, widow. AWW 20 Dec. 1800 to Effingham Lawrence. (PROB11/1351).

Willett, Thomas of NYC, merchant. Will 26 Dec. 1766 pr 20 Oct. 1768 by son John Willett. AWP. (PROB11/943). AWP.

Williams, Arthur of Boston, MA, Major in 52nd Regiment. AWW 23 Aug. 1776 to brother Rev. William Williams. (PROB11/1023).

Williams, Ayliffe, late of NC but now residing in Westminster, Mddx. Will 22 Nov. 1734 pr. 2 May 1735 by Henry Nean and James Webb. (PROB11/671). NGSQ 63/133.

Williams, Howley of Wellington, [ON]. Will pr. 7 May 1746. (PROB11/2036).

Williams, Henry of Bedford, Nassau Island, NY. Will pr. 9 Mar. 1784 by nephew John Williams. (PROB11/1115).

Williams, Jenkin of QC, Member of Executive and Legislative Councils. Will pr. 21 Nov. 1815. (PROB11/1632).

Williams, John, mariner of HMS *Nightingale* but late of privateer *Hornet* of NY who died in hospital in France, bachelor. Will 15 Nov. 1754 pr. 27 Oct. 1758 by mother Ann Williams of Deptford, Kent, widow. (PROB11/841). AWP.

Williams, John of Newport, RI, mariner, who died in hospital in France. AWW 17 Jan. 1775 to Thomas and William Maude. (PROB11/1004).

Williams, John. *See* **Tucker.**

Williams, Margaretta Mariam of Greenville, Bond Co., IL. Will pr. 6 Oct. 1857 by Rev. Clement Dawsonne Strong. (PROB11/2259).

Williams, Mary late of West FL but late of the City of London. Will 21 Jan. 1791 pr. 9 Feb. 1791. (PROB11/1202). NGSQ 63/131.

Williams, Thomas of NL. Will pr. 2 Jan. 1749. (PROB11/767).

Williams, Thomas Charles of NYC, merchant. Will pr. 14 Oct. 1784 by relict Sarah Williams and brother John Williams. (PROB11/1123).

Williamson, Elizabeth Ann, of Charleston, SC, widow. Leg: Mrs. Margaret Barron, wife of Francis William Barron and her daughters Mary Ann and Margaret Barron; nephew William Mason of Charleston; Frances Claudia and Susan Lovington Marchant, daughters of nephew Peter Marchant of Charleston. Exec: Francis William Barron. Wit: Isaac Hill, hatter, and Samuel Hill, tobacconist of Strand, London. Pr. 30 Sep. 1831 by Francis William Barron Sr. (PROB11/1791).

Williamson, William of Charles Town, SC, but lodging at Four Lions Inn in London. Will 14 Apr. 1766 pr. 30 Dec. 1770. (PROB11/962). AWP.

Willing, Charles of Philadelphia, merchant. Will 28 Jul. 1750 pr. 15 Jan. 1756 by relict Ann Willing and son Thomas Willing. (PROB11/820). AWP.

Willing, James of Bristol, soap boiler, whose brother Thomas Willing was in Philadelphia, merchant. Will 25 Nov. 1727 pr. 5 Dec. 1727 by brother Richard Willing. (PROB11/618). AWP.

Willing, James of Haverford Township, Cleveland, DE Co., PA. Will pr. 20 Sep. 1819. (PROB11/1620).

Willing, Richard of DE Co., PA. AWW 22 Jun. 1820 to Walter Stirling. (PROB11/1632).

Willison, Robert of St. Saviour Southwark, Sy., formerly of SC. Will 2 Feb. 1729 pr. 16 May 1729 by affirmation of uncle George Oldner. (PROB11/630). AWP.

Wills, Thomas of H.M. Hospital, RI, seaman of HMS *Nonsuch*, born in Morval, Corn. Will 6 Mar. 1778. Leg: brother John Wills of *Nonsuch*. Wits. James Lucas and John Richardson. AWW to said John Wills. (PROB11/1062).

Wilmshurst, John of Charles Town, SC. Will 9 Sep. 1756pr. 21 Jul. 1774 by daughter Elizabeth, wife of John Dugleby. (PROB11/1000). AWP.

Wilshear, John of Carbonair, NL, planter and fisherman. Will pr. 27 Apr. 1850. (PROB11/2112).

Wilson, Daniel of NYC, mason. Will pr. 8 Jun. 1849 by brother Charles Thomas Wilson. (PROB11/2095).

Wilson, John Francis of Gaspé Co., QC, merchant. Will pr. 8 Jun. 1854. (PROB11/2194)

Wilson, Mark. *See* **Hodgson.**

Wilson *alias* Brooks, Susanna of Montreal, widow. Will pr. 26 Apr. 1833. (PROB11/1814).

Wilton, Noel of Charles Town, Middlesex Co., NL, mariner. Will pr. 10 Sep. 1689. (PROB11/396).

Winckworth, John, of City of Louisbourg, NS, collarmaker to the Royal Artillery, bachelor. Will dated 5 Feb. 1759, witnessed by Thomas Butler, Joseph Chester and Thomas Strode, pr. by his brother Francis Winckworth 27 Feb. 1761. (PROB11/863).

Windsor, Leonard of St. Lewis Street, QC City, merchant. Will pr. 13 Sep. 1845. (PROB11/2024).

Winfield, Thomas of VA, late citizen and currier of London. Will 4 Jan. 1720 pr. 5 Mar. 1722 by John Orton. (PROB11/584). AWP.

Winslow, Isaac of Halifax, NS. Will pr. 16 Oct. 1780. (PROB11/1070).

Winslow, Joshua of QC. Will pr. Will pr. 2 Nov. 1802. (PROB11/1383).

Winstanley, Rev. Charles of Toronto, clerk. Will pr. 3 Nov. 1848. (PROB11/2084).

Wise, John, seaman of the *Golden Fleece* who died in VA. Will 27 Jul. 1684 pr. 29 Jun. 1685 by mother Anne Miller. (PROB11/380). AWP.

Wiseman, Richard of NL, bachelor. Will pr. 4 Feb. 1747. (PROB11/753).

Witham, Robert of Newport, RI, mariner of HMS *Vigilant* and widower. Will dated 22 Jun. 1745 appoints William Woodward, mariner, as sole legatee and executor. Witnessed by Sam Vernon, John Calder and Henry Ball. AWW 8 Oct. 1751 to Benjamin Wickham, attorney for William Woodward now at Newport, RI. (PROB10/790).

Wood, Edward of Steubenville, OH. Will 24 Feb. 1846. Leg: wife & exex. Susan Wood to have house and lot in Steubenville; daughter Sarah W. Pentecost of New Lisbon, [OH]. Wit: W. Spencer and N. Dike. AWW 13 Sep. 1855 to Mary Ann Wood, spinster, attorney for relict in Steubenville. (PROB11/2220).

Wood, James of Woolwich, Kent, mariner, who died in MD, bachelor. Will pr. 26 Apr. 1745 by mother Mary Harrell. (PROB11/778). AWP.

Wood, Richard of Whaddon, Gloucester City, whose cousin William Barnes had a daughter in New England. Will 7 Sep. 1650 pr. 17 Feb 1652 by relict Mary Wood. (PROB11/220). AWP. NGSQ 61/115.

Wood, Rev. Thomas of Annapolis Royal, NS, missionary. Will pr. 1 Dec. 1779. (PROB11/1059).

Woodbridge, Dudley, Rector of St. Philip's, Barbados, late chaplain of HMS *Sunderland* who died in Barbados and whose sister Mary was wife of Maj. Abel Alleyne deceased of Boston, MA. Will 15 Mar. 1748 AWW 14 Feb. 1750 to Edward Clark Parish, attorney for Nathaniel Haggett in Barbados. (PROB11/777). AWP.

Woodbridge, Ruth of Barbados but late of Boston, MA, and who died there, widow. Will 23 Dec. 1748 AWW 14 Feb. 1750 to Edward Clark Parish. (PROB11/777). AWP.

Woodfall, William, Chief Justice of Cape Breton Island. Will pr. 17 Dec. 1806. (PROB11/1453).

Woodhouse, Henry of Linhaven, Lower Norfolk Co., VA. Will pr. 24 Jul. 1688 by son Henry Woodhouse. (PROB11/392). GGE.VGE.

Woodley, Samuel of St. John's, NL, planter. Will pr. 31 Jul. 1832. (PROB11/1803).

Woods, Joseph of Philadelphia, house carpenter. Will 5 Jun. 1793 pr. 22 Jul. 1793 by father John Woods. (PROB11/1235). NGSQ 63/40.

Woodward, John of Hector, Tompkins, NY. Will pr. 25 Jul. 1850 by son John Woodward. (PROB11/2117).

Worthington, *formerly* **Laugher, Elizabeth** of Hartford, CT. AWW 19 Nov. 1813 to James Smith Hancock. (PROB11/1550).

Worthington, John of Anne Arundel Co., MD, merchant. Will 22 Oct. 1764 AWW 2 Jun. 1769 to James Russell, attorney for sons John and Charles Worthington in MD. (PROB11/949). AWP.

Worthington, William of Anne Arundel Co., MD. Will 27 Sep. 1770 AWW 3 Sep. 1771 to Silvanus Grove of London, merchant, attorney for William and Mary Hunt. (PROB11/971). AWP.

Worts, James of Toronto, miller. Will pr. 31 Dec. 1841. (PROB11/1955).

Wotton, Simon of Calvert Co., MD, surgeon. Will 13 Jan. 1696 pr. 29 Dec. 1696 by Thomas Wharton. (PROB11/435). AWP.

Wotton, William of VA. AWW 12 May 1656 to sister Mary Meredeth. (PROB11/255). AWP.

Wragg, Samuel formerly of Holborn, Mddx., but lately of Charles Town, SC. Will 14 Jun. 1749 pr. 26 Jan. 1751 by son William Wragg and Robert Henshaw. (PROB11/785). AWP. Revoked Jul. 1754 and AWW with codicil granted to the daughters Mary and Judith Wragg.

Wragg, William of Charles Town, SC, passenger aboard the merchant ship *Caesar*. Will pr. 3 Apr. 1779. (PROB11/1052).

Wraxall, Peter Esq. of NYC. Will pr. 13 Feb. 1762 by relict Elizabeth Wraxall. (PROB11/873). AWP.

Wray, George of Westfield, Washington Co., NY. Will 16 Mar. 1803. Leg: Anne Elizabeth Blake, widow, and her natural daughter Anna Blake; nephew John Wray; wife Catherine Wray who is to have land in Waterford village, Saratoga Co., NY; daughter Maria, wife of Charles H____; grandson George Wray Cuyler, son of daughter Jane deceased. Wit: Nicholas Blakney, ___?___ Goodall, Benjamin Blake and Matt. Ogden. AWW 7 Feb. 1805 to Philip Sansom. (PROB11/1421).

Wright, Benjamin of merchant ship *Levite* who died in VA. Will 12 Aug. 1706 AWW 13 Jan. 1707 to John Hunt, attorney for Robert Jones, now at sea. (PROB11/492). AWP.

Wright, Francis of Thurlow, Midland District, [ON], gent. Will pr. 18 Oct. 1836. (PROB11/1868).

Wright, John of Wapping, Mddx., who died in VA on the *Hope*. Will 18 May 1698. Leg: wife & exex. Ann Wright of Wapping. Wit: Sheppard and William Huggins. Pr.13 Oct. 1699 by relict Ann Wright. (Guildhall: Ms 9171/49/461).

Wright, Dr. John of QC, Inspector of Military Hospitals. Will pr. 22 Jan. 1828. (PROB11/1736).

Wright, John of St. James, Wasamsaw, SC, bachelor. AWW 28 Jul. 1828 to Keating Simons. (PROB11/1743).

Wright, Moses of Boston, MA, seaman of HMS *Victory*. Will 20 Mar. 1744 Pr. 15 Nov. 1744 by sister Ann Douglass. (PROB11/736). AWP.

Wright, Peter of New Orleans, LA, Lieut. in Royal Engineer Corps. AWW 6 Feb. 1816 to sister Martha Wright. (PROB11/1577).

Wright, William Esq. St. Ann Westminster, Mddx., who died in Annapolis Royal, NS. Will 21 Jun. 1715 pr. 25 Feb. 1719 by relict Sarah Wright. (PROB11/567). AWP.

Wyatt, Thomas of Boreham, Essex, yeoman who died in MD. Will 14 Apr. 1750 pr. 26 Nov. 1756 by affirmation of brother Samuel Wyatt of Boreham. (PROB11/826).

Wyborne, Thomas of New England, surgeon who died at sea, bachelor. Will 19 Nov. 1690 pr. 22 Oct. 1691 by Nathaniel Wickham, surgeon. (PROB11/406). AWP.

Wyett, Davey of St. Gregory Stoke, Som., husbandman, who died in Carolina, bachelor. Will 2 Sep. 1682 pr. 4 May 1685 by brother John Wyett. (PROB11/380). AWP.

Wylly, Margaret of St. Simon's Island, Glynn Co., GA, widow. AWW 13 Oct. 1852 to Charles Robert Simpson. (PROB11/2160).

Wyld, Daniel, formerly of Brewerton parish, York Co., VA, planter, but late of Stepney, Mddx. Will 2 Sep. 1676. Leg: daughter Margaret, wife of John Martin of Ratcliffe, Mddx., mariner, to have plantations in Brewerton; kinsman Nicholas Harrison of London, tinman; the poor of St. Andrew's, Worcester; testator's servant and apprentice Valentine Harvey in VA; Robert Rowe of Ratcliffe, tobacconist, and his wife; Capt. Richard Martin and his wife of Wapping, Mddx.; Henry Dennis and Sarah his wife; Mrs. Margaret Chichley of London, widow. Execs: John and Margaret Martin. Wit: Henry Dennis and John Martin. Pr. 25 Oct. 1676 by Margaret Martin (PROB11/352).

Wynne, Robert of Charles City Co., VA, gent. Will 1 Jul. 1675 AWW 15 Aug. 1678 to Thomas Crane attorney for relict Mary Wynne in VA. (PROB11/357). AWP.

Wyron, John of Reading, Berks., tinplate worker, whose daughter Grace, wife of William Rackstraw, was in PA. Will 29 Apr. 1688 pr. 10 May 1688 by Thomas Smith. (PROB11/391). AWP.

Ximenez *alias* **Jimenez, Jose** of Baton Rouge, LA. AWW 4 Jun. 1832 to Jose Ventura de Aquirre Solarte and Cristobal de Murrieta. (PROB11/1802).

Yale, Thomas of London, merchant, who died in Grone, Denbighshire and whose uncle Thomas Yale was in New England. WILL 29 Sep. 1697 AWW 10 Jan. 1698 to John Evans and Robert Harbin. (PROB11/443). AWP.

Yarwood, Stephen of Montreal, purser in Royal Navy. Will pr. 25 Apr. 1848. (PROB11/2074).

Yates, Charles of Spotsylvania, VA. Will pr. 28 Sep. 1809. (PROB11/1503).

Yesline, Jonas, mariner of HMS *Seaford* bachelor. Will dated NY 14 Dec. 1714 AWW 22 Oct. 1723 to Margaret Cudlipp, attorney for kinswoman, Mary Scot of Highgate, Mddx., widow. (PROB11/593). AWP.

Young, Sir Aretas William, Lieut.Governor of PE. Will pr. 16 Jul. 1836. (PROB11/1865).

Young, Edward of St. Botolph Aldgate, London, mariner of merchant ship *Daniel & Anna* who died in MD, bachelor. Will 1 Jan. 1734 pr. 4 Jul. 1734 by William Speven. (PROB11/666). AWP.

Young, George of NY, merchant aboard the brig *Mary and Eliza* in the Downs bound to Havana. Will pr. 8 Sep. 1827 by brother John Young, nephew James Young and Margaret Lyell, widow. (PROB11/1731).

Young, Nathaniel of Shadwell, Mddx., mariner of *Eagle* who died in Carolina. Will 16 Dec. 1704 pr. 8 Apr. 1706 by Mary Dearing, widow. (PROB11/488). AWP.

Young, Theophilus of Lunenburg, NS, Lieut. in 45th Regiment who died in Louisburgh, NS. Will 15 May 1758 pr. 1 Dec. 1758 by father Thomas Young of Hare Hatch, Berks. (PROB11/842). AWP.

Younie, James of Dutchess Co., NY, farmer. Will pr. 20 Mar. 1829. (PROB11/1753).

Yuill, James of Truro, Halifax Co., NS. Will pr. 10 Aug. 1812. (PROB11/1536).

Supplementary Index of Names

Brush, Naomi 14
Bryan, John 11, 26
Bryan, Joseph 75
Bryant, Francis 15
Bryant, Micah 74
Bryne, John 44
Buchanan, Alexander 66
Buchanan, Elizabeth 66
Buchanan, George 59, 102
Buchanan, Margaret 59
Buchanan, Neil 99
Buckham, Elizabeth 21
Buckler, Lucy 84
Bugdon, Mary 102
Bulkley, Edward 33
Bulkley, Gersham 33
Bulkley, Peter 33
Bull, Elizabeth 14
Bullivant, Benjamin 23
Bullock, Mary Elizabeth 3
Bullock, William 3
Bunce, John 6
Burburet, T. 9
Burchfield, Mathew 44
Burd, Richard 97
Burgen, Margaret 80
Burgen, Thomas 80
Burges, Ann 72
Burges, Margaret 72
Burgess, Isaac 40
Burgess, John 106
Burgess, William 60
Burke, Andrew 63
Burke, James St. John 43
Burke, John 44
Burnley, Charlotte 15
Burnley, John Hume 15
Burnley, William F. 15
Burrage, Barbara 15
Burrage, Robert 58
Burridge, Sarah 16
Burrowes, John 1
Burrows, Sarah 77
Burton, Richard 72
Bush, Hannah 36
Busher, Anne 37
Busher, Jane 37
Bushnell, John 1
Butcher, Sarah 15
Butler, Edmund 15
Butler, Thomas 109

Butler, William 6, 56, 102
Buttall, Mary 15
Buttell, Samuel 15
Buy, John 15*
Buy, William 16
Byfield, Robert Elliott 25
Byrne, Redmond 46
Byrom, Roger 15
Byron, Rosina 73

Cable, Joane 15
Cade, Andrew 15
Cade, Magdalen 15
Cage, William 32
Calcraft, John 11
Calder, John 109
Caldwell, Agnes 16
Callis, Henry Addison 1
Calvert, Margaret 16
Campbell, Alexander 16*
Campbell, Duncan 16*
Campbell, Helen M. 31
Campbell, John 16
Campbell, Robert 31
Campbell, William 48
Cane, Abigail 85
Cane, Francis 85
Cannady, John 97
Capell, Joane 15
Carey, John 67
Carget, Robert 16
Carpender, Helen 16
Carpender, Simon 16
Carpenter, Elizabeth 16
Carpenter, John 81
Carpenter, Nathaniel 16
Carpenter, Thomas 58
Carrack, James 77
Carre, Andrew 103
Carroll, James 40
Carroll, John 46
Carsan, James 63
Carswell, Richard 103
Carswell, Sarah 103
Carter, Ann 24
Carter, Catherine 37
Carter, Charles 24
Carter, James 44
Carter, Robert 90
Carter, Thomas 60
Carter, William 37

Cartman, John 36
Cary, Archibald 81
Cary, Esquire 15
Cary, James 54
Cary, Jane 17
Cary, Nathaniel 17
Cary, Robert 4, 92
Castle, Edmond 21
Castle, John 80
Caswall, John 17
Cathrell, Ephraim 83
Cauldwell, John 22
Causton, Henry 71
Chads, Susanna 22
Chadwick, Ebenezer 55
Chadwick, Edwin 91
Chadwick, Thomas 12
Chadwick, William 35
Chalke, William 5
Chalmers, John
Chalmers, Lionel 40
Chambers, John 38
Chambers, Mary 17
Chamier, Anthony 17
Chancellor, William 71
Chapman, Frances 17
Chapman, George 103
Chapman, Isaac 17
Chapman, John 20
Chapman, Robert 97
Chapman, William 35
Chardavoyne, Isaac 17
Chardin, George 59
Charles, George 85
Charlton, John 72
Chauncy, Lionel 23
Chauncy, Mary 23
Chauncy, William 23
Chauvin, Marianna 48
Chavasse, Nicholas W. 38
Cheny, Joane 54
Cherry, Mary 18
Cherry, Samuel 91
Chesley, Margaret 18
Chester, Joseph 109
Chester, Robert 97
Chester, William 2
Chichester, John H.R. 49
Chichester, Richard 18
Chichley, Margaret 111
Chiencultie, A. 40

Chilcott, William 90
Child, Abigail 28
Child, Davis W. 28
Child, Francis 90
Child, Joshua
Child, Lucretia 28
Chinnery, John 3
Chipchase, Robert 24
Chipman, Elizabeth 79
Chipman, William 9
Chisholm, William 5
Chosin, Mary 26
Christie, Alexander 39
Christmas, Susanna 79
Churchill, Charles 29
Clagett, Horatio 69
Clapcott, William 87
Clapham, John 4
Claridge, John 25
Clark, Ann
Clark, George 31
Clarke, Catherine 19
Clarke, Elizabeth 18
Clarke, George 76
Clarke, George Rochfort 18
Clarke, John 19*, 75, 82
Clarke, Joseph 88
Clarke, Margaret 59
Clarke, William 19*
Clarkson, Cornelia Ann 19
Clarkson, David 79
Clarkson, Henrietta 19
Clay, Elizabeth 54
Clayton, Casper 98
Clayton, Elizabeth 50
Clayton, Mary 98
Cleare, Anne
Cleaver, Mary 19
Clegg, James 45
Cleland, John 102
Clement, William 71
Clenth, Bruno 105
Cleriston, Francis Henry 61
Clerk, George 19
Clerk, Sir James 19
Clerk, John 19
Clerk, Thomas 19
Clerke, Susanna Eliz. 18
Clerke, Sir William Hy. 18
Clinton, Martha 58
Cloke, Hannah 44

Clopton, William 45
Clover, Mary 83
Clow, Andrew 17
Cloyson, Hendrick 17
Cluny, David 82
Coachman, Thomas 51
Coatsworth, John 12
Coatsworth, Susannah 72
Cochet, Anne 19
Cochet, Dorothy 19
Cochran, Catherine 20
Cochran, Margaret 20
Cochran, Robert 20
Cochran, William 20
Cock, George 102
Cockburn, James 33
Cockburn, John 20
Cocke, John Catesby 20
Cocke, William 20
Cockran, William 47
Cockshudd, Thomas 20
Coddington, Samuel 92
Codrington, Edward 58
Coffin, Abigail 20
Coffin, Richard 20
Coggins, Ann 63
Cogswell, Jonathan 20
Cogswell, Lois 20
Colcutt, Anne 20
Colden, Elizabeth 72
Coldham, George 36
Coldham, John 52
Coldwell, George 22
Cole, Henry 93
Cole, John 24, 48
Cole, Josiah 45
Cole, Mary 83
Cole, Susannah 74
Cole, William 20
Coleman, Philip 1
Coleman, Thomas 95
Coleman, William 1
Coles, John 9
Colles, Mary 20
Colleton, J. 12
Colleton, John 20
Colleton, Sir John 20
Colleton, Katherine 21
Colleton, Peter 12
Colleton, Robert 20, 21
Colley, Michael 27

Collier, Jane 1
Collier, William 78, 100
Collins, Edward 32
Collins, Francis 1
Collins, Mary 55
Collins, William 74
Collyer, Jane 24
Collyer, Thomas 24
Colpoys, John 97
Cols-, Alexander 72
Coltman, Alice 21
Colvert, William 84
Colvill, Susanna 21
Comby, Martha 30
Comport, Richard 99
Compton, William 17
Connaway, Thomas 57
Connelly, Sarah 36
Conner, Elizabeth 96
Conner, Lewis 96
Conquest, John Tucker 21
Conquest, Mary Ann
Conquest, Rebecca 21
Conquest, Ruth 21
Conquest, William 21
Conway, Robert 61
Cook, Anne 21
Cook, Ebenezer 21
Cook, George 102
Cook, Philip 102
Cook, Richard 102
Cook, Samuel 58
Cook, Susanna Lanigan 102
Cooke, Ann 84
Cooke, Charles 9, 70
Cooke, Elizabeth 22
Cooke, Judy 28
Cooke, Rebecca 22
Cookworthy, Benjamin 94
Cookworthy, Philip 94
Cookworthy, Rachell 94
Coomes, Joane 42
Cooper, Charlotte 22
Cooper, Daniel 59
Cooper, George 22
Cooper, Margaret 42
Cooper, Olive 52
Cooper, Rachel 22
Cooper, Robert 32
Cooper, Rosabella 22
Cooper, William 63

Supplementary Index of Names

Hildreth, Joseph 72
Hill, Alice 48
Hill, Anne 48 , 89
Hill, Bartholomew 84
Hill, Edward 48
Hill, Elizabeth 48
Hill, George 48*
Hill, Isaac 109
Hill, Joan 48
Hill, Martha 48
Hill, Mary 48*
Hill, Samuel 109
Hill, Thomas 48
Hill, William 48
Hilton, Richard 80
Hind, Isaac 20
Hind, James 20
Hingman, John 101
Hinton, Anne 37
Hinton, Thomas 37
Hiscutt, Silas 67
Hitcham, Joseph 48
Hitchcock, Elianor 74
Hitt, William 100
Hoare, Samuel 78
Hobbs, Catherina 48
Hobbs, Elizabeth 48
Hodges, Elizabeth 49
Hodges, Dame Mary 15
Hodges, William W. 80
Hodgson, John 46
Hodgson, Marina 27
Hodgson, Peter 23, 30
Hodgson, R. 43
Hodshon, William 79
Hoffman, William 40
Hogg, Robert 20
Holland, Elizabeth
Holland, John 49
Holland, Niel 70
Holland, Thanks 49
Holland, William 6
Hollier, Elizabeth 45
Hollier, Nathaniel 45
Hollyday, Ann 46
Holmes, Andrew 44
Holmes, Anthony 52
Holmes, Henry 77
Holmes, Hugh 17
Holmes, Jane 59
Holmes, John 31

Holmes, Katherine 77
Holmes, Margaret 52
Holt, Henry Frederick 7
Holt, William 35
Home, Rod. 46
Home, William 49
Honeychurch, Mary 100
Honnor, Isaac 36
Hooke, Nathaniel 51
Hooker, Cornelius 49
Hooker, Elizabeth 49
Hooker, Mary 49
Hoole, Edward 41
Hooper, George 40
Hooper, Samuel 100
Hooper, Susannah 40
Hopes, Ann 49
Hopkins, John 26
Hopley, Randolph 46
Hopton, John 49
Hornbe, Elizabeth 49
Horne, John 72
Horsepool, William 25
Horsmonden, Anthony 97
Horsmonden, Mary 34
Horsmonden Warham 34
Horsnell, James 69
Horwood, Henry 50
Houlden, Agnes 38
Houlden, Elizabeth 38
Houlden, Katherine 38
Houlden, Margaret 38
Houlden, Richard 38
Houseal, Frances 89
Houseal. John Bernard 89
Howard, Francis 50
Howard, Michael Cashio 73
Howard, Patrick 73
Howard, Sarah 81
Howard, Thomas 73
Howe, Richard, Lord 50
Howes, Jeremiah 34
Howett, Thomas 50
Howson, Mary 50
Hubbard, Nathaniel 108
Hubbard, St. John 30
Hubbersly, Hannah 57
Hubbersly, Stephen 57
Huckstep, Jane 50
Hudleston, Rebecca 76
Hudley, Mathew 86

Huggins, Sheppard 110
Huggins, William 110
Hughes, Juliana 11
Hughes, Mary 50
Hughes, Peter 61
Hughes, William 30, 50
Hulen, Eleanor 37
Hulen, John
Hulen, Sarah 37
Hull, Edward 30
Hulls, Nancy 68
Hume, Joseph 15
Hume, Joseph Burnley 15
Hume, Maria 15
Hume, Robert 104
Humm, Ferdinand 9
Humphreys, John 60
Humphreys, Sarah 60
Hunt, Andrew 50
Hunt, John 110
Hunt, Mary 110
Hunt, Richard 97
Hunt, William 72, 110
Hunter, Catherine 41
Hunter, John 62
Hunter, Robert 64
Hunton, Elizabeth 51
Hunton, Matthew 51
Hurd, John 75
Hurdd, Mary 6
Hurry, Elizabeth Ann 51
Husenbeth, Frederick
Charles 63
Hutchings, William 51
Hutchinson, Ann(e) 51*
Hutchinson, Bridget 51
Hyndman, John 85, 92
Hyne, Maria 8

Ilmore, Henry 95
Ingate, Charles Colville 51
Ingate, James Wright 51
Ingleby, Sir Charles 86
Ingram, Merriam 51
Irby, Olive 52
Iredell, Rebecca 101
Ironside, Isaac 15
Isaacson, John Frederick 31
Isham, James 37, 52
Isham, Mary 52
Isham, Thomas 52

Kirkpatrick, Anne 102
Kistell, Charles 37
Kistell, Edward 37
Kistell, John 37
Kistell, Philip 37
Knewstubb, Richard 69
Knight, Hannah 101
Knight, Robert 57
Knight, William 73
Knowles, ------ 67
Knowles, Ellinor 28, 74

La Rocque, Joseph Felix 65
Lacely, William Henry 7
Lacy, Moses 88
Lade, Stephen 90
Lake, Harriot Elizabeth 90
Lamb, Daniel 57
Lamb, Joseph 57
Lamb, Sarah 57
Lamb, Thomas 68
Lambe, Joshua 40
Lambe, Susan 40
Lambert, Caroline 99
Lambert, Edward 57
Lambert, George 99
Lambert, John 45
Lanchester, William 43
Landon, Thomas 26
Lane, John 103
Lane, Thomas 57, 71, 86
Lanfar, Ambrose 34
Langborne, William 25
Langhorne, Sir William 58
Langley, Margaret 58
Langley, Thomazine 58
Lanigan, Susanna 102
Lapage, Elizabeth 30
Lapage, George 30
Lapage, Samuel 30
Lapage, Sarah 30
Larrick, John 26
Lasall, P. 59
Lassock, John 26
Latham, Thomas 107
Laurens, Henry 58
Laurens, Mary 58
Laver, John 60
Lawrence, Ben 26
Lawrence, Effingham
　　　　13, 41, 93, 108

Lawrence, George 51
Lawrence, J. 46
Lawrence, Mary 58
Lawrence, Thomas 61, 63
Le Clerc, Elias 8
Le Cocq, Elizabeth 58
Le Counte, Ann 7
Le Mesurier, Abraham 27
Le Sage, John 24
Lea, William 13
Leam, Edward 50
Lean, Alexander 52, 53, 97
Leary, John 17
Leask, Ann 58
Leask, Barbary 58
Leask, Ellison 58
Leaver, Mary 89
Leckie, George 89
Lee, James 62
Lee, John Francis 59*
Lee, Lettice 59
Lee, Martha 59
Lee, Sarah 59
Lee, Thomas 198
Lee, William 49
Lees, John 70
Leeth, Jane 59
Leger, Elizabeth 59
Legh, John 64
Legoe, William 104
Leigh, Judith 60
Leighton, Susan 73
Lejean, Francis 50
Lenthall, John 59
Leonard, Thomas 56
Leslie, Alexander 59
Leslie, Archibald 59
Leslie, William 59
Lever, Ezekias 24
Levitt, Sybilla 10
Lewis, Elizabeth 46
Lewis, James 30*
Lewis, John 2
Lewis, Morgan 60
Lewis, Sarah 71*
Lewis, Selina Percy 77
Lias, Henry John 2
Lidderdale, John 16
Lidderdale, William R. 81
Lidlow, Edward 103
Lightfoot, John 58

Lillie, Isabel 60
Lilly, John 48
Lilly, Samuel 48
Limbre, William 27
Linacre, Ann 60
Linch, Thomas 104
Lindsay, David 74
Lindsay, Robert 93
Linsey, Alice 62
Lister, Joseph Jackson 30
Littlepage, Joseph 60
Littleton, William 41
Livingston, Ann 4
Livingston, Robert R. 99
Livingston, Wm. 4, 98, 107
Lloyd, Ben 5
Lloyd, Edward 8
Lloyd, Elinor 12
Lloyd, Grace 60
Lloyd, John 48, 62, 97
Lloyd, Joseph 5
Lloyd, Katherine 60
Lloyd, William 60
Lluellin, Anne 60
Lluellin, Margaret 60
Lluellin, Martha 60
Lockey, George 24
Lockley, Margaret F. 61
Lodwick, Charles 89
Logan, George 92
Long, Alice 61
Long, Barbary 58
Long, Susannah 21
Longe, Richard 67
Longley, John Edward 61
Longley, Robert 61
Longly, Ann 103
Longman James 16
Longman, Richard 1
Longstreet, John 74
Lonsdale, Susanna 64
Lord, Dan 105
Lord, Daniel 23
Lorimer, John 38
Loring, Benjamin 61
Loring, Hannah 61
Loring, John 61
Loring, Joseph Royal 61
Loring, Joshua 61
Loring, Mary 61
Lothrop, Susan 106

128 Supplementary Index of Names

McGillivray, James 95
McGillivray, Simon 65
McHugh, Cormick 70
McIntosh, Alexander 65
McIntosh, Elizabeth 66
McKay, James 7
McKenzie, Anne 64
McKenzie, Colin 76
McKenzie, Hugh 65, 67
McKenzie, James 64
McKillop, James 14
McLeod, Alexander 66
McLeod, Hannah 66
McLeod, John M. 65
McLeod, Roderick 70
McLeod, Susanna 66
McNaught, Dugall 66
McPherson, M. 85
McTartan, Mordecai
McTavish, Isabel 67
Mead, John 59
Meadows, William 67
Medhurst, Robert 67
Medhurst, William 67
Meese, Ann 67
Meese, Frances 67
Meese, Henry 67
Meese, John 67
Mercalfe, John 87
Mercer, Grace 68
Meredeth, Mary 110
Merrefield, Vernon 68
Merricke, Giles 93
Merydale, Richard 75
Messenger, Maria 68
Metcalfe, Thomas 68
Methuen, William 3
Mew, Ellis 68
Mew, Mary 68, 97
Mew, Sarah 68
Michau, Abraham 54
Michie, James 102
Mico, Joseph 50
Middleton, Benjamin 68*
Middleton, Henry 52, 104
Middleton, James 104
Middleton, John 104
Middleton, Peter 72
Middleton, Sarah 68
Middleton, Susanna M. 72
Middleton, Thomas 41

Middleton, William 68
Mifflen, Edward 13
Mifflen, -iennes R. 13
Mifflen, John 13*
Milburn, Joseph 97
Miles, George 44
Miles, Henry 44
Miles, Martha 42
Miles, Thomas 42
Mill, John 61
Mill, Sarah 68
Mill, Stanhope 57
Millechamp, Timothy 91
Miller, Ann 109
Miller, Isabella 54
Miller, John 95
Miller, John Smith 99
Miller, Richard 81
Miller, Robert 26
Millett, Thomas 39
Mills, Eleanor 68
Mills, Henry 81
Mills, Honor 68
Mills, Richard 35
Mills, William 10, 68
Milner, Job 102
Minet, Isaac 62
Minor, Mary 3
Minterne, John 43
Mitchell, John 38, 68
Mitchelson, James 68
Moar, Isabella 54
Mobrye, Edward 104
Moffat, Thomas 16
Molleson, William 37
Molyneux, William
Hargraves 69
Moncke, Edward 38
Money, John 18
Monk, Peter 15
Monk, William 69
Monsey, Messenger 57
Montgomrey, Rosina 69
Montresor, Frances 72
Moone, Alice 69
Moone, Thomas 48
Moor, George 92
Moor, Paul 25
Moore, Alexander 38
Moore, Daniel 102
Moore, Elizabeth 27

Moore, Thomas 24
Moores, John 96
Moorson, George 17
More, Elizabeth 27
More, H.J. 53
Morecroft, Elizabeth 69
Morgan, Evan 94
Morgan, James Francis 69
Morgan, John 21, 69
Morley, John 69
Morris, Elizabeth 69
Morton, John 70
Morwick, James 86
Mosley, Sir Anthony 75
Mosse, Benjamin 67
Motteux, John Anthony 70
Moule, Elizabeth 50
Moulson, Foulke 70
Moult, Francis 70
Moultrie, John 41
Mousell, William Thos. 76
Movelty, Nathan 3
Mow, Richard 108
Mowland, Richard 93
Moxon, John 70
Muir, Barbara 14
Mulcaster, Frederick W. 26
Muller, Lyder 70
Mundell, William 70
Munro, Simon 70
Murcott, Henry 30
Murdock, William 18, 39, 40*, 54, 69
Murine, Charles 102
Murray, Grace 36
Murray, John William 40
Murray, Joseph 22
Murray, Mungo 94
Murrell, John 76
Muse, Lawrence 64
Musgrave, Peregrine 30*
Musgrave Thomas 71
Mustard, Christian 28
Myers, Dame Elizabeth 65
Myers, Naphtali Hart 17
Mynterne, Alice 71
Mynterne, Byngey 71
Mynterne, Nathaniel 71
Mynterne, Samuel 71
Mynterne, William 71
Myrick, Anna 71

INDEX OF PLACES

London & Middlesex (cont'd)
Edmonton 57
Enfield 53, 60
Fenchurch Street 97
Fishmongers' Hall 95
Fleet Prison 8
Four Lions Inn 109
Furnival's Inn 16
Goodmans Fields 3
Gracechurch Street 71
Grays Inn 63
Great Poultney Street 31
Great Stanmore 69
Gutter Lane 72
Hackney 1, 18, 48, 95, 96
Hammersmith 14
Hanover Square 20, 72
Hayes 80
Hendon 6
Highgate 111
Holborn 25, 58, 110
Hoxton 74, 102
Inner Temple 40, 43
Islington 4, 16, 34, 49, 82, 100
Kensington 82
Kingsbury 42
Knightsbridge 40, 106
Laleham 36
Leicester Fields 88
Limehouse 10, 23, 42, 43, 46, 49, 60, 75, 78*, 94
Lincolns Inn 75
Little Tower Hill 108
Ludgate Hill 21
Manchester Square 27
Mark Lane 98
Marsham Street 78
Middle Temple 36
Mile End 35, 83
Mincing Lane 79, 96
New Brentford 90
Old Broad Street 61
Pimlico 16
Poplar 35
Princes Square 107
Ratcliffe 20, 21, 25, 39, 45, 63, 67, 107, 108, 111,
Ratcliffe Highway 31
Ruislip 80
Shadwell 3, 4, 7, 10, 13, 18, 20, 21, 24, 27, 40, 43, 49, 54, 61, 63*, 67, 71, 76, 77, 80*, 83, 85*, 87*, 89, 98, 100, 111
Shoreditch 25, 26, 74, 102
Southall 37

London & Middlesex (cont'd)
Spitalfields 35, 47
St. Andrew Holborn 30, 48
St. Andrew Hubbard 52
St. Andrew Undershaft 103
St. Ann 30, 71
St. Ann Westminster 111
St. Augustine 93
St. Bartholomew by the Exchange 101
St. Bartholomew the Less 70
St. Benet Fink 83
St. Benet Gracechurch 87
St. Botolph Aldersgate 57
St. Botolph Aldgate 22, 27, 34, 41*, 49, 61, 73*, 96, 97, 98, 106, 111
St. Botolph, Bishopsgate 11, 30, 38, 53, 85, 106
St. Bride's 32, 60
St. Catherine Creed 21
St. Clement Danes 7, 9,12, 36, 48, 58
St. Clement Eastcheap 108
St. Dunstan in the East 36, 56, 87
St. Dunstan in the West 59, 73, 102
St. Edmund Lombard Street 75
St. Edmund the King 38
St. Faith 85
St. Gabriel Fenchurch Street 8
St. George 60
St. George, Hanover Square 15, 18, 33, 88
St. George in the East 8, 51
St. George the Martyr 25, 90
St. George Westminster 1
St. George's 49
St. Giles Cripplegate 8, 19, 29, 103
St. Giles in the Fields 7, 39, 101
St. Gregory 9, 98
St. Gregory by St. Paul's 1
St. James Westminster 21, 50, 53, 60, 74, 103
St. John the Baptist 90
St. John the Evangelist Westminster 70, 78
St. Katherine by the Tower 39, 41, 56
St. Katherine Creechurch 67, 98
St. Katherine's Precinct 21, 74
St. Leonard Eastcheap 46
St. Luke 88, 107
St. Margaret Moses 39
St. Margaret Westminster 6, 31, 46*, 71*, 74, 80, 103, 105
St. Martin in the Fields 6, 24, 29, 57*, 58, 65*, 75, 80, 82, 89
St. Mary Abchurch 87, 95
St. Mary at Hill 49, 108
St. Mary le Bow 26
St. Mary Woolnoth 64

Index of Ships

www.ingramcontent.com/pod-product-compliance
Lightning Source LLC
Chambersburg PA
CBHW050526270326
41926CB00015B/3089